Pursuing The Mission of God in Church Planting

The Missional Church in North America

Compiled By John M. Bailey

Thank you for acquiring a copy of *Pursuing the Mission of God in Church Planting: The Missional Church in North America.* Our prayer is that the content of this resource would lead you and your church to explore some very difficult issues regarding lostness in North America. We believe this book will provide its greatest contribution to the kingdom of God if it is read and discussed in the context of a small group within a local church or network of pastors.

Therefore, we have developed a discussion guide to assist you in exploring the issues raised within each chapter and the book in its entirety. The discussion guide has two sections. One is a series of questions for a small group within a local church. The second section is written for a network of pastors who want to not only connect the issues raised within the book to their respective churches, but also to their entire community.

To download a copy of the complimentary discussion guide to use with this book, please go to *www.churchplantingvillage.net/missionalchurchbook*

Also at this web site, you'll be able to download free copies of the book, *Pursuing the Mission of God in Church Planting*, for everyone in your group.

For more information, please e-mail The Enlistment & Missional Networks Team at *DiscoverChurchPlanting@namb.net*

A missional church is a biblically faithful, culturally appropriate, reproducing community of Christ-followers who abandon themselves to passionately pursue the living out of God's mission to reach all peoples.

Today, across North America there is a renewed emphasis upon the *sending* of believers into the world to live as missionaries who seek to fulfill the Great Commission. But this time it is the local church who is sending everyday Christ-followers to live as missionaries, often without crossing geographical barriers or going through mission agencies. Everyday Christ-followers are being commissioned to live as missionaries across town, in the workplace, apartment buildings, and organizations.

Are these churches *missional*? Would it be better to describe them as indigenous? Culturally engaged? Incarnational? Missionary sending? Missionary producing? Immersed in culture? First century? Biblical? Acts 1:8? Normal? All of these terms, including *missional*, "could" describe a church with a passion for sending everyday Christ-followers into the harvest to intentionally engage those who are not yet Christians.

How do you raise up an army of everyday Christ-followers who passionately seek to reach the lost by planting churches? What skills will they need? What process shall they follow? The Church Planting Group of the North American Mission Board has developed a resource to guide churches in the enlistment, equipping, and sending of everyday Christ-followers into their communities and around the world to live as missionaries.

To review this resource please visit *www.churchplantingvillage.com/Epoch* or contact the Enlistment and Missional Networks Team.

North American Mission Board
Enlistment and Missional Networks Team
(770) 410-6223
DiscoverChurchPlanting@namb.net

Dedication

This book is dedicated to
those leaders yet to be sent
into the harvest for God's glory
and worship among all peoples.

Table of Contents

Acknowledgements

Foreword

PART ONE

1: Ronnie Fox: *The World Around Us* 3

2: Van Sanders: *The Mission of God and the Local Church* 13

3: George Thomasson: *The Church – Bigger, Better, Broader?* 27

4: John M. Bailey: *The Missional Church* 39

5: Jack Allen: *Redeeming the Culture Through Missional Living* 55

PART TWO

6: *Sending… Same Activity… Same Mission…* 69

7: *The Father's House* 71

8: *The Journey Church* 81

9: *Western Alberta* 91

10: *Japanese International Baptist Church* 103

11: *Cuyahoga Valley Church* 115

12: *Peace Baptist Church* 127

13: *The AnchorPoint* 137

14: *Hope Community Church* 147

15: *Brentwood Baptist Church* 157

16: *Forerunner Baptist Church* 167

Conclusion 177

Acknowledgements

Special thanks to the authors who shared their wisdom and passion for the Lord's glory by contributing to this project.

To Sherri Jachelski who made the production of this project a reality. Thank you for your effort and for going above and beyond the call of duty.

To those who read and edited the chapters. Your ability to take a good start and help bring it to a great finish is deeply appreciated.

To Bryan Taylor who worked diligently on the research and contributed in numerous ways we give thanks.

To the entire Strategic Resourcing Unit of the Church Planting Group for guiding us through the process. Thank you for being such faithful servants.

To Dr. Richard Harris for allowing us the freedom to explore issues. We praise God for your leadership.

FOREWORD

Pursuing the Mission of God in Church Planting is an initial foray by the Church Planting Group of the North American Mission Board of the Southern Baptist Convention into a discussion concerning God's mission, the term *missional*, and the understanding of a *missional church*. At the time the authors were selected for this book, none of them realized the depth to which they would go in this pursuit. Lengthy discussions and searching of Scripture resulted as they attempted to clearly articulate the biblical mission of God. The authors humbly acknowledge that they have only touched the hem of the garment and that much more missiological investigation is needed. Careful study and writing are necessary to properly assess the term *missional* and the emergence of the *missional church* in light of the biblical revelation concerning the mission of God, hundreds of years of mission practice, and current church mission practices in the North American context.

Today, the sad reality in North America is that lostness continues to increase more quickly than do the number of Christians and churches. Therefore, the authors agree that we must do whatever it takes to mobilize Southern Baptists to more effectively embrace God's mission for North America. Our belief in God's mission for His glory among the *ta ethne* (all peoples) of North America through His Church is the unifying perspective of this book.

The authors though have varying perspectives on the best use and meaning of the term *missional*. Partly, this is due to current variety of usages of the word *missional*. Thus, each author reflects portions of some of these current meanings or may even use the word *missional* in ways that differ completely from current popular usage.

Each author writes from different backgrounds of ministry experiences such as: pastors, seminary teachers, church planters, missionaries, associational directors, and state leaders. This contributes to the book's lack of uniformity concerning the meaning of *missional*.

The authors conclude that their various uses of the term *missional* does not lessen the value of the book's purpose to address North America's need for more churches to fully embrace God's mission for all peoples. It is to this end that this book is devoted. It is the intent of the authors to inspire and motivate their readers to continue their quest in the pursuit of God's mission through their churches. Each chapter stands on its own; yet, all chapters seek to describe and exemplify obeying God's mission mandate for local churches. In this regard, *missional* is not the focus of the book. Instead, the focus is on God's glory, as we seek to honor Him with our obedience to further His kingdom among all peoples.

Part 1

CHAPTER ONE

The World Around Us

By Ronnie Fox

Church Planting Group

North American Mission Board

Alpharetta, Georgia

It was Labor Day weekend and the girls at my house "needed" some things from the mall. We drove a few miles up the road to the small town of Dawsonville, Georgia, approximately 55 miles from downtown Atlanta.

The stores and sidewalks at the outlet mall were crowded with people. Yet it was obvious that many of them were "not from around here," as the locals might say. While the girls shopped, I found a seat in the shade and began to watch the people as they made their way from store to store. A few minutes of people watching revealed a surprising variety.

One of the first things I noticed was the different way people responded when their path intersected with someone else's. There were those who marched ahead making no apparent effort to adjust to allow others to pass. Staring straight ahead, they never made eye contact with those they passed. Their posture seemed to force oncomers to yield the right-of-way. Others moved along as if they were looking to let someone pass by in front of them. They always paused to allow others to go by. Their temporary halt was accompanied by a smile and a nod. Their wordless communication was not deterred if the others did not respond. Their expression remained equally pleasant.

Some appeared oblivious of those around them; while others seemed keenly aware of everyone they encountered. The diversity signaled something deeper, a difference in the way they think.

Clothing was equally varied. There were those who wore color coordinated outfits, with everything carefully matched from the shoes to the earrings and everything in between. Others seemed as if their wardrobe was an afterthought. Many in the younger crowd clearly wanted to make a statement with their choice of attire. A few of the teenagers looked as if they were dressed in their pajama bottoms, a T-shirt, and flip-flops. They were certainly comfortable, but had my mom or her friends been seated next to me, they might have suggested they put on some clothes the next time they leave their house. Sprinkled among the customers that day were some who were obviously out-of-towners. It was more than just those whose baseball hats promoted schools from "up north." It went beyond baseball, football, and basketball and included replicas of the jerseys from national teams that competed in the recent World Cup. Some stood out even more noticeably because the clothing they wore was from another country where the dress is radically different. These and other visible distinctions point to customs, attitudes, and values that determine not only their wardrobe, they influence every aspect of their life.

As I reflected on the scene that afternoon, I realized that this crowd was more diverse than even I would have imagined. There was a mix of cultures, languages, and ethnicities. Yet, there were other differences even among those who looked and talked alike.

Unless you are one of those "folks who don't get out much," as some would say, you certainly have noticed that North America is filled with many different peoples. It goes beyond those speaking a different language and those born in another country. There are many things that run much deeper. Values and customs are different, even among those who look and talk like you or me.

Cultural Change is Evident

Cultural change has swept across the United States and Canada. If there ever was a day when our culture was more uniform, it has long since passed. The scene I saw at the outlet mall represents only a fraction of the diversity that now exists. Immigration has resulted in a shifting of beliefs and values that has influenced every facet of society. These changes have added new dimensions to the mix. At the same time, they have allowed much of the diversity that was disguised beneath the surface of "America" to bubble to the surface. The result is an increasing number of cultures and subcultures that provide multiple opportunities and challenges to the communication of the gospel message.

In 1981, Joel Garreau published his book, The Nine Nations of North America. His work sought to address the multiplicity of cultures by grouping the North American population into nine broad geographic categories. He readily recognized the cultural complexity that existed and sought to provide a practical solution. However, he also conceded,"Yet the existence of interstate highways, dense air connections, cheap long-distance rates, ubiquitous television, and the celebrated franchised hamburger has lulled many, incorrectly, into some sense that North America has become utterly homogenized, if not bland."[1]

This same lulling effect exists two and a half decades later. Many "Americans," especially evangelicals, believe, or at least want to believe, that North America is a "melting pot" of cultures. Many continue to hold on to the idea that the vast majority of the U.S. and Canadian populations is homogeneous, and consist of those who share a common set of values and beliefs that is so monolithic that it has washed over anyone else who might have a differing cultural viewpoint. Yet the evidence of the increasing diversity, even among Anglos, is undeniable. The change is much more than new products and technology. It is more than new languages and new ethnic groups. The more consequential changes are in beliefs and values that determine how those around our churches respond to the gospel message.

In the wake of increasing cultural diversity, new business markets have emerged, providing opportunities for companies that have the agility to respond. Success is determined by their ability to connect with new or changing clients. Those that fail to adapt are left to fish in the shrinking client pools that once held great promise.

[1]Joel Garreau, *The Nine Nations of North America,* (New York, NY: Avon Books, 1981), 6.

Grocery stores have responded by continuing to add more and more specialty sections. There is a natural food section for the health conscious, complete with organically grown produce that is not only marketed for its health benefits, but also for the minimal impact on the environment. I remember when the Mexican food section in my neighborhood store was small and the only Spanish words were "taco" and "burrito." Today, the same section is much larger and many of the products offered have labels entirely in Spanish. The mega-stores, with their one-stop-shopping, appeal to the hurried lifestyle that values time as money. The finely tuned product selection and marketing plan respond to the values and culture of the changing community.

Harley Davidson is an example of exceptional marketing to the culture and values of aging baby boomers. A friend of mine, who owns a "Harley" and participates in some of the gatherings offered by the local dealership, describes the events as "costume parties for Hell's Angels wannabes and those who dream about wilder days (theirs or somebody else's)." Harley Davidson sells more than motorcycles, accessories, and apparel; they market an image.

Developing markets produced by the new and changing facets of cultures and subcultures provide new business opportunities. On the other hand, for some industries, the challenge to provide products and services to an increasing number of different clients is more of a burden than an opportunity. Schools, hospitals, and other social services struggle to respond to this rapidly changing landscape.

Many public school systems are scrambling to educate the rapid influx of students whose native language is not English. English as a Second Language to Overseas Learners (ESOL) programs are essential components in almost every district. Public school teachers often have students in their classrooms that are so new to the area they speak little or no English. Educators and administrators grapple with curriculum for "Values Education" in an effort to respond to the obvious need to instill values in our children. Yet, their task is increasingly more complex as they serve the demands of an increasingly pluralistic society.

The communication of the gospel is one of the many areas that have been significantly impacted by the changes in society. If a church seeks to "make disciples" of those around them, they, too, are faced with many of these same opportunities and challenges.

Some churches have and will continue to successfully engage segments of the new and changing cultures in their midst. To the attentive, the changes will provide a wide range of opportunities. Others may become overwhelmed with the complexity that exists in the multitude of cultures and subcultures present in their community and limit their ministry to those who are like them.

The implications are far more serious for churches than for businesses. Eternity is at stake, not just reduced profits or loss of market share. If a company fails to identify a new or changed segment of the population, it may simply miss an opportunity to increase its profits. For the church, failure to identify and reach a new or changed segment of the lost in their community is disobedience to the command to make disciples of all "*ta ethne*" or people groups.

Cultural Diversity is More Than Language and Ethnic Origin

When we encounter someone who speaks a different language, we immediately recognize the cross-cultural nature of the encounter. The barrier of language is unavoidable. Interaction with someone of a different ethnic origin is also easy to identify as cross-cultural. Yet, when someone looks like us and talks like us, our natural response is to assume they have similar views and opinions. In today's world, this is often a false assumption.

Recent elections illustrate the range of opinions and values that coexist in the United States. Not only has the divide between political parties widened, the parties themselves struggle with competing internal factions. As issues are debated, a proliferation of opinions emerges. The underlying values may or may not become apparent, yet visible or not, there is a vast array of standards, morals, and ideals that drive these competing ideologies.

Language and ethnicity are factors that contribute to the cultural diversity that exists in North America. Deeply held beliefs and values, the ones that influence behavior, also play a role. The result is a complex mix of people groups, each with unique attitudes and beliefs that cause them to respond differently to the gospel message.

Understanding Worldview is the Key

Worldview is described as the way people understand their world. It is the set of beliefs that determines how they act and live. It defines what is important and what is not. It identifies what is right and what is wrong. Worldview is formed through growing up in a culture, a group that shares common beliefs and values. Learning a language as a child, living in a family, being corrected, and being affirmed all blend together to form the values that influence our behavior. From our worldview we know how to live and relate to others.

Culture is the outward expression of beliefs and values, in other words, the outward expression of one's worldview. For example, worldview influenced the interaction I observed at the outlet mall. For some, pausing to allow other patrons to pass was the "right thing to do." In a similar way, one's worldview determines if the lack of eye contact by others was "normal" or "a little rude." Because beliefs and values act as a lens through which every experience of life is viewed, they have a powerful impact on how a person hears and understands the gospel.

Worldview is often at work subconsciously. Unless someone makes a conscious effort to identify their own worldview, it generally remains an unconscious influence. Most people cannot tell you what their worldview is. However, this does not diminish the powerful influence it has on their life. For some it is perceived as "just who I am." The potent impact of an individual's worldview influences two interdependent areas of each church's ministry: the communication of the gospel and the making of disciples.

Worldview Impacts the Communication of the Gospel

Each time the gospel message is presented to someone, it passes through the filter or lens of his or her personal worldview. As cultural diversity increases in the U.S. and Canada, so does the number of distinct worldviews through which the gospel is sifted.

At the risk of oversimplification, perhaps an example will illustrate the potential problems. Take Sally for instance. Over the course of her life she has come to believe that nature or the natural order can adequately explain everything. As a child she learned about Mother Nature and even marveled at the complexity of the world around her. In school, she was exposed to evolution as a scientific explanation of how the world began. In the media, she heard about scientific studies that explained some of the things she wondered about. Therefore, she came to the logical conclusion that science has an answer for everything. All this seemed reasonable to her and, moreover, many people she respects hold similar views.

Although God is not really relevant to her daily life, spiritual things interest her greatly. She believes she has experienced many significant spiritual moments. One was when the wind was caressing her face as she and some friends stood on top of a mountain looking at a beautiful sunset. Another was a peaceful moment of bliss that came over her as she sipped coffee by the hearth at a friend's house. She went to church a few times as a child, but the memories are now very vague.

Sally always respects other's ideas and opinions, and appreciates those that do the same. She always seeks to be honest and trustworthy. Deep down, she knows she is a good person.

She has a coworker, Bill, who attends a new church start that is meeting in a nearby hotel. Sally has worked with Bill for some time and sees him as honest and trustworthy. He seems to respect others, just like she does. Therefore, although most of her conversations with Bill have related to their work, she intuitively believes they share similar beliefs.

Bill is courteous and polite as he strikes up a conversation. He mentions his church and how much he enjoys it. Reading Sally's receptiveness, he tells her how much his relationship with Christ means to him. He talks openly about his faith and shares his testimony clearly.

As they talk, somewhere deep inside Sally realizes that she enjoys talking with someone who is spiritually sensitive like her. At the same time, Bill is excited about the fact that Sally was so open to his testimony of faith in Christ and hopes she will soon respond by accepting Christ. As Sally turns to go to her desk, she thinks to herself, it is great to work with people who share the same beliefs I have.

Sally had processed everything Bill communicated, verbal and non-verbal, through the filter of her worldview. As a result, she believes Bill shares her views on life and spiritual matters. She views Bill as intelligent and articulate. Without consciously thinking about it, she assumes that they share very similar beliefs.

Encounters like this are a common occurrence. Bill's words were filtered by Sally's worldview. As a result, she did not hear a testimony about faith in Christ, instead she heard a reasonable and intelligent person talk about spiritual experiences she thought were much like her own. As a result, two people with different worldviews often have radically different interpretations of the same event or conversation.

Bill's unintended mistakes are common. He failed to consider Sally's worldview as he witnessed to her about faith in Christ. Using a method that has worked many times before, he failed to truly present the gospel message to her in a way she could understand.

Worldview Impacts Disciple Making

In our churches, the worldview of each person in attendance acts as a filter for every sermon and for everything that is taught. Often, the result is an unintended distortion of the message.

Therefore, in the church, worldview has a significant impact on the process of "making disciples." The disciple making process is essentially helping someone replace their worldview with a biblical worldview. Each of our personal beliefs must be aligned with the Word of God. Failure to address the underlying belief system will result in layers of conflicting beliefs.

After truly understanding and receiving Christ, individuals like Sally in the previous illustration have significant worldview issues that must be addressed if they are to fully adopt a biblical worldview. The Great Commission gives us the responsibility of "teaching them to observe everything I (Jesus) have commanded you." Situations like Sally's are not just common, they are the norm. As a result of the diversity of cultures and subcultures, each individual has a unique blend of beliefs and values that must be addressed to truly be transformed. Scripture states it this way; "Do not be conformed to this age, but be transformed by the renewing of your mind" (Rom. 12:2, HCSB).

Worldview is the primary focus of George Barna's book Think Like Jesus. He states: "While most people never think about their worldview on a conscious level, everyone has one."[2] The book encourages us to "think like Jesus" by replacing our personal worldview with a biblical one. As an analogy, Barna describes a biblical worldview as a pair of eyeglasses that enable us to see things from God's point of view, thus allowing us to "think like Jesus". [3]

In his book, Barna also sounds the alarm by revealing what research shows about the percentage of born-again adults who have a biblical worldview:

> For years we have used a standard battery of six questions that begin to reveal people's adoption of central biblical principles. Specifically, we examine the following beliefs:

---

[2]George Barna, *Think Like Jesus*, (Brentwood, Tennessee: Integrity Publishers, a division of Thomas Nelson, Inc., 2003), 5. Used with permission.

[3] Ibid., 4.

- God is the all-knowing, all-powerful Creator of the universe who still rules the universe today.
- When Jesus Christ was on earth He lived a sinless life.
- Satan is not just a symbol of evil but is a real, living entity.
- A person cannot earn his or her eternal salvation by being good or doing good things for other people; that salvation is the free gift of God.
- Every person who believes in Jesus Christ has a personal responsibility to share his or her faith in Him with other people who believe differently.
- The Bible is totally accurate in all that it teaches.

> These six statements are, of course, an incomplete inventory of a person's belief system. There are many additional elements that we would ideally include in a full profile of someone's spiritual perspective. To more completely think like Jesus we would have to consider views on worship, love, obedience, stewardship, service to the needy, accountability, forgiveness, and so forth.
>
> Using even this limited scope of indicators, however, we find something very disturbing. Let's say we define a biblical worldview as one in which a person believes that the Bible is the moral standard, believes that absolute moral truths exist and are conveyed through the Bible, and the person possesses an appropriate point of view regarding each of the six belief statements listed above. By that definition we discover that only 9 percent of born-again adults have a biblical worldview![4]

Based on this and other similar statistics, Barna states: "A final conclusion that these statistics lead us to is an appreciation for why the Christian Church is having such limited discernible impact on American culture."[5]

Failure to Address Worldview Often Results in Syncretism

Syncretism is the result of adding or blending new beliefs or concepts into one's worldview without changing the underlying values and beliefs that are not consistent with the new belief. The result is layers of conflicting beliefs.

A classic example is a people whose belief system is based in animism (the belief that things in nature have souls or consciousness). Their belief system allows them to add beliefs about Christ to what they already believe without discarding other animistic beliefs. Belief in Christ is simply added and becomes another part of their belief system rather than a life changing experience.

Syncretism may explain part of the reason Barna's research found that only nine percent of born-again adults have a biblical worldview. Yet it may run deeper. In January 2004, The Barna Research Group published the results of a study that concluded "that only half of the country's Protestant pastors—51%—have a biblical worldview."[6]

---

[4] Ibid., 22, 23.

[5] Ibid., 27.

[6] George Barna, "Only Half Of Protestant Pastors Have A Biblical Worldview", (The Barna Update, January 12, 2004). Used with permission.

Many who identify themselves as born-again Christians have adopted a mixture of various beliefs. They have selected generous portions of appealing beliefs as if they were serving themselves at a grand buffet. The result is often a plate full of inconsistent or even conflicting concepts. Churches and seminaries have failed to adequately address the underlying worldviews of their members and students, often allowing competing ideas to coexist.

Syncretism impacts what many "missional" writers describe as "authentic Christianity." The failure to be authentic is often not the root problem; it is instead, the failure to address a person's beliefs and the resulting syncretism.

The "Panta Ta Ethne"

The proliferation of cultures and subcultures that are increasingly evident across the North American continent each represent different worldviews. Each people group's worldview contains barriers to the communication of the gospel and the making of disciples.

Scripture addresses this diversity and the barriers it creates in the Great Commission. Jesus commanded; "Go, therefore and make disciples of all nations" (Matt. 28:19, HCSB). The phrase "all nations" or "*panta ta ethne*" is also translated "all people groups." These people groups are the diverse cultures and subcultures that exist.

A worldview based people group approach to making disciples is essential to adequately address the many cultures and subcultures that exist. Dr. James Slack, in a list of "Missiological Issues of Today", includes the following: "Worldview is at the heart of "*ta ethne*" engagement, yet is hardly a known, understood and utilized concept by today's evangelizers."[7]

Peoplegroups.org, an evangelical Web site that lists the people groups of the world and their status of evangelization, defines a people group based on the flow of the gospel. It states: "For strategic purposes, a people group is the largest group through which the gospel can flow without encountering significant barriers of understanding and acceptance."[8] This definition serves as a means to identify peoples based on their worldview. This definition centers on the flow of the gospel, and is therefore, both strategic and practical. Worldview based people group strategies seek to take the gospel to everyone within each people group. Because they share a common worldview, the strategies and methods used among them are more readily transferable to others within their group.

It is through individual believers, gathered into local churches, that the gospel passes from one person to the next. However, when the flow of the gospel reaches someone with a significantly different worldview, there are barriers that can obstruct the natural flow. Barriers fall into two primary categories: 1) understanding; and 2) acceptance.

Language is a common example of a barrier to understanding. Cultural values, social structures, and belief systems can also block understanding. When we send missionaries

[7] James B. Slack, "While Europe Slept, America Sleeps, and God Pleads!", (Ridgecrest, NC, SSLM Presentation, August 2006).

[8] FAQS, "What is a people group?", (*www.peoplegroups.org/faqs.aspx#WhatIsPG*).

to another country, we logically expect them to learn the language of those they desire to reach. As a missionary explained to a church group how difficult it is to learn a new language, someone reportedly responded, "I guess it is easier than teaching them all to speak English." Yet, communication in a cross-cultural setting is more than just knowing the vocabulary. It requires knowledge of their culture, social norms, and other beliefs that may block or distort the message.

Barriers of acceptance can include cultural attitudes, prejudice, social pressure, and more. Jesus encountered one of these barriers in his interaction with the Samaritan woman at the well. "'How is it that You, a Jew, ask for a drink from me, a Samaritan woman?' she asked Him. For Jews do not associate with Samaritans" (John 4:9, HCSB). The implications are clear; there is a social norm that prohibits Jesus, a Jew, from associating with her, a Samaritan woman.

Churches with a burden for the lost will adapt their methods to address worldview issues first within their own people. They discover the worldview issues that impact the communication of the gospel within each different people group around them and then determine the best approach to engage them with the gospel. This adaptation is essential to fulfill the Great Commission to make disciples of all *ta ethne* (all people groups).

Summary

Reggie McNeal presents a scathing indictment of the church in his book The Present Future. He asserts, "We have failed at missiology. We don't know how to function in a culture of religious pluralism. We own God, and others have no right to him except on our terms."[9] Many churches have failed to respond to the increasing cultural diversity surrounding them. Others have and will renew their commitment to the Great Commission with a clear understanding of the cross-cultural nature of the task in their neighborhoods, in their community, in their state, across North America, and to the ends of the earth.

The root issue that clouds our perception and complicates our interactions is that there are more than two worldviews involved when we encounter someone and seek to "make them a disciple of Christ." Becoming a disciple can be summed up as replacing ones' current worldview with a biblical worldview. In every situation, there is the worldview of the recipient, there is the biblical worldview, and there is a third worldview, our own, which has not yet been fully transformed into a biblical worldview. If you do not consciously identify and speak to their worldview, by default you will speak to your own.

The challenge in North America is the immense diversity that exists. Roger Greenway reminds us that, "People from all nations are coming to America. They crowd our cities. In short, the ends of the earth have come to town. And many of them know little or nothing about Christ and salvation."[10] The American culture, even if it ever really existed, has long since fractured into many pieces. The foreigners, and even those much like the Anglo

[9] Reggie McNeal, *The Present Future: Six Tough Questions for the Church* (San Francisco: Jossey-Bass, 2003), 60. Used with permission.

[10] Roger S. Greenway & Timothy M. Monsma, *Cities: Missions' New Frontier* (Grand Rapids: Baker Academic, a division of Baker Publishing Group, 1989, 2000), 82. Used with permission.

majority (which given regional differences is probably a myth), think different thoughts and have beliefs and values very different from our own. Yet, a simple approach can be effective in helping kingdom-focused evangelicals identify and manage the complex mix of cultures. We must consistently, even relentlessly, ask two questions; "Who has not yet been reached?" and "Is there a church that is pursuing them?"

CHAPTER TWO

The Mission of God and the Local Church

By Van Sanders

Church Planting Group

North American Mission Board

Alpharetta, Georgia

The North American Church[11] is probably the most educated, best resourced, and most mobile group of Christians in world history. Yet with all these advantages for spreading the gospel, most evangelical churches are struggling to move beyond maintaining their current church membership. While most of these churches would agree that evangelizing the ever-increasing numbers of lost people all around them should be one of their top priorities, few have had success in reducing the level of lostness in their community. How can it be that the Church in North America is not even evangelizing its own population?

No doubt a variety of factors contribute to the anemic mission condition that exists among many North American churches. Much could be written about these factors and many people are writing about them. But the focus of this chapter is on examining God's mission as seen in the patterns and practices of Scripture and applying them to the local church. God has shown us in Scripture and in history, that if His people will return to His ways for fulfilling His mission, then He will expand His kingdom and many new believers and churches will result.

Too often churches pattern their structures and processes for mission after the cultures they find themselves in rather than seeking to conform themselves to biblical patterns and practices. Churches that follow the biblical patterns and practices of God's mission are more likely to see new converts and new churches among unreached peoples.

This chapter emphasizes that God's mission must be fully embraced by local churches in order for all the people groups and people group segments of North America to hear and respond to the gospel in a way that results in new churches. Multitudes of North American churches need to return to God's ways of doing His mission. The gap that exists in many churches today between God's way of mission and their actual practices can be overcome. When churches strive to embrace God's mission practices and patterns in the power of the Holy Spirit, individual Christians are renewed to be faithful witnesses of Christ and churches corporately demonstrate the missionary nature of Christianity.

[11] Throughout this chapter, "Church" with a capital "C" refers to the entire body of Christ, the universal Church, and "church" with a lower case "c" refers to an individual local church.

God's Mission: It's More than the Popular Meaning of the English Word Mission

It may sound strange, but churches must wrestle with what the Bible tells us concerning the meaning of the word mission. This is not as easy as it seems at first glance. One difficulty lies in the fact that the English word *mission* is used in a variety of contexts today. These contexts influence the meaning of the word. In the aerospace industry we hear about *the mission to Mars*. In the military world we hear about a *successful training mission*, a *waterborne mission, performing one's mission*, and *articulating the military mission.* In the business world we hear about *creating a personal mission statement, the organization's mission*, and *a corporate mission statement.*

Christians hear these common uses of the word mission in American society every day. The meanings associated with these uses influence how English-speaking churches in America understand the word mission.

For example, some churches are beginning to use mission in much the same way that businesses do. They are writing one sentence mission statements to explain the entire purpose of their church. Such mission statements become a slogan for helping that church, and its community, understand a specific purpose for which that church exists. The mission statement becomes an executive summary through which all that the church does is filtered.

It is true that church mission statements can help unite a local church to focus on accomplishing its ministries. And they can also provide non-attendees a user-friendly handle for identifying a church's unique ministry focus. Unfortunately though, mission statements can also prevent churches from understanding the full meaning of God's mission.

The point here is not to evaluate the validity of church mission statements. Instead, it is to point out the challenge that the popular culture's use of the English word *mission* brings to the local church that is trying to follow God's *mission*. Even the discussion in the rest of this chapter on God's *mission* reflects this challenge. When you read the word *mission*, your mind will automatically define that word with a meaning that you most commonly associate with mission.

Churches that follow and teach God's mission cannot allow American cultural meanings of mission to shape their understanding of the biblical meaning of God's mission. Church leaders must intentionally strive to understand God's mission from within the theological context of Scripture and apply that understanding to their churches.

A strong temptation for twenty-first century American Christians is to settle for a conceptual definition of mission and then move on with living our lives and doing church without giving any further thought to the meaning of God's mission. Nevertheless, we must have a clear definition of God's mission if our churches are to fully embrace it. This definition must be lived out in daily experience or it will have no practical meaning for our churches. Applying the biblical patterns and practices of God's mission to the structures and ministries of local churches is the best protection against our tendencies to know without doing. With this caution in mind, the following section briefly discusses two primary aspects related to defining God's mission.

God's Mission: One People, the Church, from All Peoples

The fact that the Bible does not contain one word that directly parallels our term mission complicates our desire to understand God's mission. Sometimes it seems that God could have made things easier for us by putting a glossary of terms at the end of Revelation. In reality though, God's way of revealing His mission to us through Scripture is better than a glossary of terms. God demonstrates His mission through His actions and words over a long period of time. He paints a clear picture for us concerning His mission.

Historically, evangelicals have distinguished between the Church and the Church's God-given mission task. The Church is entrusted with the message of the gospel, for the sake of the world. By its nature, the gospel carries a definite purpose, i.e., to invite all to accept God's offer of redemption to become a new creation and a part of His family. So then by extension, the essence of the mission of the Church is defined by its gospel message.

The mission of the Church is to expand the Church into the world by living and declaring the gospel through witnessing and disciple making among all *ta ethne* or peoples of the world. Faithful participation in this mission, by submission to the Holy Spirit, results in new churches being started among all peoples. The sum total of all believers in these churches is the Church universal, God's body, bride, and temple. When Christ returns and this world ends, the worldwide disciple-making mission of the Church also comes to an end.

The Church's mission then, is a temporary task. The Church in eternity will cease witnessing to non-believers and starting new churches for them. John Piper illustrates well the temporality of the church's mission task to make disciples of all *ta ethne*:

> Missions is not the ultimate goal of the church. Worship is. Missions exists because worship doesn't. Worship is ultimate, not missions, because God is ultimate, not man. When this age is over, and the countless millions of the redeemed fall on their faces before the throne of God, missions will be no more. It is a temporary necessity. But worship abides forever.[12]

So in defining God's mission we need to recognize that the Church redeemed for eternity is distinct from its temporary mission task. Church is not synonymous with mission The Church, Christ's body which consists of all believers, is an eternal entity and the Church's mission task is a temporal activity.

However, the temporal nature of the Church's mission task in no way lessens its eternal significance. Just the opposite is true. This temporal mission task influences the makeup of the eternal Church so much so that every local church is vital to seeing God's mission for the Church accomplished. Eternity is affected both negatively and positively by each

[12] John Piper, *Let the Nations be Glad! The Supremacy of God in Missions* (Grand Rapids: Baker Academic, a division of Baker Publishing Group, 1993), 11. Used with permission

local church's response to the mission task they have been given. Therefore, the Church as a whole, and every local church in particular, has the same mission task which they can either obey or disobey.

So what is this mission task that affects eternity and for which every local church and every Christian has responsibility? *God's mission task for the Church is to be His instrument through which He creates one, called-out, holy people, the Church, for His glory and worship, from all the* ta ethne *(all peoples) of the world.*

Scripture records the fact that the early churches struggled with embracing this task. God's movement of His kingdom from Hebrew Christians to Gentile pagans as described in the book of Acts led to the meeting known as the Jerusalem Council. The Hebrew Christians were unsure about how Gentiles could be experiencing salvation as they had. They examined Peter, Barnabas, and Paul's testimonies of Gentile conversions in the light of the Old Testament. The Council then concluded that God had "visited the Gentiles (*ethnos*) to take out of them a people for His name" (Acts 15:14, NKJV). Later in verse 18, James states that this work of God, gathering a people for His name, was known by Him from eternity.

Consequently, from Genesis to Revelation, God's mission for His people is progressively revealed. In Genesis 12:1-3 God calls Abram and his descendants to become God's special people in order to be a blessing to all the clans or families of the earth. Paul wrote that Abraham's blessing comes "upon the Gentiles in Christ Jesus" (Gal. 3:14, NKJV). John at Patmos shows us that in eternity God, through Christ's atonement, will have His one people for Himself, "a vast multitude from every nation, tribe, people, and language, which no one could number, standing before the throne and before the Lamb" who was "slain from the foundation of the world." (Revelation 7:9, 13:8, NKJV)

Because the formation of one people for God's name from all peoples is God's mission for the Church, Christ commands and sends the Church to make disciples of all *ta ethne* (see Matt. 28:19; John 17:18; Acts 1:8). All local churches are given this task. Practically this means that every local church is entrusted with God's mission mandate and responsible for figuring out how to obey it.

God's Mission: God's Glory and Worship from All Peoples

Later in this chapter we look at biblical patterns for obeying God's mission in the local church, but first it is important to discuss one other aspect related to defining God's mission. That is, a definition of God's mission must include the truth that God is bigger than the mission task which He has given to the Church.

God and mission are not synonymous. It is true that God demonstrates what we would call a missionary nature throughout the Bible. Scripture shows God seeking out the lost and sending Christ to redeem a people for His name, and then sending the Church in the power of the Holy Spirit with His mission to all peoples. All of these activities reflect God's missionary nature, but they cannot all be explained solely in terms of His missionary nature. God's nature is not just and only missionary. God is also holy, sovereign, righteous, love, truth, life, a God of justice, the name above all names, the only wise God, immortal, invisible, inapproachable light, bread, father, judge, shepherd, consuming fire, a God of vengeance, and much more.

Neither the Church nor its God-given mission is the ultimate purpose of God's mission. Instead, God in His entire splendor is the ultimate focus of His own mission. His mission is about revealing the mystery and wisdom of God's multi-sided grandeur as demonstrated through Christ's redemptive sacrificial life. And this revelation of Himself results in worship and praise to Him. Paul writes of this when he says that God has given him the grace to declare among the Gentiles:

> ... the unsearchable riches of Christ and to make all see what is the fellowship of the mystery, which from the beginning of the ages has been hidden in God who created all things through Jesus Christ; to the intent that now the manifold wisdom of God might be made known by the church to the principalities and powers in the heavenly places, according to the eternal purpose which He accomplished in Christ Jesus our Lord. (Ephesians 3: 8-11, NKJV)

The fulfillment of the Church's mission task demonstrates and proves God's worthiness to be forever worshiped and praised. God will be universally worshiped when, at Christ's return, all creation realizes the glory He alone deserves and demands because of what Christ did through grace, to redeem a people, the Church, His bride, through His own life and blood.

Essentially, God's mission is for His glory among all peoples. The Church brings glory to God as she obeys her mission task out of love for her redeemer bridegroom, Jesus Christ. God must be the ultimate focus in any definition of God's mission. His glory, honor, and worship are the heart of the reason for the mission task He has given to the Church.

The mission task of every local church is to make disciples of all the *ta ethne* in the earth. The remainder of this chapter examines biblical patterns and practices that local churches follow in carrying out their mission task to bring about God's glory, honor, and worship in eternity from all *ta ethne*.

Biblical Patterns for God's Mission

Our consideration of God's mission and the local church forces us back to the Bible and its patterns that demonstrate how God grows His kingdom throughout history. The patterns of God's mission are revealed in the context of the entire Bible. These patterns are foundational for discerning effective mission practices that fulfill God's mission mandate for the Church.

Patterns of God's Mission in the Old Testament

The Old Testament is seminal for understanding not only the meaning of God's mission but also God's way of carrying out that mission. Early in Genesis, after the fall of Adam and Eve, we see humankind as a homogenous race with one language. Then at the tower of Babel, humankind is divided into different language groups. Later God reveals Himself to

Abram and calls him to follow His commands. God sends Abram to another land in order to make him a great people.

By the time Abraham's descendants have grown very numerous in Egypt, God calls them out of Egypt. He tells them to go to the land of Canaan. God sends Moses to lead them out of Egypt. In the process of leading the Hebrews out of Egypt, God reveals His message to both the Hebrews and the Egyptians that Yahweh is the only true God to be worshiped.

On the way to Canaan, God reveals to Moses His covenant with Israel. God sends Moses back to the Hebrews from Mt. Sinai to declare the message of His covenant with them. Israel is to be God's special treasure above all other peoples. Through their obedience, He would manifest His glory to the other peoples around them as they functioned as a kingdom of priests; holy and set apart for God's glory.

Throughout the Old Testament, God continues to strive with the Hebrews to form them into his cherished chosen people, set apart for Him, to worship in His glory. To the extent that they obey God's covenant with them, to that extent God is able to demonstrate His glory through them to the surrounding peoples.

God repeatedly calls out faithful and anointed messengers to deliver His special revelation to the Hebrews. God's intent with these sent ones is to enable the Hebrews to fully experience the blessings of His covenant promises. The essence of God's communication is about Himself, who and how great He is, and His desire to have a special relationship with them because He loves them.

The barrier between the Hebrews and God is sin. Immediately after God communicates His covenant relationship with them, He begins to reveal to them their need for atonement. He is a holy God. He is YAHWEH, I am that I am. He is totally unlike the gods of the people around them because those gods are only demons (see 1 Cor. 10:20). There is only one Creator God. He can only be approached on His terms, through His means. He reveals to them the way for them to have relationship with Him. That way is through special God-designed sacrifices and offerings and the Law.

The Old Testament word *shalach* conveys the Hebrew concept of one sent from God as an *authoritative messenger.*[13] Abraham, Moses, Joshua, Joseph, the judges, the prophets, and even Israel herself, demonstrate by their practices the meaning of *shalach*. They are sent by God with a message and purpose which when obeyed brings God's blessing to all who hear the message.

On a different level, we see that God's activities to reveal Himself to the Hebrews and form them into His special people actually provide the foundational meaning of *shalach*. In this sense, God Himself acts as a *shalach*. The stories in the Old Testament of God's *shalachs* (Abram, Moses, Samuel, etc.) simply illustrate God's basic pattern for communicating His message to His people. The Old Testament *shalachs* show us that God's messengers are most effective in their God-given mission when they most resemble God's nature and ways of communicating His message.

[13] See Karl Heinrich Rengstorf, *Apostleship,* 1933, for a full discussion of this concept.

The Bible gives us a history of God's self-revelation to one people group, the Hebrews. Of course there is a lot more to the Bible than this. But in terms of understanding God's mission and His patterns for accomplishing that mission, much of the Bible deals with God's activities among the Hebrews.

As onlookers, so to speak, we get to "look in on" God's ways of bringing the Hebrews into relationship with Himself. In this regard, the Old Testament provides prototypical patterns that apply to God's people of all eras. The New Testament follows and further develops these patterns. In Jesus Christ, all people groups, Hebrews and Gentiles, are the explicit focus of God's mission.

Patterns of God's Mission in Christ

The ultimate revelation of God Himself occurs in the incarnation of Christ. In the incarnation we see how Immanuel, God with us, reveals the complete truth of God and His kingdom to the Hebrews. Jesus, born into Hebrew society learns Hebrew and Aramaic. He grows up in and learns the Hebrew culture. Jesus fully understands the Hebrew worldview and its Old Testament roots. Therefore, He was able with both His teachings and His actions, to simultaneously reveal with perfect clarity the nature of God and His mission.

Jesus' life fully demonstrates in the flesh the Old Testament concept of *shalach*, one sent from God as an authoritative messenger. God the Father acted as *shalach* to the Hebrews via prophets in the Old Testament. Now, in the Gospels, we see how Jesus fleshes out the meaning and purpose of God's messenger as the message Himself.

The incarnation pattern flows out of God's messaging patterns in the Old Testament. The continuity between Jesus' life and God's use of *shalach* in the Old Testament accentuates the importance for churches to follow God's patterns as revealed in Scripture.

Jesus Christ demonstrates the heart of God's pattern for communicating the gospel among any and all *ta ethne* for His glory and worship. Christ's command to make disciples of all *ta ethne* is doable if local churches follow the incarnation pattern of witnessing. Simply put, churches must learn how to practice Jesus' incarnational pattern of witness if they are to fully participate in God's mission.

The full range of this pattern is revealed after the coming of the Holy Spirit in the book of Acts. God's pattern of mission in the New Testament churches is discussed in the next section. But for now we must distinguish the different types of applications that the incarnation pattern holds for the local church that engages in her God-given mission task.

Jesus' pattern of witness has application at three different levels. A good way to visualize this is by picturing a three-tiered chess board. This type of chess set has one chess board set up on top of another chess board which is on top of yet another chess board. In a similar way we can picture the three levels of application with the incarnation pattern of witness. Unlike the three-tiered chess board though, these three levels are interdependent and build upon each other.

The first level of application from the incarnation pattern relates to the individual Christian in a local church. In this level, Christ's life demonstrates how every believer, in the normal course of daily life, witnesses the gospel and makes disciples among his or her own kind of people. Jesus as a Hebrew witnessed and discipled other Hebrews because He spoke their language, lived in their culture, and held their worldview. Likewise, every Christian in every local church is a member of a population group that speaks the same language, lives in a similar culture, and holds a common worldview. Every Christian then, in their daily life routines, is responsible to follow Christ's incarnational pattern of witnessing among their own kind of people.

The second level of application focuses upon groups of Christians rather than individuals. The first level of application is still in view and in fact makes the second level application possible. In the second level, Jesus demonstrates the nature and practices of community witness and disciple making. Jesus' interaction with His small group of disciples reveals the pattern for discipling groups into mature communities of faith. Obviously, the effectiveness of second level practices depends upon each one in the group practicing the first level.

The sphere of application with the second level is among a common population group, just as it was in the first level. With Jesus, this population group was the Hebrews. In America many different population groups exist. But each Christian in every local church will be a part of a population group with whom he or she most naturally relates. It is within this group that Jesus' pattern of maturing disciples is applied and reproduced. Significant reproduction creates growing communities of faith, i.e., local churches or in New Testament terms, *ekklesia*. If churches continue practicing Christ's discipling pattern among their own kind of people, eventually the entire population group of which they are a part, can be discipled. Christ demonstrates with the Hebrews, how reproducible His pattern is among a group of people, who speak the same language, live the same customs, and hold to a similar worldview.

The third level of application is not visible in Jesus' pattern of ministry until the Holy Spirit comes in the book of Acts. This level of application relates to reproducing Christ's pattern among all kinds of people. Jesus demonstrated this pattern among one people group, the Hebrews. But Christ's pattern of witnessing and discipling must also be replicated by His followers among people who are culturally different. Paul, as the first, post-resurrection missionary, follows Jesus' pattern and illustrates making disciples of those who were culturally distant from him and his witness of the gospel. To this we now turn.

Patterns of God's Mission in the New Testament Church

As we look briefly at God's patterns of His mission in the New Testament, we see that they are a continuation of what God has revealed in the Old Testament and in the incarnation. This is to be expected. How could the Holy Spirit do differently than the Father and the Son?

God's manner of progressively revealing to us His ways for His mission is instructive. We realize that it takes time for His people to learn His ways, conform to His ways, and then practice His ways. Jesus perfectly demonstrates how individual Christians and assemblies of Christians (*ekklesia*) are to pattern their lives as His witnesses among all peoples. Yet even the early churches often struggled to put into daily practice God's mission patterns.

Acts to Revelation shows us even more clearly God's mission pattern. First, God reveals the gospel message to individuals who become His people. Then as they mature in Christ they witness and disciple among their own kind of people, i.e., people of their own language and culture. At some point in their maturation process, they begin taking the gospel message to groups of people that are different from themselves, i.e., people with different languages, cultures, and worldviews.

The emphasis here is not on the chronological sequence with which God's mission progresses with and through His people to other unreached peoples. Churches can participate in all three levels simultaneously. Instead the focus here is on the patterns which the early churches practiced as they engaged in God's mission to make disciples of all *ta ethne* for His glory and for His worship.

First, the eyewitness disciples of Christ practiced witnessing and disciple making among fellow Jerusalem Hebrews. They followed Jesus' pattern of disciple making. Sometimes they witnessed to large crowds, sometimes to small groups, and sometimes one-on-one with individuals.

Soon this witnessing and disciple making turned into groups of new believers who began meeting together. Again, the eyewitness disciples of Christ followed His pattern for developing local maturing communities of faith, i.e., local churches.

These *ekklesia* spread rapidly among people of their own kind, the Hebrews. Culturally near people like the Hellenists, who were Greek speaking Jews, were also converted. Groups of both types of these believers rapidly multiplied in Jerusalem. Members of these groups were learning how to follow Christ's pattern of witnessing and discipling other individuals. Group leaders emerged who did the best they could to follow Christ's pattern of discipling groups into maturing communities of faith.

The purpose of the general outline above is to highlight the most basic pattern of God's mission. That pattern is Jesus' way of witnessing and discipling people who were culturally and linguistically near to Him. The explosive reproducibility of this pattern in part stems from its simplicity. But even more it stems from the fact of following this pattern in the power of the Holy Spirit. The Jerusalem Christians witnessed exponential growth of churches through the power of the Holy Spirit. As they followed Christ's pattern for God's mission, the Spirit expanded God's kingdom among the Hebrews and among Greek-speaking Hebrews.

In Antioch, another pattern emerged for expanding the kingdom of God. That pattern was the missionary team structure. Until Antioch, the only structure was the local *ekklesia*. But at Antioch, God spoke to the leadership of the local church there and set apart Paul and Barnabas for the work to which He called them (see Acts 13:2). Immediately the Antioch church obeyed and sent them out.

Paul and Barnabas followed Jesus' incarnation pattern as they traveled through various cities witnessing and discipling groups into growing communities of faith. In every city of their first journey, they go first to the synagogues to witness of Christ the Messiah. Some receive and others refuse their invitation to the gospel.

Eventually, Paul and Barnabas encounter non-Hebrew people who have no Old Testament understanding of God. Instead, their belief system consists of many gods with many conflicting teachings. Paul and Barnabas learn quickly that Gentile pagans, the *ta ethne* of God's mission mandate, have difficult cultural and linguistic barriers between them and their gospel message (see Acts 14:8-18; 17:16-34).

The missionary team structure introduced at Antioch is God's pattern for moving the gospel between population groups that are culturally distinct and distant from each other. Missionary teams though follow Christ's incarnation pattern of witnessing and discipling among each culturally distinct people group or people group segment.

A close study of Paul's approaches to different groups clearly shows that he followed the three application levels of Christ's incarnation pattern. First, he witnessed and discipled individuals. Second, he discipled groups of new converts into maturing communities of faith just as Jesus did with His disciples. Third, he identified within the churches he started, those like himself who were called to be missionary church planters. He took them with him and discipled them by following the incarnation pattern. They were discipled as witnesses and disciple makers by witnessing among unreached people and discipling the converts into transformational communities of faith.

As a result, the gospel spread quickly to the Hellenists and Samaritans who were near neighbors of the predominately Hebrew churches in Jerusalem. Likewise, the gospel spread to the Mediterranean peoples who were culturally and linguistically distant from the original Hebrew churches in Jerusalem.

Embracing God's Patterns of Mission in Local Churches Today

The formation of one people for God's name from all peoples is God's mission for the Church. Christ therefore commands the Church to make disciples of all *ta ethne.* Ultimately, the Church's mission exists so that God's name is known and glorified among all peoples. This should be the heartbeat of every church no matter where they are located and no matter who attends their church.

Unfortunately, most churches fail to fully grasp the privilege of their God-given mission task. The biblical meaning and patterns of God's mission are largely hidden from them.

Therefore, they fail to see the need to align their structures and ministries with the biblical meaning of God's mission and its patterns.

Churches that are disconnected from their God-given mission task distort the fundamental nature of the local church. They lose sight of God's mission patterns. This leads them to adopt cultural meanings of God's mission. Eventually God's mission message is diluted.

Evangelism becomes a peripheral component of church life. Such churches may support missions and missionaries and do missions activities, but at the same time fail to grasp and follow God's mission to disciple the world's unevangelized *ta ethne*.

Churches that find themselves in such a situation must take deliberate action to regain the biblical focus of the mission task that God has given her. This is not just a matter of instituting new mission activities. The heart of the problem lies in the church's spiritual condition.

Devoted worship and prayer are at the heart of a church that lives out their God-given mission mandate. The lack of devoted mission practice indicates the lack of devoted worship.

The brevity of this chapter does not allow for an adequate discussion of all of the biblical teachings related to the daily lifestyle of the Christian. But it is the practice of biblical admonitions that allows God to create in the hearts and minds of Christians a willingness to give their lives away for the sake of God's glory among all peoples.

Obedience to the commands of Christ is essential for experiencing the power of the Holy Spirit. The power of the Spirit is in turn a prerequisite for living out God's mission task in and through the church.

Obeying God produces godliness, and godliness leads to further obedience. As our relationship with Christ grows through obedient godliness, we are transformed in the inner man to the point where we desire more and more to experientially identify with the missionary character of Christ in all circumstances of our lives.

Most of this chapter has discussed God's mission patterns. But it must be emphasized that practicing these patterns apart from the power of the Holy Spirit is vain. The patterns and practices of God's mission flow out of and depend upon transformational relationships with Christ and others.

Today the gospel can still spread rapidly through local churches when God's mission patterns are practiced in the power of the Holy Spirit. The Holy Spirit enables churches to fruitfully participate in God's mission to glorify Himself through the Church among all peoples. Churches submitted to the Holy Spirit strive to practice the mission patterns briefly outlined above.

First, individual Christians within these churches are faithful witnesses and disciples of Christ. They follow Christ's pattern of witnessing to others and discipling them. Second, these churches reproduce other churches among unevangelized people that are culturally near to them. Third, these churches recognize those who are called by God to follow Paul's missionary pattern. They send these missionaries out and support them in their efforts to start new churches among unreached peoples that are culturally distant to their church.

Paul-type missionaries pattern their witnessing and discipling practices after Christ just like every Christian does. But their God-given objective in witnessing and discipling is to start new communities of faith among groups of people who are culturally and/or linguistically distant from the witness of existing churches.

Christians who are not missionaries though, witness and disciple to expand the church among people that are like themselves. They are not called and gifted to cross cultural and linguistic barriers for the purpose of starting new churches. This does not mean that they never witness to people that are culturally different. They may if both parties speak a common language. But that is not the norm.

Churches must constantly work to develop structures and ministries that reflect the biblical patterns of God's mission. Every church faces conflict to conform itself to the cultural ways of the world. The very nature of the church's mission task requires intentional engagement with peoples whose cultures and worldviews are demonically inspired. The source of this conflict then is not flesh and blood, but the spiritual powers and wickedness in high places (see Eph. 6:12). The New Testament is clear that any church that obeys God's mission must be prepared to fight spiritual enemies with God's spiritual weapons (1 Cor. 10:3-6).

God's Mission and Being Missional

The absence today in many churches of a tangible understanding of God's mission is alarming. Fortunately, many Christians, both lay and clergy, are realizing that there is more to Christianity than simply attending church services each week. Praise the Lord for the increasing number of churches making this discovery.

Throughout history, the Church has wrestled with understanding and obeying God's mission task for her. Satan does not want the Church to fully comprehend the glorious nature and privilege of participating in God's mission for his glory among all peoples. Sadly, the history of the Church indicates that more often than not she has failed to consistently carry out God's mission faithfully.

A significant attempt to reconnect the Church with its mission occurred in the first half of the twentieth century. The phrase *missio Dei* was used to address the Church's anemic mission practice of that time.

In 1934, Karl Hartenstein, a German missiologist, coined the phrase *missio Dei* (Latin for the sending of God) in response to Karl Barth and his emphasis on actio Dei (Latin for the action of God). For Hartenstein, *missio Dei* meant that the "mission of the church finds the ground of its existence and its limits in God's mission."[14]

When kept in the context of the Scriptures, *missio Dei* correctly emphasizes that God is the initiator of His mission to redeem through the Church a special people for Himself from all of the peoples (*ta ethne*) of the world. He sent His Son for this purpose and He sends the Church into the world with the message of the gospel for the same purpose.

[14] Gerold Schwarz, "Karl Hartenstein 1894-1952: Missions with a Focus on 'The End'" in *Mission Legacies: Biographical Studies of Leaders of the Modern Missionary Movement.* ed. Gerald H. Anderson, Robert T. Coote, Norman A. Horner, and James M. Phillips. (Maryknoll: Orbis Books, 1994), 593. Used with permission.

But the attempt to point European churches back to God's mission was short lived. Just a few years later, *missio Dei* began to be used primarily in a manner that went beyond the bounds of Scripture. In the 1950's and 1960's, ecumenicists and others following them, decided that *missio Dei* meant that Church and mission are synonymous. *Missio Dei* came to mean more than just the task of making disciples of all *ta ethne* by the Church. Dutch missiologist Johannes Hoekendijk said the "mission of God was to establish Shalom-'peace, integrity, community, harmony and justice'-or humanization in this world." The World Council of Churches (WCC) adopted this understanding of *missio Dei*. This interpretation fostered a sociopolitical view of *missio Dei* and "meant that the church should act in partnership with the sending God, not by world evangelization and church planting, but by directly promoting political and economic human good."[15]

The ecumenical definition of mission holds that everything a church does is mission because the mission is church and the church is mission. This definition of mission is unbiblical and denies the true meaning of God's mission. Emphasis is placed on the sent nature of the Church, but without holding on to the specific purpose and message with which it was sent.

The ecumenical meaning of *missio Dei* strongly influences current discussions about the meaning of mission. This influence on the meaning of mission comes from many of those who are writing about being missional.

Many missionalist writers consistently use the word *missional* to basically claim that *missional* and *biblical* are synonymous terms. In truth, *missional* is simply an English word that needs qualification to be of value to the local church. Recognizing the grammatical function of the word *missional* is pivotal to our discussion on being a missional church.

Grammatically, the function of the word *missional* is clear. *Missional* is the adjectival form of the word mission. According to the common rules of English grammar, the suffix al converts a noun into an adjective.[16] *Mission + al* = missional. Adjectives function "to restrict, qualify or limit the meaning of other words or word groups."[17] *Missional* then, no matter what noun it is modifying, must qualify the meaning of that noun by referencing God's mission as defined by Scripture. More specifically, *missional* limits any noun that it modifies to the temporary mission task of the Church to make disciples of all *ta ethne* for God's glory and worship. If the word *missional* is used in a way that does not reflect the biblical meaning of God's mission, then it fails to communicate the purpose of God's mission to form one people for His glory and worship from among all peoples. Therefore, a local church is *missional* when it intentionally pursues God's mission for His glory among all peoples by following His patterns and His ways of expanding His kingdom.

[15] John A. McIntosh, "Missio Dei" in *Evangelical Dictionary of World Missions*. Gen Ed, A. Scott Moreau. (Grand Rapids: Baker Books, 2000), 632.

[16] John C. Hodges and Mary Whitten, eds. *Harbrace College Handbook*, 7th ed. (New York: Harcourt Brace Jovanovich, Inc., 1972), 40.

[17] Ibid., 39.

Conclusion

Scripture is not a linear, step-by-step plan for doing God's mission. Instead, Scripture over broad spans of time comprehensively reveals patterns and practices that, with the guidance of the Holy Spirit, lead churches to be God's mission force in their community.
The Bible reveals God's ways and patterns for His people to proclaim His message to non-Christian groups of people so that new, reproducing groups of believers multiply into many new churches. These patterns reflect different, but integrated practices of God's mission. When followed, they provide local churches the best opportunities to fully experience God's mission in His way.

CHAPTER THREE

The Church — Bigger, Better, Broader?

By George Thomasson

Senior Associate Pastor

Bell Shoals Baptist Church

Brandon, Florida

"Have we become so preoccupied with the wedding trappings that we've overlooked the Groom? The path to reigniting the church's passion for Jesus isn't the next program, the next conference, or the next book. White-hot passion in the church begins when we rediscover a love relationship with Jesus and allow that relationship to shape everything we do." [18] — Steve Ayers

Pastor Steve Ayers, in the above quote from his book, *Igniting Passion in Your Church*, is obviously reacting to methodological approaches to growing a church. He is not alone. Many are taking a hard look at the implications of the church growth and church health movements, especially in light of the sad state of the church in North America.

Most would not be surprised by the painful reality that approximately 80 to 85 percent of all Protestant churches in the United States are either plateaued or declining.[19] In a recent chapel service at the North American Mission Board of the Southern Baptist Convention, Thom Rainer, prolific author and president of LifeWay Christian Resources, indicated that 62 percent of all Southern Baptist churches are in "rapid decline!" How can this be when Jesus said, "On this rock I will build My church, and the forces of Hades will not overpower it." (Matt. 16:18b, HCSB)? This simply should not be. The Lord's church should be growing, thriving, impacting, transforming—but by and large it is not. Many are attempting to explain the reasons for this dilemma and even offering solutions. The problem is, however, the reasons and solutions differ widely depending upon whom you are reading.

We will examine three movements in this chapter which have given reasons and offered solutions to address the decline of the church in North America. The church growth movement concerned itself with the church becoming *bigger*. Somewhat in reaction to this emphasis, the church health movement focused on the church becoming *better*. In reaction to both, the missional church groundswell pleads for a church that is *broader*.

Perhaps we should begin by asking the question, "What is the church?" The word in the New Testament translated "church" is *ekklesia. Ek* means "out of" and *kaleo* means "to call." It was used in the first century to refer to any assembly of people. As the word began

---

[18] Steve Ayers, *Igniting Passion in Your Church,* (Loveland, CO: Group Publishing, 2003), 12. Used with permission.

[19] James Emery White, *Rethinking the Church,* (Grand Rapids: Baker Books, a division of Baker Publishing Group, 1997), 16. Used with permission.

to be commonly used to refer to an assembly of Christians it obtained the meaning, "called out ones."

Many refer to the church as an institution or organization. It should be more accurately called a living "organism." Why? The church is not brick and mortar with a steeple, pews, and carpet. The church is made up of people who have turned from their sinful lifestyles, trusted in Jesus Christ alone for forgiveness, followed Him in believer's baptism, and identified with a local body of believers—not a building, but a body or community. Hence, the church is a living organism composed of born again, baptized believers who have been called out of the world and into personal relationship with God and with one another. More than 90 percent of the occurrences of *ekklesia* in the New Testament refer to a local church.

What is to be the purpose of this living "organism" known as the church? Many passages could be cited, but I will just mention my favorite. In His high priestly prayer recorded in John 17:21 (HCSB), Jesus prayed to the Father, "May they all be one, as You, Father, are in Me and I am in You. May they also be one in Us, *so the world may believe You sent Me* [emphasis added]." God has a heart for His world—all the peoples of His world. He wants His church to love Him and to love one another with authentic oneness. Through this oneness the lost world will believe in Christ and His mission.

With this foundational understanding of God's church, let us explore how these movements have possibly contributed to His purpose for the world.

Church Growth

"We stand in the sunrise of missions." This is perhaps the most characteristic phrase proclaimed through the years by Donald A. McGavran, regarded by many as the twentieth century's premier missiologist… McGavran was born of missionary parents in India before the turn of the century . . . He was the director of a missionary agency… He is fluent in Hindi and Chattisqarhee… He was the founding dean of a prestigious missiological institution. He has written twenty-three books on missions and church growth. His travels have taken him to virtually every nation of the world… McGavran will most likely be remembered chiefly as the father of the Church Growth Movement.[20]

After McGavran had invested many years in India, the result was only 20 or 30 small churches that were not growing. Many missionaries settled for this result feeling that the people were just resistant. McGavran, however, believed there were more effective ways of reaching people and planting churches. In the 1930s he stated that he had dedicated himself to "discarding theories of church growth which do not work, and learning and practicing productive patterns which actually disciple the peoples and increase the household of God."[21]

The Church Growth Movement was launched in 1955 with his new book, *The Bridges of God*. The book was widely read and discussed for its new and controversial ideas.

[20] C. Peter Wagner, *Church GROWTH State of the Art, (Wheaton, Ill.: Tyndale House Publishing Inc.,* 1986), 15. Used with permission.

[21] Ibid., 16.

McGavran focused on four key issues: theological, ethical, missiological, and procedural. He held that disciple-making, and not merely getting decisions, should be the goal. He also demanded that mission efforts must be evaluated based on results and not excuses. McGavran was among the first to recognize that each people group had to be understood individually and then approached contextually. He talked about the homogeneous unit principle. He believed that people desire to become Christians without crossing racial, linguistic, or class barriers. He also saw a clear distinction between discipling and maturing in the believer's life.

McGavran established the Institute of Church Growth at Northwest Christian College in Oregon and later became the founding dean of Fuller Seminary School of World Mission. It was here that C. Peter Wagner was taught and eventually led the work after McGavran's retirement. In expressing personal concerns as to where the Church Growth Movement should go in the future, Wagner states, "We need to develop ways to measure church *quality* as well as measuring membership growth. We need to aim for biblical *balance* in evangelism and mission."[22] Wagner here provides a hint into the concerns of church leaders today. His concerns are refreshing because, frankly, the Church Growth Movement mutated greatly from McGavran's missiological foundations.

It should be mentioned here that Peter Wagner has been a great proponent of church planting as a priority method for church growth. In fact, in his book *Church Planting for a Greater Harvest*, Wagner states that planting new churches is "the most effective evangelistic method under heaven."[23]

I began my vocational ministry in the mid-70s. As a result, I have been greatly influenced by various streams of the Church Growth Movement. I have been to the conferences, been certified in the training, read the books, and tried the methods. God put a hot passion in my heart to see people and families transformed by God's power through the sharing of the gospel. I have tried to lead my people to do the same for three decades. Like most pastors who are always pressed for time, I have often looked for practical, workable tools to build up the churches I pastored.

Unfortunately, most of the church growth influence I received had degenerated from the holistic, contextual, biblical focus that McGavran initiated. Many of the authors and conference leaders encouraged me to "do it exactly as I have indicated and your church will grow." The emphasis was on slavishly implementing a methodology because it "works." It seemed as though biblical theology and ecclesiology were an afterthought and methods that "work" took center stage.

Apparently other pastors were experiencing similar struggles. David Fisher says, "I was vaguely suspicious of that early form of Church Growth but was unsure why. Now I think I understand. It was the sheer pragmatism and methodological certainty…" He goes on, "The Bible becomes a source book used to find texts that support the methodology… Bigger is assumed to be better, so focus is placed on quantity, regardless of quality…

[22] Ibid., 34, 35.
[23] C. Peter Wagner, *Church Planting for a Greater Harvest, (Ventura, Ca.: Regal Books, 1990), 7-8.*
Used with permission.

Growth itself seemed to excite them… If church growth can be engineered and managed by me, at the end of the day, how can I know if it is God's work or mine?"[24]

In spite of these criticisms, I do need to report that God blessed my efforts over the years. Every church I led grew significantly as well as the churches we helped to plant. Our focus was on evangelism, discipleship, worship, fellowship, and ministry. I do look back, though, with regret that I did not know how to lead God's churches intentionally in an effort to transform entire communities. There was no help to identify unreached people groups and engage them at the point of their worldviews. I often wish I could go back and "do church" over again. I would employ McGavran's teachings of communicational effectiveness, theological contextualization, and cultural sensitivity.

Church Health

Ed Stetzer observes that, "Despite all the good the church growth movement provided, its influence waned in the 1990s. Church leaders stopped looking to professors (most of the early writers were seminary professors) and started looking to successful pastors. They looked to pastors who had grown large churches . . . They flocked to their conferences. These mega-church pastors did not emphasize church growth but rather church health. They explained that healthy churches built around certain key values and a passion for the lost would grow."[25]

Even though these mega-pastors warned against it, many aspiring pastors tried to "clone" the exact methods of pastors like Rick Warren and Bill Hybels. For some, who happened to be in a similar context and demographic, it was successful. For others, however, their efforts failed. Hybels and Warren studied their context and designed ministries and methods that were relevant to their audience. God has blessed their work beyond imagination. Anyone who is familiar with Warren's ministry is aware that he has led Saddleback to plant many churches over the years. His relatively new P.E.A.C.E. Plan is aggressively leading his people to identify and reach out to unreached people groups in their own neighborhoods with contextually relevant approaches. His church and the network of "Purpose Driven" churches have also begun adopting certain people groups around the world as well as developing resources for them designed to be compatible with their worldviews.

In my opinion, the most significant observation Rick Warren made in this regard was as follows: "Read this book like you'd eat fish: Pick out the meat and throw away the bones. Adopt and adapt what you can use. One of the most important skills of leadership is learning to distinguish between what is essential and what isn't. The method must always be subservient to the message. Whenever you read a book about church health or growth, don't confuse primary issues with secondary ones.

---

[24] Paul E. Engle and Gary L. McIntosh, *Evaluating the Church Growth Movement,* (Grand Rapids: Zondervan Publishing House, 2004), 255, 256. Used with permission.

[25] Ed Stetzer and David Putman, *Breaking the Missional Code,* (Nashville: Broadman & Homan Publishers, 2006), 47. Used with permission.

The primary issues of church health and growth:

- Who is our master?
- What is our message?
- What is our motive?

Secondary issues of church health and growth:

- Who is our market?
- What are our models?
- What are our methods?

We must never become so enamored with methods that we lose sight of our mission and forget our message."[26]

Coming on the scene the very next year was Christian A. Schwarz's *Natural Church Development*. Robert E. Logan, in the foreword to the book, states, "Critics of the church growth movement have often emphasized the need for quality congregations. 'Don't focus on numerical growth, concentrate on qualitative growth.' Christian Schwarz agrees wholeheartedly! Through careful research, Christian Schwarz has verified the link between church health and growth… To my knowledge, there has never been such an extensive, statistically valid, worldwide church growth research project ever conducted. The research results confirm what many leaders have known intuitively—that healthy churches are growing churches, making more and better disciples in loving obedience to Christ."[27] Schwarz identified eight quality characteristics of healthy, growing churches. They are: empowering leadership, gift-oriented ministry, passionate spirituality, functional structures, inspiring worship service, holistic small groups, need-oriented evangelism, and loving relationships.

J. Robert White, executive director of the Georgia Baptist Convention, addresses this topic of church health in his book, *Healthy Kingdom Churches*. His approach is not scientific like Schwarz, but rather experiential. He states, "The qualities of healthy Kingdom churches that I have brought together in this book are assembled from personal experience and observation over the course of my lifetime. This is not intended to be a book of scientific research on the theme of healthy churches, nor is it exhaustive of the subject …You are certainly free to disagree with my list of ten qualities of Healthy Kingdom Churches. I am strongly convicted about these ten, however, and I expect that, while the list is not exhaustive, many will agree with the necessity of these ten qualities… Let us remember that Jesus established the church to be healthy so that its mission might be accomplished.[28]

White's 10 qualities are: preach and teach the gospel of Christ; worship that inspires; priority on prayer; conscientious, visionary leadership; engage in church multiplication; an environment of unity and joy; cheerful stewardship; on mission for Christ; a good reputation in the community; and people being added to the church.

[26] Rick Warren, *The Purpose Driven Church*, (Grand Rapids: Zondervan Publishing House, 1995), 71. Used with permission.

[27] Christian A. Schwarz, *Natural Church Development*, (Carol Stream, IL: Smart Resources, 1996), 2. Used with permission.

[28] J. Robert White, *Healthy Kingdom Churches*, (Friendswood, TX: Baxter Press, 2002), 21, 22. Used with permission.

The lists of characteristics of healthy churches will vary with every author you read. For example, Schwarz lists quality characteristics (four of which are similar to some of White's), while White lists both characteristics and actions necessary for a healthy church. White's list includes elements that the Missional Church Movement emphasizes: priority of prayer, church multiplication, an environment of unity and joy, and being on mission for Christ. I am convinced that the critical difference between characteristics of healthy churches listed by Schwarz and White is "church multiplication." I am not sure how the extensive research of Schwarz could have missed this component of a healthy church. One of the favorite statements of Dr. Richard Harris, vice president of the Church Planting Group of the North American Mission Board is, "Anything healthy reproduces." If a church is not planting churches with a similar DNA or predisposition to plant more churches, it is merely adding. When new churches are planted, multiplication is engaged.

I was also influenced by the Church Health Movement. I embraced, for a while, the ideological view that if I would help my church to become healthy it would grow naturally. As a result I set out to preach, teach, disciple, shepherd, and nurture our folks. The people loved it, but there was one problem. The number of transformed lives declined significantly. We did what the gurus said, but it didn't work. Why? We began to navel gaze. We turned inward and took our eyes off of the fields that are ripe unto harvest. Our intentional efforts to evangelize were no longer the priority.

Many pastors have had similar experiences and have objected to the Church Health Movement feeling that it is too inwardly focused. They point out that these churches are oblivious to the lost peoples around them and that community and world transformation is not even on their "radar screens." Their thinking seems to center on how to make the church healthy rather than examining the diverse peoples in their communities and designing contextually relevant approaches to reach them.

Once again I must admit, however, that the Church Health Movement was much needed and it has had a positive impact. A proper emphasis on serious discipleship, holiness of life, nurturing family relationships, and Christ-centered worship honors God and brings His blessings upon a congregation.

We should not choose either church growth or church health. It is not either/or; it is both/and. A community of believers in love with Christ and one another should be passionate about sharing Him with everyone. But it takes intentional leadership.

Missional Church

The most recent movement involves what many are calling the missional church. In some ways it almost seems as if we are coming full circle back to McGavran's tenets. There are, however, divergent views of what a missional church is. In my opinion, some of what is being espoused is good but some is also dangerous. Without being exhaustive, let me point out a few things I have observed.

Many "missionalists," if we can coin a new word, put major emphasis on missionary activity as opposed to the traditional "attractional" approach. Generally speaking this seems to be a good directional change, but is every Christian a "missionary?" Certainly every Christian should be involved in disciple-making according to Matthew 28. There is, however, a legitimate calling to missionary service as one enters the world of an unreached people group and is used by God to bring the gospel to them contextually.

Missionalists use the word "incarnational," but do they use it correctly? Jesus was the incarnate God-man. He was born into the Hebrew nation, learned the Hebrew and Aramaic languages, embraced the culture and Old Testament teachings, and communicated in a way that was relevant to the people. He also, however, confronted the hypocrisy of the religious leaders and called the people to repentance openly. He refused to conform to sinful practices and even pointed them out. Some missional church leaders today tend to be so intent on connecting with the lost in their context that they have smudged black and white into indefinite gray. They want so desperately to resonate with the lost that they are in danger of allowing the values of the world to infiltrate and infect their lives.

If the New Testament teaches anything, it clearly points out the need for a balanced Christian life and a balanced church. We are to allow God to love people unconditionally through our available lives. But we cannot endorse or engage in their sinful practices. Even though pastor Douglas Webster is speaking to the church growth movement, his comments are germane to this point. "The question… is how far we should go in shaping the gospel message to fit the expectations and thought forms of the culture. When does the 'seeker' become a 'consumer' and begin demanding from the church an accommodation that distorts the gospel?" He adds, "By catering to self-interests and felt needs, the church is held hostage by the tyranny of desire… It is one thing to understand cultural trends and attitudes in order to discover meaningful starting points for penetrating a culture with the gospel. It is quite another thing to frame the gospel to fit the expectations, aspirations, and dreams of the consumer."[29]

The insistence of missionalists to break out of our outdated forms of church and try to look at our communities as mission fields is a breath of fresh air. As pointed out above, the church in North America is dying rapidly. We must listen to this cry to take a fresh look at God's mission and how His Church should respond to the mission mandate in our context.

Erwin McManus seems to achieve balance in *An Unstoppable Force* as he is explaining the need to "go back to zero" in order to transition a church to become relevant in its context. "For those of us who are followers of Jesus Christ, going back to zero means putting aside all of our assumptions and allowing *the Scriptures* to speak to us afresh. In other words, we need to go backward before we go forward. We need to deal with the 'why' of our theology and ask ourselves the question, *Why are we doing what we're doing?* We need to ask whether the approach we're using is the best and most appropriate for the present context."[30] He continues, "The difficulty in going back to zero and the process of transitioning a

[29] Paul E. Engle and Gary L. McIntosh, *Evaluating the Church Growth Movement,* (Grand Rapids: Zondervan, 2004), 259, 261. Used with permission.

[30] Erwin Raphael McManus, *An Unstoppable Force,* (Orange, CA: Yates & Yates, LLP, Literary Agents, 2001), 188. Used with permission.

congregation is that the very things that need to be changed are not rooted in evil or even in wrong decisions or actions. They're simply rooted in applications that are now outdated . . The preservation of a particular tradition, methodology, or style can move beyond preference and take on an element of sin. This happens when we choose the practice over the principle. When the prophetic leader begins to expound the purpose of God, he begins to expose the heart motivation in God's people."[31]

McManus strikes a strong note of caution to church leaders who would aspire to transition a congregation from church growth or health to missional—though he does not use this specific term. "Effective re-engineering happens when you wrap yourself in the Bible. If you cannot defend the *why* from the Scriptures, you are not ready to lead a change process. You need to develop a clear theology of change—a theology that demands transition and transformation. Before you can begin to call God's people to a new way of living and action, you must clearly establish for them the purpose for so painful a process . . . When the people of God see in their spiritual leaders a willingness to sacrifice for the sake of others and to be the first to change for the sake of the Gospel, they're more likely to make the changes that they need to make . . .The ultimate outcome of the change process is not the implementation of any one single change, no matter how significant. It is to move the people of God through a journey that leads them from transition to transformation."[32]

What should this transformation look like in the church? It should be a people wholly passionate about and committed to the mission of God. As stated in a previous chapter *the mission of God is the formation of one people for God's name from all peoples.* This mission was first clearly seen in Abraham's call (see Gen. 12:1-3). Tragically, however, just as the Hebrews turned inward and focused on themselves, so has the institutionalized church of the modern era. Having lost its focus on God's mission for the peoples of the world, the church has poured enormous resources into extravagant edifices and expended most of its energy on programs for its members. The missionalists are trying to reverse this wrong direction. An example is a series of questions asked by Milfred Minatrea in *Shaped by God's Heart*. "What does God desire for our church? What is on His heart?" That should prompt a strategic question: "What would He have us to do, as individuals and as a Body?" Only then can you ask, "How should we structure our ministry to best accomplish those strategies?"[33]

God does seem to be engineering circumstances toward the fulfillment of His mission through the church. Jerry Rankin, president of the International Mission Board (IMB) and co-author of *Missiology*, comments on this movement. "More and more discussion focuses on completing the Great Commission. Many people are discerning that God is moving to fulfill his purpose of repentance and forgiveness of sin through Jesus' name being proclaimed among all the nations and a remnant gathered from every tribe and people and tongue and nation to worship our Lord and sing his praises (Matt. 24:14; Rev. 7:9, HCSB)."[34] Clearly, the top priority of the IMB is a worldview-based people group-focused church planting effort to the ends of the earth.

[31] Ibid., 188.
[32] Ibid., 189, 198.
[33] Milfred Minatrea, *Shaped by God's Heart,* (San Francisco: Jossey-Bass, 2004), xviii.
[34] John Mark Terry, Ebbie Smith and Justice Anderson, eds., *Missiology: An Introduction to the Foundations, History, and Strategies of World Missions.* (Nashville, TN: Broadman & Holman Publishers, 1998), 31.

I think we have said that there are both strengths and weaknesses in all three movements. We should embrace the strengths and reject the weaknesses as we attempt to address God's mission.

What's a pastor to do?

At this point a critical question comes to mind. "How is the average local pastor in an established church or a church planter aspiring to start a new church supposed to respond to all of this?" Should he ignore the realities of a church in trouble and continue business as usual? Should he attempt to transition his church from outdated, ineffective forms through a process of revitalization? If so, what would the process look like? Does the pastor take his people back to "zero" as McManus suggests? Should he take a realistic look at the current reality of his church in terms of church growth and health indicators? If he goes this route, should he follow Schwarz, White, Wagner, Warren, Minatrea, McManus, or whom? If he is starting a new church, what is he to teach his core group? What kind of functions should the new church perform? How should the new church be structured?

The pastor of an established church may be forced to face an even more fundamental question. As he stands in the valley of "dry bones," otherwise known as his church, should he move forward with the conviction that "these bones can live again" or, as many recommend, should he give up on this corpse and plant a new living organism all together? If he plants a new church, how can he ensure that it will be a balanced church that effectively pursues the mission of God?

Let's think again about the pastor who is attempting to transition his congregation into a transformational, balanced church that is focused on God and His mission. If he will put his glance on the strategic mechanics and put his *gaze* on the spiritual dynamics, he can be used of God to mobilize his church to address the mission.

A close look at Acts 1:6-14 reveals a biblical process for transitioning an established church into an effective church. After His resurrection, Jesus instructed his disciples to wait in Jerusalem until they were empowered from on high (see Luke 24:49). The disciples asked Him, "Lord, at this time are You restoring the kingdom to Israel" (Acts 1:6, HCSB)? After three power-packed years of intense discipleship with Jesus, the disciples still did not understand the mission of God. They were looking for a military or political leader to deliver them from Roman bondage. Just like those first century disciples, the churches of North America must *rethink the mission.*

Jesus responded to His disciples' obvious confusion by saying, "It is not for you to know times or periods that the Father has set by His own authority" (Acts 1:7, HCSB). In other words, "Don't spend your time on conjecture but commitment." He wanted them to take their minds off of the hypothetical and *refocus their attention* on the mission. A church today must honestly evaluate everything it is doing in ministry in light of this laser focus on God's mission.

Jesus then spoke His last earthly words to His disciples. We know them as Acts 1:8. "But you will receive power when the Holy Spirit has come upon you; and you will be My witnesses in Jerusalem, in all Judea and Samaria, and to the ends of the earth" (HCSB). If a church today is to transition into an effective mission-focused church, its members must *receive power* and follow the revealed strategy of Jesus.

After Christ was taken up into heaven right before the eyes of His disciples, two angels assured them that just as Jesus had departed so He would return (see Acts 1:10-11). Then the disciples obeyed the Lord and returned to wait for His empowerment to make possible their witness. Verse 14 records that the first thing they did was to enter into united prayer. It was through prayer that God would *release His presence*. If the presence and power of God do not rest upon a body of believers, their ministry efforts are useless. The old hymn says it best, "All is vain unless the Spirit of the Holy One comes down!"[35] His presence in the church that permeates a lost world like salt and light is released through extraordinary, believing prayer. A balanced, effective, powerful church that pursues the mission of God will be a praying church.

The graphic which follows shows how an established church can follow this biblical pattern and become a congregation that effectively pursues the mission of God.

Transitioning a Church to Pursue God's Mission
Acts 1:6-14

All the Peoples of the World

[35] "Brethren, We Have Met To Worship"

Pulling it All Together

If there ever was a time when we need to *rethink the mission* to obtain a clear understanding of God's mandate and *refocus our attention* on how we do "church," it is now. There is no redemptive value in criticizing the church growth, health, and missional movements. Each made positive contributions to help the church reach lost people and build up the body. The missiological concepts promoted and practiced by McGavran, for example, form a solid, biblical foundation upon which churches can find their moorings. I appeal, therefore, to pastors and authors to resist the temptation to step on former leaders, unless you acknowledge that you are standing on their shoulders.

As we conclude this chapter, flash back with me to something Rick Warren said about primary issues of church growth and health. He asked three critical questions: 1. Who is our *Master?* 2. What is our *Message?* 3. What is our *Motive?* Any church, if it is to effectively pursue the mission of God, must come to grips with these three primary issues.

Our *Master* is Jesus Christ, the Son of God, the Creator of the universe, the King of kings, the Lord of lords, the Prince of Peace, the Lamb of God slain from the foundation of the world, the Way, the Truth, and the Life. He and He alone is the Head of the Church, the Groom, and we are His Bride! Our *Message* is about Him—the only true Savior who bore our sins on Calvary, was buried, and rose again that we might receive the free gift of eternal and abundant life. Our *Motive* is one of love. The Groom loves his Bride, the Church, and gave Himself for her (see Eph. 5:25). More than anything our Groom wants His Bride to submit to Him as Lord and to demonstrate our love for Him in unquestioned obedience to His revealed will.

Could it be that we have missed the primary motivation for being the church and doing God's mission? Look afresh at Matthew 28, but do not begin at verse 18 as we usually do. Begin with verses 16 and 17: "The 11 disciples traveled to Galilee, to the mountain where Jesus had directed for them. When they saw Him, *they worshiped…* "[emphasis added] (HCSB). Jesus then voiced His Great Commission in the context of their worship! The implication is that *mission is to be the overflow of worship*. Love for our Groom should be so deep, so intimate, so personal that it becomes the driving motivation for all we do.

When Jesus encountered the woman at the well, he opened up to us the Father's clear mission. "But an hour is coming, and is now here, when the true worshipers will worship the Father in spirit and truth. Yes, *the Father wants such people to worship Him*" [emphasis added] (John 4:23, HCSB). The Father is after worshipers—men and women, boys and girls who love Him with all their hearts.

Jesus intentionally prepared His disciples for His departure when He said, "If you love Me, you will keep My commandments… The one who has My commands and keeps them is the one who loves Me. And the one who loves Me will be loved by My Father. I also will love him and will reveal Myself to him" (John 14:15, 21, HCSB). A post-resurrection appearance of Jesus with His disciples at the Sea of Galilee emphasizes this same primary motivational issue. Three times Jesus confronted Peter desiring his affirmation of love.

Each time He said, "Feed My lambs… Shepherd My sheep… Feed My sheep" (John 21:15-17, HCSB).

Steve Ayers, in *Igniting Passion in your Church*, brings this issue into the spotlight. "The church's life is the relationship between a committed Groom and a loving bride. And that's what our disconnected world needs to see: a loving bride. A culture disenchanted with cold formality and calculated decision needs a passionate church. The adjectives that'll describe the church of the twenty-first century are *loving, connected, authentic, passionate, risky, mysterious, messy, beautiful, brave, fluid, fun, and honest*… You're Jesus' bride, and these are marital must-haves. It's time for the church to replace corporate language with passionate language. It's time we say 'I do' to Jesus again and leave our business-clad suitors behind."[36]

Secondary issues will vary among all churches. You will see great diversity among the churches highlighted in the following chapters. Other churches you have encountered may also come to mind. They may have very different expressions of ministry, structure, and focus. This is to be expected when churches take seriously God's mission to engage the unreached peoples of the world.

All of them, however, will have some things in common.

- They all desire to please their *Master*, the Lord Jesus Christ.
- They are all committed to communicate His *Message* to all the unreached peoples in their unique contexts and beyond with relevancy and effectiveness.
- They are all *motivated* and driven because of an intimate, love relationship with their Groom.

Their passionate and obedient pursuit of the mission of God is their highest expression of worship.

[36] Ayers, *Igniting Passion in Your Church*, 12.

CHAPTER FOUR

The Missional Church

By John M. Bailey

Church Planting Group

North American Mission Board

Alpharetta, Georgia

Several months ago, I and a seminary student began a quest to define the term *missional church* and identify common characteristics or values which seem to set these churches apart from the rest. We examined many published works on the *missional church* and writings posted on the Web. We identified churches who claimed to be *missional* and dialogued with their pastors. We spoke with individuals who have served as missionaries around the world about their journey as missionaries. We filtered all of this activity through Scripture and our Southern Baptist distinctives.

My personal journey began with a search for the *missional church* and ended up focusing on the mission of God to gather for Himself a people out of all peoples. I struggled with the term *missional.* Was its usage merely a fad? Did it have biblical roots? Would its usage or application of its values one day introduce a fresh movement of God across our continent? Does it clearly connect with God's mission purpose for the local church as identified by Van Sanders in the second chapter of this book, "*God's mission task for the Church is to be His instrument through which He creates one, called-out, holy people, the Church, for His glory and worship, from all the ta ethne (all peoples) of the world?*"

As I journeyed through the process, I settled on this definition of a missional church: *A missional church is a biblically faithful, culturally appropriate, reproducing community of Christ-followers who abandon themselves to passionately pursue the living out of God's mission to reach all peoples.* Cam Roxburgh, in *Discipling Our Nation: Equipping The Canadian Church For Its Mission*, describes a missional church this way: "Being missional is not about putting on more programs, or giving more money, or even putting more time into trying to reach out to the neighborhood. Being missional begins with a profound conviction that we are invited to join in the mission of God and that the church does not exist for itself, but rather for the world around us that God so desperately loves."[37]

Beyond the formation of a definition, I noted four major characteristics which seemed to be held by these churches:

- A passion to reach the lost with the gospel of Jesus Christ
- An appropriate connection or adaptation to the culture in which they serve
- A faithfulness to God's Word
- A desire to see new churches planted throughout North America and around the world

[37] Murray Moerman editor, *Discipling Our Nation: Equipping The Canadian Church For Its Mission* (Delta, BC Canada: Church Leadership Library, 2005), 151. Used with permission.

If you are like me, you may have already asked these questions, "Should these not be the characteristics of every local church which follows the teachings of the New Testament? Should not every church be involved in reaching across cultural barriers to reach the lost?" Therefore, should not every evangelical church be described as being missional and thereby eliminate the distinction of a *missional church*? Forgive me for this answer but here it goes… "yes" and "no." Yes… the definition I came up with should be used to describe every church that believes and teaches the New Testament. But based upon the activities and effectiveness of the church in North America, we are faced with the reality that not all churches are living up to the teachings of Scripture regarding God's missional purpose for them.

Many of our churches are missions minded but few are *missional.* Our baptisms as a denomination reflect that we are reaching less than one-fourth of one percent of the unchurched population in North America. Less than eighteen percent of our churches are engaged in church planting activities. If we were to plant 2,000 churches in the next year, each church would have to reach more than 1,500 people in their first year just to keep up with the projected population growth for North America. Here in North America a large number of people groups and their sub-cultures remain unreached with the gospel. There are places throughout North America where no evangelical church exists.

I have concluded that a *missional church* does not reflect a new model or way of doing church. It is simply church doing church as God intended. Every church can be *missional* regardless of their model or approach to doing ministry. Being *missional* therefore is a choice. My prayer is that the dialogue and emphasis upon the *missional church* ushers in a fresh movement of God that focuses our attention on reaching all peoples with the gospel of Jesus Christ and brings God glory by reducing the level of lostness amongst all peoples.

The Values of a Missional Church

As I traveled on our journey, I identified certain values (actual or aspired) which made up or defined these *missional* communities of faith. Although the majority of the churches I examined affirmed the values, few, if any, have integrated all of them into their ministries. The following pages will explore the values I identified, keeping in mind that this proposed list is not exhaustive. If anything, it is a work in progress!

Passionate for the Mission of God

The first and foremost value of a *missional church* is a passionate commitment to carrying out the mission of God, the formation of one people from *all* peoples, within their communities and around the world. This is the demonstration of their love for God and for others. His love toward us compels us to continue (see 2 Cor. 5:14) to pursue the mission of God. It is the single focus of a missional church. It is the essence of who they and of who *we* are.

> Mission is not merely an activity of the church. It is the very heartbeat and work of God. It is in the very being of God that the basis for the missionary enterprise is found. God is a sending God, with a desire to see humankind and

> creation reconciled, redeemed, and healed. The missional church, then, is a sent church. It is a going church, a movement of God through His people, sent to bring healing to a broken world. North America is as much a mission field as any other nation or people group on the face of the earth.[38]

Therefore in the *missional church* there must be a shift from just a programmatic and attractional approach of doing church. The church should put priority emphasis upon developing disciples to witness in the culture in which they live. At the same time, it should be sending out God-called missionary teams to cross cultural barriers in order to reach the lost and establish indigenous New Testament churches. In essence, the followers of Christ become an extension of God's mission in the world as missionaries and/or as a witness. *They become partners with God, entrusted with the message of reconciliation* (see 2 Cor. 5:18-19), *participating passionately in God's redemption of humanity*. For the m*issional church*, the mission of God is based upon faithfulness to God's Word, upon an accurate understanding of one's culture and/or cultures, and a passion to communicate the gospel in the heart language of the listener.

At the heart of a *missional church* seems to be a movement away from a philosophy of church where people outside the family of God are invited into the world of the church and encouraged to adopt its culture. The trend now is moving toward an approach where God's people are sent to live a life which displays the transforming power of God in the world, in the network of relationships in which they live and work. Scripture also gives us an additional pattern where teams, aware of a calling and giftedness to cross-cultural ministry, engage in world-view based evangelism and church planting amongst unreached peoples.

God's mission flows out of worship as the church, filled with the Holy Spirit, obeys His mission mandate to make disciples of all peoples (see Matt. 28:19). The mission is not to be focused upon drawing a larger and larger crowd into a *sacred space* where their needs or wants are the focus of the church's existence. In other words, the members of a missional church "come" in order to "go."

A missional church seeks to take the message of hope to the entire world (see Acts 1:8), one people group at a time. They simultaneously and intentionally work among specific people groups in their own community, across their region and continent, and among groups overseas. They call out and send mission teams to assist in the reaching of people groups in places far from their Jerusalem, as well as in the midst of their own community. They support the Cooperative Program.[39] They partner with other Southern Baptist churches to proclaim the gospel of Jesus Christ and plant churches.

For many in the missional church, their partnerships do not stop with Southern Baptist churches. Out of necessity from the enormity of the task, many partner with other evangelical churches to reach the lost wherever they join God on mission. Knowing that they cannot handle the unfinished task on their own, they build strategic partnerships

[38] Michael Frost and Alan Hirsch, *The Shaping of Things To Come* (Peabody, Massachusetts: Hendrickson Publishers, Inc., 2003), 18. Used with permission.
[39] For more information on the Cooperative Program visit *www.cpmissions.net.*

with like-minded evangelical churches and para-church organizations in different levels of cooperation.

Called to Authentic Christian Living

A second value in the *missional church* is a call for all believers to live *authentic Christian lives*—a call for all believers to be like Christ (see Rom. 8:29). They are called to empty and humble themselves, to become obedient to the point of death for the glory of God the Father (see Phil. 2:5-11). A *missional church* is a place where the life and mission of Jesus Christ is held up as the model of authenticity and people are challenged to journey toward that standard. Once Christ has been established as the standard, they can then clarify the process which aids their members in their growth and development as followers of Christ. This is why the church exists: to make disciples—*authentic* disciples.

This calls for a radical shift from a self-focused lifestyle to a Christ-centered life of service to others. A shift from being a consumer to a multiplier of disciples to a life dedicated to fulfill the mission of God. Missional churches, therefore, strive to move from a place where individuals come primarily to have their needs met, to a place where disciples find life and health, and then are equipped and released into the harvest for the glory of the Father.

The *missional church* "disassembles itself and seeps into the cracks of a society in order to be Christ to those who don't yet know Him."[40] As Christ's disciples *seep* into the cracks of society, they seek to interact, to be incarnational in places where they can have meaningful relationships with those who are not yet followers of Christ. This requires both vulnerability and humility. As the transforming power of Christ is displayed via their lives before the disconnected, the world is attracted to God Himself. Missional churches expect to see the world transformed through the ways their disciples live their lives among the people they are called to reach. However, life without a verbal witness is inadequate. Christ-followers must be committed to proclaiming the gospel, sharing with others how they too can experience the presence and power of God in their life (see 1 Pet. 3:15).

It is vital that we understand that all disciples are called to live cross-culturally whether they serve in their hometown or across the ocean. This world is not our home! We are called to be different (see Rom. 12:2). We are called to not be conformed to this world. We are called to be imitators of God (see Eph. 5:1). God has chosen us to be holy and blameless in His sight (see Eph. 1:4) while we "eat, drink, and talk like the natives, and love and serve them in Jesus' name."[41] Missional living therefore cuts against the grain of culture while at the same time being appropriately contextual. The call to authenticity requires denial of self (see Matt. 16:24) and a passion to become all things to all people so that we may win some (see 1 Cor. 9:19-22). This must be done without compromising the truth. The call to authenticity also requires a connectivity to the culture they (Christ-followers) are called to serve, while maintaining separation from the things of this world… remaining faithful to the Word of God.

[40] Frost and Hirsch, *The Shaping of Things To Come,* 12.
[41] Ed Stetzer, *Planting Missional Churches* (Nashville, TN: Broadman and Holman Publishers, 2006), 17. Used with permission.

The focus upon authenticity includes more than an emphasis upon how an individual lives life. When the followers of Christ gather as a community, as they experience biblical community, the world is attracted to God. In Acts 2, we read that God added daily to the church as they lived life together. As they focused on discipleship, worship, evangelism, mission, and fellowship the world took notice. Therefore a *missional church* can be, and will be, attractive to the world, as it functions as an authentic biblical community.

Readily Seeking and Responding to the Call of God

A third value of the *missional church* is an emphasis upon seeking and responding to the call of God. When one does, God offers guidance and direction for life and mission. Jesus said in John 5:19 (HCSB), "I assure you: The Son is not able to do anything on His own, but only what He sees the Father doing. For whatever the Father does, the Son also does these things in the same way."

If a *missional church* is characterized by a passion to live out the mission of God, it must have a passion to be in relationship with God Himself. This passion will be evidenced by a hunger for His direction. The church must earnestly seek the heart of God, listening attentively to the leading of the Holy Spirit. The call of God is where ministry begins.

Seeking the heart of God is directly connected to knowing and experiencing Him in His Word and through prayer. Some followers of Christ struggle to discern if their thoughts and feelings are being shaped by Scripture. They hunger for the certainty of knowing it is God leading them. They struggle with determining if what they "feel" and "sense" is the will of God.

They would question the dependence of many upon research and strategy development as sole means for setting direction for the local church. They might contend that God's will cannot be predicted by human planning, that Scripture cannot be used to support or justify their plans.

The tension between knowing the will of God and the ability of pastors to conduct research and create church growth strategies presents a healthy state of tension. Some would place a heavy emphasis upon research and strategy development. Some would focus heavily upon discerning God's will and understanding the cultural context in which the church serves. Kingdom growth requires both. At times we need to do strategic planning—to identify what we can do to facilitate church growth. But there are times when we need to stop and understand that only God can provide the answer, the direction we need. Therefore, we wait for the Lord to guide and direct our efforts. We wait for a calling from God. There are seasons where both are required.

Embracing Simplicity in Purpose, Process and Programming

A *missional church* embraces simplicity… simplicity in purpose, process, and programming.

First, a *missional church* has a clear, simple purpose: to glorify God by living out, by participating in His mission in their Jerusalem, Judea, Samaria, and beyond. The apostle Paul stated, "... but one thing I do, forgetting those things which are behind and reaching forward to those things which are ahead, I press toward the prize of the upward call of God in Christ Jesus" (Phil. 3:13, 14, HCSB). Focus. Clarity. Simplicity in purpose.

Second, a *missional church* has a simple, intentional process for developing disciples who serve as witnesses or as missionaries in their context. In many cases, the process would look something like this:

Connect People To One Another
Connect People To God
Connect People With Those Needing Christ

Disciples are expected to attend a worship service, participate in a small group, and incarnate the gospel in the world. From our earlier characteristics we find a simple purpose: Live out the mission of God. We also find within *missional churches*, a simple process that moves people through the progression of life transformation that enables them to participate in the mission of God.

In *Shaped By God's Heart*, Milfred Minatrea states, "Missional churches provide both the pathway and the expectations of membership with consistency and excellence."[42] Therefore the goal of a *missional church* is not necessarily to grow larger, but rather to equip individuals to live as authentic disciples and release them into the world to live out the mission of God. Simple purpose. Simple process.

Geiger and Rainer in their book *Simple Church*, say that for a process to be effective, it must be clearly defined. People know what the church wants them to become. They know and understand the process for becoming an authentic follower of Christ. It is sequential and it is clear. The process is visually illustrated. Progress is measured. They have a system that evaluates the effectiveness of the process and the progress of individuals who participate in the journey. Finally, it is discussed constantly by the leaders of the church. It is lifted up frequently.[43]

Third, a *missional church* understands that if they are to fulfill their purpose, they must remove or avoid adding programs and events which distract Christ-followers from living out the mission of God. Some churches have calendars full of endless activities in spite of the hurried lives of their members. Others have too many events or programs which reinforce only one of their values. The issue is clearly aligning the purpose of the church with God's mission and reviewing all activities in light of that purpose. For every church there must be a healthy balance between programs and events which are for the growth and development of the membership and those that are designed to connect the body of Christ with nonbelievers. Minatrea states, "Consumer or maintenance-minded churches tend to design most of their events for members. Missional churches exist to reach those not yet part of the church, and so design activities that connect them with people outside

[42] Milfred Minatrea, *Shaped By God's Heart* (San Francisco, CA: Jossey-Bass A Wiley Imprint, 2004), 36. Used with permission.

[43] Eric Geiger & Thom S. Rainer, *Simple Church* (Nashville, TN.: Broadman & Holman Publishers, 2006), 109-128. Used with permission.

the church."[44] Again, it is not one or the other. A balanced church values both. Simple purpose. Simple process. Simple programming.

Expressing Unconditional Love for All People

Our fifth value is an unconditional love for people which is marked by a passion to see lives transformed through a personal relationship with Jesus Christ and strengthened through life in authentic biblical community. A *missional church* has a genuine love for all people regardless of ethnicity, income, or lifestyle… A genuine love for people that is reflected as Christ's followers establish relationships with those who seem to be the farthest from God. Roxburgh states, "Being missional includes caring for the least, the lost and the lonely."[45] The greatest expression of their love for people may be their willingness to adjust their church (not their convictions or values) in order to connect with the disconnected, with the culture in which they serve.

Glenn Johnson, pastor of Veritas in Oxford, Ohio, stated in an e-mail, "One of the lamest bits of advice I got as I was readying to enter the planting field was to 'watch out for the messed up people.' In other words, keep them away. These were the rejects, the needy, the losers of society. When God started bringing those to us and we realized that was the kind of make up our church would have, I had to reject that notion. It is Jesus' church. He brings to us whomever He pleases. We count it as an honor that God would trust us enough to incubate the 'least of these.'"

Frost and Hirsh in *The Shaping of Things to Come* connect the practical expression of God's love by the church with God's love for people:

> The missional-incarnational church starts with the basic theological understandings: God constantly comes to those who are the most unlikely. For example, the Hebrews were the world's outcasts. God chose them. The Old Testament story of Ruth is profoundly missional. It is part of the continuing story of God's future plans emerging through the strangest and most unlikely people and places. In that story God revealed that His future for Israel was to be fulfilled in and through a Gentile (Ruth). If we are to take incarnational mission seriously, then we must see that God's future—his new creation—is not just among 'his people' (churchgoing Christians) but it is among the 'ordinary' people—the lost, strugglers, and listless ones of the world.[46]

For the *missional church*, people outside the family of God (the disconnected) are valued and affirmed. Hospitality is extended. Relationships are established. In the midst of these relationships, people are not seen just as being in or out, but as being closer or farther from God. They understand that discipleship is a process and the process begins as people begin to ask questions when they become seekers. Certain lifestyles or behaviors can only be changed as an individual experiences the transforming touch of Jesus Christ. The journey begins as they seek to understand the things of Christ. As individuals are drawn closer to God, the church patiently waits for God to bring His work to completion, living an

[44] Minatrea, *Shaped By God's Heart,* 107.
[45] Moerman, *Discipling Our Nation: Equipping The Canadian Church For Its Mission,* 152.
[46] Frost & Hirsch, *The Shaping of Things To Come,* 42.

authentic Christian life and community in front of the seeker. At the appropriate time a verbal witness is given, inviting individuals to receive Christ as their Lord and Savior.

On a recent visit with a *missional* pastor in Virginia, I saw this love being expressed first hand. The pastor and his wife gave me a tour of their city, stopping in a dance club to affirm an individual playing in a band. While in the midst of these partiers, I saw a couple totally in love with people just as I believe God is. They were dwelling among them. Talking, affirming… interacting with them on their turf. Stetzer and Putman in *Breaking the Missional Code* make an important observation when they state:

> Those outside the church need a safe place and safe people to help them on their journey toward faith. In cultures like ours, simultaneously pre-Christian and post-Christian, life change is a process that often involves conversion from a radically different worldview to a biblical one. In some cases, that conversion can be instantaneous. In most cases, God draws people to himself through a journey that includes making connections with a Christian community.[47]

They go on to state, "There are two conversions—one temporal and one eternal. The first conversion is the *conversion to community*. With few exceptions, people come to Christ after they have journeyed with other Christians—examining them and considering their claims."[48]

A *missional church* strives to build relationships with those disconnected from God. They seek to connect with them, and then to connect them to their faith community, believing that genuine conversion may come best when it is preceded by belonging.

> A gospel for a postmodern context must recover the New Testament emphasis on individuals finding a new identity within a loving and healing community of faith. This suggests, for instance, a more corporate theology of evangelism, enacted by the entire community into which women and men are invited to participate. A gospel that is "preached" by the shared life of the people of God. Genuine loving relationships will give our message a stamp of authenticity. This dovetails closely with the story told in Acts of a church whose loving embodiment of the gospel and care for one another became a compelling form of evangelism (Acts 2:43-47).[49]

Committed to Appropriate Cultural Adaptability

Imagine a missionary couple moving to Africa or South America. Upon their arrival they notice that the housing is not up to their standards so they use mission groups to build a home similar to what they had back in the states. They also note that the local churches are not much more than huts with dirt floors so they use teams to build a nice sanctuary with proper fixtures… pews and pulpit furniture. Once worship begins they import an organ

[47] Ed Stetzer and David Putman, *Breaking the Missional Code,* (Nashville, TN: Broadman and Holman Publishers, 2006), 123. Used with permission.
[48] Ibid., 124.
[49] Dean Flemming, *Contextualization In The New Testament: Patterns for Theology and Mission* (Downers Grove, Illinois: Intervarsity Press, 2005), 316. Used with permission.

and a piano and teach their congregation the hymns of their childhood. Immediately they begin teaching the locals proper dress (Sunday best) and behavior. Is this missional?

Imagine it is the late 1950's and early 1960's. People from Kentucky and Tennessee are moving to places like Ohio and Michigan to find employment in factories. Their greatest struggle is finding a church like they had back home. Well-intentioned individuals see this as an opportunity to plant churches, to reach people with the gospel, so they rent a building and begin to cruise the local factories and restaurants for license plates from the south. Soon large Southern Baptist churches are built and filled with people from back home. It looks like, sounds like… even feels like church back home. In the 1980's and 1990's those buildings, once filled with people from the south, are empty. What changed? Why the struggle to fill the pews?

It is 2004 and a church planter, fresh out of a seminary in the south, moves to northern Minnesota to plant a church. He has been in church since his childhood and knows just what he wants his new church to look like, how it will operate. He dreams of success and large crowds but discovers that church planting in this environment is difficult. After three years of nothing but pain and anguish he and his family move back home to pastor an established "First Baptist" church. Why did he not succeed?

Imagine it is 2010 and a new church is being planted in an urban setting in North America. The young planter wants to be sensitive to the culture into which he feels called by God to plant his church so he works hard to learn their language and their music. He learns to eat the local food and enjoys hanging out with his new friends. He lives among them and begins to craft a church which looks like and feels like the inner-city God has called him to reach. People feel comfortable with the pastor and the new church. In an effort to be sensitive to the culture in which he now dwells, he decides to not make a big issue over the consumption of alcohol. Wine is served in their small group Bible studies, even an occasional beer. One day the pastor hears of a small group that went away for a long weekend, who partied too hard. People were intoxicated. Is this activity acceptable? Have they taken being contextual too far? What does God say in His Word?

Missional Churches see that their structures, customs, and language are possible barriers to the gospel. Therefore they seek to penetrate the culture in which they are called to serve with the gospel by becoming bilingual, speaking the language of their context in worship, community, and discipleship while maintaining faithfulness to the Word of God. Not only are they bilingual, in many ways they are bicultural. They are living both in the presence and authority of God while living in the world in which they are striving to reach. In our final example above we noted that you can take cultural adaptability too far. If you are not careful, you can sacrifice previously held values in an effort to be connected with the culture. Note that our distinctiveness as the people of God can and will be attractive to the world.

The problem is that as *missional churches* begin to serve in their communities they discover not one, but many cultures, each with their own set of values and behaviors. Today, Canada has people from more than 200 nations, 500 languages and dialects, and more than 1,000 tribes dwelling within its borders.[50] Overseas mission fields have come, and continue to come, to North America. If we are going to be faithful to God's mission to reach all people groups we will have to send missionary teams, called by God, into our own communities to reach these identified people groups while maintaining a witness within our personal world.

Moerman contends that the people groups of Canada are a microcosm of the world. "Canada is unique among the nations in that it officially espouses multiculturalism, seeks increasing numbers of immigrants and has seen Toronto designated by a UN agency as the most multicultural city on the planet."[51] Is Canada a mirror of what the United States is becoming? If so, what does this say to us as church planters? How do we adapt to the culture or cultures God has called us to serve while maintaining integrity? What does this say to organizations and a denomination that are committed to reaching our world with the gospel?

Stetzer states, "A church becomes missional when it remains faithful to the gospel and simultaneously seeks to contextualize the gospel (to the degree that it can) so the gospel engages the hearers and transforms their worldview."[52] Tim Keller notes that a missional church would adapt and reformulate absolutely "everything it does in worship, discipleship, community, and service – so as to be engaged with the non-Christian society around it."[53]

"Every church in every particular place and time must learn to do theology in a way that makes sense to its audience while challenging it at the deepest level."[54] A *missional church* must be indigenous if it is to thrive. It develops slowly as it learns the heart language and behaviors of its focus audience, as it is rooted in its environment. Planters must come into new areas without preconceived notions of what their plant will look like. Issues like choirs or praise bands are determined by the culture. Dress code? Building and interior design? The day, time, or style of worship? Even programs are determined by the culture.

Living Incarnationally

In a missional church, its style of worship, community, and discipleship are appropriately contextualized. Its language, methodologies, and behaviors reflect the culture, and yet they understand it is impossible to reflect each and every culture in their community. Because of the number of cultures or people groups that make up their community, they understand that connection occurs best outside the church within the culture by people who have an understanding and appreciation of the culture—by people from within the culture itself. Mission, therefore, is "not about where the church is, but who the church is, and what it is here to accomplish. It is not location-based, but relational-based. Wherever believers are, those among whom they live and work constitute the mission field. Being missional is not

[50] Moerman, *Discipling Our Nation: Equipping The Canadian Church For Its Mission,* 15.
[51] Ibid., 5.
[52] Stetzer, *Planting Missional Churches,* 25.
[53] Tim Keller, *"The Missional Church" (www.gracepeace.com/articles-for-ministry),* June, 2001, 1.
[54] Flemming, *Contextualization In The New Testament: Patterns for Theology and Mission,* 14.

first about ministering among those we do not know, but living authentically among those we do know."[55]

The church in the past has functioned in many ways as an alternative culture, living as an island unto themselves. Members, when they ventured "off the island", made an effort to "rescue" people from society, returning them to *their* island and indoctrinating them to *their* culture. In the *missional church*, the emphasis is not placed upon withdrawing people from society and introducing them to a new culture. Rather, individuals are connected to the faith community, then to Christ, and then sent back into their network of friends and families to duplicate the process, to *incarnate* the gospel.

Jefferson Calico, pastor of The Church at Cedar Creek, stated in a recent e-mail, "The incarnational idea for me is that we are immersed in the culture yet on many points we stand against the culture. We appear 'normal' at first glance but there ought to be something deeply different about us. It is that point of difference that should be intriguing to others. That point of difference is our totally deep, attachment and love for God in Christ Jesus."

Missional churches must enlist, equip, and commission those who commit themselves to incarnational living. This is true *missional living*. They must become the body of Christ in society. Enlistment includes not only helping people see the lostness of their friends and communities, it must help disciples see how God has created them for service. All are called to be and give a witness. Some are called to minister cross-culturally.

The incarnation of Jesus is our model, our example. Not only was He a man; He was a Jewish man. He worshiped as a Jew with Jews. He spoke their language. He used words and examples from their world. He wore their dress. He worked among them. He lived and shared life with the weak; the despised of society. He fit in so well that many of His contemporary's did not know that He was not one of them; that Israel was not His home. "The incarnation of Jesus makes contextualization not just a possibility but an obligation."[56]And yet Jesus challenged the sins of the religious leaders, the woman at the well, Peter and others. He refused to tolerate their sin or adapt to their culture.

Planting Churches

If being missional requires a church to reflect the culture they are seeking to reach, then church planting must be a natural expression of their ministry. Why? As a missional church seeks to reach its community, it will identify multiple people groups with different worldviews and cultures from their own. Their church discerns they can no longer truly reflect their community, can no longer speak the heart language of *all the people*. They will need to plant churches designed to reach these identified peoples, understanding that there are barriers that prevent people from hearing the gospel even in their churches! Different methodologies, different languages, different life experiences, and different churches are required to reach different peoples. Therefore, the natural response for a missional church is the planting of strong, effective, churches to reach identified unreached peoples who will

[55] Minatrea, *Shaped By God's Heart,* 92.
[56] Flemming, 21.

then duplicate the process. Missional churches see church planting as a natural ministerial expression of a New Testament church.

Some churches strive to plant churches in locations within their community using those that make up their body as a core group. Securing a church planter, they send out a launch team, commissioning them to reach a specific people group similar to their own in an under-reached location. Ideally each daughter church would multiply herself as she establishes herself and attains stability. This is a productive strategy for planting churches but it is limited by the number of professional church planters available.

While not every church sees itself as being capable of being the sole sponsor of a new church plant, every church can be involved in church planting. Some churches form clusters with sister churches to plant churches, while others provide financial support, prayer support, or mission group support on an as needed basis.

Here in North America a growing number of individuals are starting house church networks to facilitate the multiplication of leaders and churches. Larry Kreider states, "Hungry for community and relationship, people are learning the values of the kingdom by first-hand participation. They meet in small groups in homes, offices, boardrooms or restaurants. For them church has become a way of life where discipleship and growth occur naturally as everyone develops his or her gifts and 'learns by doing,' under the mentorship of spiritual fathers and mothers. I like to call this fledgling grassroots phenomenon 'house church networks.'"[57]

A large number of church plants in North America begin in homes. Eventually they may move to a larger facility and conduct worship services and other ministries from that location. A church that meets in a house is different. Their intent is to stay small, to multiply when the group gets too large for meaningful relationships within the entire group. Typically their ministries are not smaller, home-based versions of churches meeting in commercial buildings. Networks are formed, partnerships are created among the churches to enhance their ability to live out the mission of God in their community, region, and around the world.

There is a growing trend among our churches to combine the two models for church planting. A church planter establishes the church around a strategy that calls for weekly gatherings, and then disperses into homes for community and mission throughout the remainder of the week. Therefore, they are attractional and incarnational at the same time.

Randy Frazee in *The Connecting Church* sees connecting the disconnected to God as the mission or purpose of the home group. It is here where a small group of individuals are encouraged to live out the Christian life. It's not just a Bible study, but rather a group who covenants together to live out the following seven principle functions of biblical community: Spiritual formation, evangelism, reproduction, volunteerism, international missions, care, and extending compassion.[58] Some will be formed because of geographical

[57] Larry Kreider, *House Church Networks: A Church for a New Generation* (Ephrata, PA: House to House Publications, 2001), 1. Used with permission.

[58] Randy Frazee, *The Connecting Church,* (Grand Rapids: Zondervan Publishing House, 2001), 82-83. Used with permission.

reasons. Some will be established along affinity lines while others will be connected because of income or education.

This approach requires that the church not offer competing events on the main campus, affirming the ability of the home group to live out God's mission within their community, among their own people group. Christ-followers are allowed to simplify their lives through participation in this one group. This works best when these groups are of the same ethnicity or takes into account the multiple ethnicities represented to the point where a people group focus is adopted. Competition amongst the groups is reduced when worldview issues are addressed.

The Church Planting Group of the North American Mission Board dreams of a day when there will be a New Testament church for every person in every community. We pray that one day there will be a church pursuing every people group in North America and beyond. If we are to see this as a reality in our day, we will need to plant a wide variety of churches across North America.

Intentionally Crossing Cultures

Then Jesus came near and said to them, "All authority has been given to Me in heaven and on earth. Go, therefore, and make disciples of all nations, baptizing them in the name of the Father and of the Son and of the Holy Spirit, teaching them to observe everything I have commanded you. And remember, I am with you always, to the end of the age" (Matt. 28:18-20, HCSB).

But to what people do we reach out? As stated in our second chapter, the command of Christ is to make disciples of all nations, all people groups. Is our focus to be on reaching those most like us (possibly the easiest to reach)? Or does our text require us to make sure that people from every tribe, every tongue have an opportunity to receive eternal life through Jesus Christ and glorify God (see Rev. 5:9-10)?

John Piper, in *Let The Nations Be Glad: The Supremacy of God in Missions*, makes the argument that God is not calling us to reach as many people as possible but rather His command is that we would reach people from all the people groups of the world.[59]A *missional church*, therefore, must be marked by cross-cultural intentionality if every people group in their Jerusalem, Judea, Samaria, and to the ends of the earth are to be reached with the gospel (see Acts 1:8). The calling is to reach all unreached people groups in the world. This requires the planting of indigenous communities of faith with the passion and ability to reach their people group with the gospel of Jesus Christ. Missional churches must be sending teams to minister cross culturally, to facilitate the planting of indigenous churches within unreached people groups. These new churches are to be equipped and committed to reaching all people groups in the world as well, not just their own people. They must intentionally plant churches committed to planting churches amongst all people groups for the glory of God. The issue is not just about reaching as many as possible; it must be to reach people through church planting with the gospel within all people groups.

[59] John Piper, *Let The Nations Be Glad: The Supremacy of God in Missions* (Grand Rapids: Baker Academic, a division of Baker Publishing Group, 1993), 167. Used with permission.

Piper concludes *Let The Nations Be Glad* with this statement, ". . . God's call for missions in Scripture cannot be defined merely in terms of crossing cultures to maximize the total number of individuals saved. Rather, God's will for missions is that every people group be reached with the testimony of Christ and that a people be called out for his name from all nations. Our responsibility is to define missions his way and then obey."[60]

It is critical to note here that for centuries we in North America had to travel across the seas to reach the nations. Today, the nations live in our world. "In Los Angeles, migration has created the world's second largest Mexican city, the second largest Salvadorian city, and the largest Korean city . . . Today the call to cross-cultural ministry doesn't even require going; it just requires staying with a purpose."[61]

Modeling Missional Leadership

A missional church is a biblically faithful, culturally appropriate, reproducing community of Christ-followers who abandon themselves to passionately pursue the living out of God's mission to reach all peoples. As I reflect upon my theological training and the previous mentioned values, I realize that I was not trained to lead this type of church. To be honest, I do not recall ever talking about or acknowledging such a church even needed to exist.

Roxburgh and Romanuk write in *The Missional Leader*, "For more than a century, North American churches were at the center of culture; they were an essential part of most people's belief and value systems. Therefore, leadership skills and capacities were developed around how to most effectively engage people when they came to the church. It was about training men and women who would faithfully run effective branch plants of the denomination so that when people came they would be well served with a set of expected resources, experiences, and programs. Leaders who ran these churches really well grew [sic] in prestige, respect, and influence."[62]

Our world has changed. As a young boy, I loved playing baseball. Today, my children dream of playing soccer. Different game. Different world. It does not make me or them better. It makes us different. Our seminaries trained godly men to serve their churches; to serve within *their* context. Our world however has changed. Additional leadership skills are required.

The challenge for those wishing to lead a missional church is, "How do you move from a model of conducting church where effective pastoral leadership was honored, to an incarnational approach of conducting ministry where Christ-followers are equipped to function as servants and as missionaries? To a place where the pastor serves less as a teacher and more as a coach?" The implications are tremendous for our colleges and seminaries. How do we retool those serving in the field? How do we train leaders for tomorrow… for today? What characteristics or skill sets are required to advance the kingdom of God?

60 Piper, 222.

61 Erwin McManus, *An Unstoppable Force* (Loveland, CO: Group Publishing, 2001), 45. Used with permission.

62 Alan J. Roxburgh and Fred Romanuk, *The Missional Leader* (San Francisco, CA: Jossey-Bass 2006), 8. Used with permission.

As I reflect upon the values of a missional church, I have developed the following list of skills and values needed by the leaders within a missional church:

1. The ability to lead a body in doing an exegesis of a community aimed at identifying people groups and their world views
2. Bilingual: Having the ability to speak the language of the culture and God's kingdom
3. Bicultural: Having the ability to dwell in the focus community while dwelling in the presence of the Father; connecting with the culture while staying grounded in God's Word
4. The ability to listen and ask good questions when relating to the disconnected
5. The ability to assist people in discovering their giftedness for ministry and to connect those gifts with viable ministry in the harvest
6. The ability to create an environment where people have the freedom to dream and are encouraged to develop God-sized dreams regarding their role in living out the mission of God
7. The ability to identify, equip, and release indigenous people to participate in kingdom activities and plant new churches
8. Authenticity
9. The sensitivity to involve God's people in the development of contextual strategies that flow out of purpose, values, prayer, God's Word, the needs of lost peoples, and so on
10. Hospitality for the unchurched
11. The ability to anticipate and navigate rapid change; having the ability to see the present and the future at the same time
12. The ability to guide the formation and practice of authentic Christian community
13. Creativity
14. A powerful passion to see lives transformed through a personal relationship with Jesus Christ

McManus states, "His (an apostolic pastor's) entire calling is wrapped up in the calling out of God's people to fulfill God's purpose."[63]

Summary

I have defined a missional church as a Biblically faithful, culturally appropriate, reproducing community of Christ-followers who abandon themselves to passionately pursue the living out of God's mission to reach all peoples. Their emphasis? Engaging culture in such a way that language and cultural barriers are removed (while maintaining a commitment to the Word of God) to enable them to connect the disconnected with God.

[63] McManus, *An Unstoppable Force,* 76.

The values identified are:

1. A passion to carry out the mission of God
2. A call to authentic Christian living
3. Responding to the call of God
4. Simplicity in purpose, process, and programming
5. An intentional, unconditional love for all people
6. Cultural adaptability
7. Incarnational living
8. Church planting activity
9. Cross-cultural intentionality
10. Missional leadership development

As I have reflected upon these values and the derived definition, I am convinced that being *missional* is not a new model for conducting church. Whether a church follows a traditional, purpose driven, house, or some other model for operating their church, they can choose to be missional. It is not an additional program or add-on to their schedule of events. It must become the very essence of who the church is.

The essence of every New Testament Church must be to reach every person, from every tribe and nation, with the gospel in their heart language as the highest expression of their love for God. They must be contextual. They must be faithful to the Word of God. Church planting must be seen as the most effective way to reduce lostness in North America and around the world.

CHAPTER FIVE

Redeeming the Culture Through Missional Living

By Jack Allen

Professor, New Orleans Baptist Theological Seminary

New Orleans, Louisiana

The past fifty years were not kind to Southern Baptists. The number of growing Southern Baptist churches shrinks every year. Research conducted at the Leavell Center for Evangelism and Church Health at New Orleans Baptist Theological Seminary found that 89 percent of Southern Baptist churches sit at plateau or fall in decline. Baptisms have never reached the high water marks of the mid 1950s.[64] Data reflect that, as a group, the SBC lost its focus on God's mission of delivering the Gospel to every people group in North America.

While the Southern Baptist Convention succeeded over the past three decades in reclaiming the verbally inspired Bible as our authority, we became less missional. It seems that while the Conservative Resurgence fought to regain lost ground in our churches, the prevailing church-challenged culture moved farther away from us. Believers today live in a hot war raging for the souls of people enslaved by sin. The prevailing culture reflects its devotees' drive toward destruction. The question today is not how will we reestablish biblical authority in our churches, agencies, and institutions; but what will we do now that biblical authority stands? Will we protect the Word, but not do what it says? Sound theology should lead to sound missiology. Why, then, do the evangelism statistics of the North American evangelical church (specifically the SBC churches) show us to be theologically alive but missionally dead? Why do we see so little evangelism in our churches?

The purpose of this chapter is to explain three behavioral models that believers employ when evangelizing nonbelievers in the prevailing, North American culture, and to help believers become effective evangelists by adopting missional behavior.

Evangelism and Culture

Evangelism is first a spiritual exercise that is governed by the sovereignty of God. Evangelism is not done outside of God's will. He draws persons to Christ (see John 6:44). He gives believers appropriate words to say at appropriate times and the faith to say them faithfully.

Second, evangelism is a cultural exercise that one's words and delivery style affects. When one chooses culturally sensitive words, he cares for the needs of others as well as his own (see Phil. 2:4). If, however, he chooses insensitive words, he makes it more difficult for his hearers to receive the Good News.

---

[64] Personal interview with Bill Day, 12 Sep 2006.

The nature of the Gospel offends and confronts people. It plainly proposes that all people are all wrong, born with glass souls, have smashed their souls to irreparable bits, and will spend their forever days in hell. God, however, graciously offers a miraculous recreation of the wrecked soul. God provides a way for the all wrong to become alright through the sacrifice of His Son. If the hearer understands it, the Gospel is Good News, if he does not understand it or he ignores it, the Good News is bad news indeed. It would seem therefore, that a believer has some responsibility to deliver the news intelligibly. Missional evangelism recognizes that people respond to God's graceful message more easily when it is good news delivered by a good neighbor. Openness to share one's home and possessions, soft words at stressful times, or helping clean the neighborhood park exemplify missional acts that lead to opportunities to express the Gospel verbally.

Richard Niebuhr and Harvie Conn can help us understand the need to find the right words to develop relationships with people of different cultures who do not yet know Christ. Niebuhr taught Christian ethics at Yale Divinity School from 1931 until his death in 1962. His most well-read book remains Christ and Culture (1951), wherein he describes the various ways that churches respond to culture.[65] Harvey Conn taught missions at Westminster Theological Seminary from 1972 until his death in 1999.[66] Conn's chapter in *Planting and Growing Urban Churches* uses three of Niebuhr's types to understand how churches engage culture in urban settings.[67]

To clarify Conn's and Niebuhr's views, when the church deals with the world, it can be looked at as the universal Church (upper case C), and, therefore not easily compartmentalized. In truth, the Church is made up of many different local gatherings that North Americans refer to as churches (lower case c). Local churches, in turn, consist of individual believers. The set apart, holy ones of God (church members) deal with the world antithetically, paradoxically, and in ways that transform culture, often simultaneously.

Three behavioral models emerge to inform us from Niebuhr's and Conn's individual work. In the first model, Christ stands against culture, maintaining strict separation between the church and the prevailing culture because the latter is not redeemed. Within the second model Christ and culture exist in a paradoxical relationship where the Church simultaneously wants to partake of the culture and expects it to be Christianized. Third, Christ transforms the culture by the Church's direct influence—its redemptive acts from *within* the culture. Each model will receive further treatment later in the chapter. For now, it helps to understand that all North American churches interact with the prevailing culture in one of the three mentioned models.

Many churches adopt something from the culture such as PowerPoint slides or contemporary music. Other times, churches try to keep the culture outside the church (immodest clothing or explicit language for example). Ultimately, the relationship between the cultures inside and outside the church boils down to relationships. The focus becomes

[65] Wikipedia, s.v. H. Richard Niebuhr, http://en.wikipedia.org/wiki/H._Richard_Niebuhr, accessed 4 Oct 2006.
[66] Westminster Theological Seminary, "Dr. Harvie Conn Home with the Lord (1933-1999)," *http://www.missiology.org/EMS/bulletins/conn.htm*, accessed 4 Oct 2006.
[67] Harvie M. Conn, ed., *Planting and Growing Urban Churches: From Dream to Reality,* (Grand Rapids, MI: Baker Books, a division of Baker Publishing Group, 1997), 192-202. Used with permission.

how individual believers will deal with individual non-believers. These relationships determine how believers either deliver or withhold the Good News from non-believing individuals.

Individuals tend to gather in groups. Sometimes those groups segregate themselves along nationalistic lines: Koreans, Indians, Saudis, Mexicans, Haitians, Guatemalans, Chinese, etc. Other groups gather by economic status or a particular affinity: graphic artists, neo-bohemians, real estate brokers, political mavens, monogamous homosexuals, musicians, neo-barbarians—the list seems endless in North America today. Each of the groups mentioned act like a distinct people group. Christians can wall off from the Gospel an entire people group by cultural insensitivity with regard to their presentation. Yes, how we present the message matters!

Believers gather in churches, so, while individual believers differ in many ways, it is unlikely that a church can move forward missionally unless its believers unite in the way they express the Gospel to outsiders. Models of engagement and discipleship become ingrained in the lives of the individual believers and then flow into the life of the church becoming, if you please, the DNA of that church. If one gathers a significant number of missional believers, one will have a missional church. Missional believers generate missional churches.

Moreover, missional churches more completely reflect the biblical picture of God's self-revelation to humanity; the first missional act. God spoke to Abraham, Jacob, Moses, and the other prophets with a mission on His mind. God came to humanity in the person of Jesus to reveal His mission of redemption for a humanity separated from Him by depravity.

The converse also holds that when apathetic, ignorant, selfish, or otherwise simply misinformed believers gather as a church, the church dysfunctions. A church that slides through the surrounding culture as an irrelevant afterthought (or non-thought), misrepresents the missional nature of God.

In a non-missional (or anti-missional) church, the Good News ceases to be good. Simply stated, a non-believer immersed in a non-Christian culture cannot understand Christ's message when its bearer uses unfamiliar or offensive language or style (nonbelievers do not speak Christianese). For instance, if one attempts to communicate the Gospel by assuming that his or her hearer believes the Bible to be absolute truth, but the other person thinks within a postmodern framework, the message will not hit its mark. Nor will a believer find a receptive audience if he or she tries to reach persons accepting of the prevailing North

American culture by first criticizing their lifestyle choices. Believers commit a crime against the Kingdom when they communicate the best news in a way that diminishes its value.[68]

Believers on Mission

If the Gospel promises one thing, it promises to add value to one's life. God gives people inherent value by making us in His image. The Son of God valued people so much that He gave His life for us. God will tell people how to live the best possible life on earth, how to endure the natural suffering that comes with life on a broken planet, and how to overcome evil, each of which is valuable. Because of Jesus' action in a specific place at a specific time, people can trust God. People can actually live forever in a perfect place. All these propositions mean something good has happened to humanity. God revealed Himself, and He draws His children to Himself (see John 12:32). No one knows how many people or exactly how He draws them, just that He draws them to Himself and that He is consistent.

As missional followers of Christ, we engage people from increasingly anti-Christian cultures. We learn their language so that we may tell them about the God we know. We pray the Lord draws enough people to Himself that they recreate the culture to reflect His goodness to more people. The culture follows the people in the culture, so we can logically say that as missional believers help people find a relationship with Christ, the culture will become easier on people. One might think of a culture with less pain; one that better cultivates Christ's equity, justice, kindness, tolerance of frailty, and intolerance of brutality.

---

[68] Sometimes, one hears postmodernism flippantly referred to as the idea that the only absolute truth is that there is absolutely no way to know the truth. This is fun to say at parties, but not an accurate portrayal of postmodernism. Postmodernism is a reaction against the past 500 years of modernism. Postmodernism is not so much anti-Christian as it is a-Christian, that is, it removes Christianity's uniqueness and renders it lifeless, meaningless, irrelevant. In postmodern thought, Christianity is non-Christianity.

Neither system—postmodernity nor modernity—is particularly friendly to Christianity. Modernism tries to take the mysteries out of life by making sure every truth claim first filters through a sieve of sensory perception; i.e., nothing miraculous happens. Reality is what is true, and what is true is universally measurable.

Postmodernism loves life's mysteries. Most postmodern thinkers believe in a god, though they have trouble explaining which one and they certainly will not criticize your view of any god except an exclusive one like the One in the Bible. Postmodernism claims that one's personal experiences color his or her perception of truth. Therefore, his truth is relative to hers. Truth does not necessarily represent reality because while reality is foundational, the truth is colored by one's perception of it. Modernism logically implies that one cannot accept miraculous Bible stories as historically accurate.

Modernism allows one to hold a position that Christ did not rise from the grave and still call himself a Christian. One might call such persons at best confused and at worst hypocrites. Modernism can exacerbate another human tendency—that of putting too much stock in the eternal value of our good deeds—by its desire to replace God's miraculous grace with humanity's measurable works. The former misrepresents Christianity as intellectually untenable; the latter represents it as legalism.

The postmodern fellow is less hypocritical than his modern brother. He will not accept a biblical, monotheistic God as absolute truth because the reality that the Bible claims to represent is (he thinks) adjusted by the perceptions of its writers and its reader. He goes about his day creating his own mystery to grab onto when things will not work out to meet his goals. He creates his own theology and worships his own finite, impotent, unknowable, and often capricious god(s). Postmodernism allows for nothing certain and demands that its followers accept competing truths. The logical conclusion is that competing truths cancel one another out so that nothing is true. If nothing is true, then everything is meaningless.

At this point, it will help to look more carefully at the behavioral models of how believers engage the culture around them. The first model exaggerates reality to make the point that Christ does not want believers to disengage from their prevailing anti-Christian culture.

Believers Against Culture

A believer living in opposition to his surrounding culture thinks of Christianity as the answer to the societal problems he sees. He becomes zealous for cultural change, and in his zeal, criticizes assorted non-Christian elements in a few of his surrounding cultures. He cannot hit all the bad in all the places he sees it. He tends to make generalizations and tries to hone in on a few areas that highlight his displeasure; i.e., abortion, homosexuality, or alcohol abuse. His presupposition is correct; Christ can improve the human condition, but his methodology for causing change demonstrates very few effective results. The model pits a believer against a culture, and by extension, his or her church against the prevailing culture. To take the model to its logical conclusion, Christ stands against any culture not fully accommodating a Christian worldview.

Christ did not oppose his surrounding culture. He sought to transform individuals. Jesus told his followers to be salt and light (see Matt. 5:13-16). He wants believers involved in culture. He traveled to Samaria and spent time talking to a woman who was clearly outside His culture. He spoke openly with her, was sensitive to her needs, and told her the truth. As a result, He drew many persons from her culture to Himself—He saw a great conversion of lost souls (see John 4:1-42).

In reality, few believers stand fully against their prevailing cultures either. Who can imagine a North American with no cultural engagement whatsoever? Who could possibly live without ever finding herself entertained by television, movies, or plays; never eating at popular restaurants; never laboring at a secular job?

More typical is the believer (and by extension the church) who adopts a church-friendly subculture that stands in condemnation of the prevailing church-unfriendly culture. So, rather than a church against a culture, one more likely finds a church that is very unsure about its willingness to love nonbelievers. A believer acting against culture will say something like, "The world is going to hell. There's no point in witnessing to those people, Jack! They're animals. Pray for them; yes we will, but we're wasting our time with anything further. The best thing we can do is teach the Bible to our church, and take care of each other. That's it."

Sin is nasty, a thing from which believers rightly want separation. Many believers adopt a fortress mentality thinking they will guard themselves against sin. They strive for purity by standing against a prevailing culture, which may be a good motive, but it almost always comes across as condemnation, which is a sin.[69] Moreover, Christian condemnation of those outside the faith turns into self-condemnation when so many church members participate in the very things we decry (see Lk. 6:37; Ro. 2:1; 1 Cor. 6:11). The attitude of condemnation is exactly what pitted Jesus against many of the Pharisees.

[69] By condemnation, we mean the level of judgment that the Lord reserves for Himself. Believers can and should judge behaviors (1 Cor 2:14), but we are not to condemn someone as irredeemable.

Condemnation results in a pro-Christian-subculture with virtually no meaningful contact with persons in the prevailing culture. Believers spend most of their time with other believers and rarely, if ever, have a non-believing friend with whom they can discuss Jesus. Believers do not have liberty to condemn people. The Against Culture model takes liberty where Christ has not granted it.

When one offers Christ while simultaneously raving against the prevailing culture, he produces more obstacles than disciples. If one engages a culture as an outsider and spikes unbelievers with a pounding volley of tracts or misunderstood phrases, has he not left the nonbeliever thinking of Christ as angry, harsh, and uncaring rather than redemptive?

Evangelism in a separationist model hits and runs. Because the believer does not remain in the culture, his method cannot be called missional. Missional believers share their lives with the people in the prevailing culture to make disciples. Believers living in opposition to their culture remain distant. They find no need to be a witness to their communities; their desire is to separate from non-believing cultures.

Perhaps the reader thinks the problem is overstated. Many mission-friendly churches hate the culture outside their church walls, but at least they pay missionaries' salaries (like mine), pray for missionaries, and often treat their missionaries better than they treat their own pastors. They take periodic mission trips, observe needs, do some very helpful things, and then go home. Such active, mission-friendly churches do not live angrily or completely separate from their prevailing non-Christian cultures. They try to represent Christ, but just cannot get themselves to love persons of different cultures. We cannot rightly condemn these mission-friendly churches, nor can we call them missional.

While believers immersed in their Christian subculture want to be evangelistic, their evangelism is abnormal. It is something for which one girds himself and goes out to do, rather than the normal result of knowing Christ. The believer against culture focuses his concern on his needs and ignores the pragmatic reality that reaching people for Christ demands that the message make sense to them. He says, in effect, "Those people really need Jesus, but first they need to think like me." His method offers peanuts to people with a peanut allergy. He sees people starving to death, and knows that his peanuts may kill them, but he is not really worried about their death. He worries about handing out more peanuts.

It seems that more believers stand against culture as the culture gets more offensive to Christianity and more tolerant of unchristian views. Modeling a harsh separation from the culture seems easier to justify today, and presents a dangerous environment for the future of Christ's church in North America. Evangelism becomes ineffective in proportion to the measure that believers separate from the people who live within the culture apart from Christ. Over the past several decades, as the prevailing culture tolerated Christianity less, believers separated from it more. Simultaneously, effective evangelism ebbed. Still, few believers hate the prevailing culture or the unbelievers who populate it. A more common model is the believer who lives in paradox with the prevailing culture.

Believers and Culture in Paradox

Believers living in paradox with their neighbors see their Christian lives as better than their neighbors' non-Christian lives, want to help their neighbors find Christ, and do not want to condemn their neighbors. Believers in paradox have a good bit of contact with their prevailing culture, but have neither the will nor the tools to help the people around them know Jesus. The church in paradox exists alongside its godless neighbors, within the culture they created together, but the church does not understand its role in the culture.

The paradox model makes evangelism much easier than the model that goes against culture. But the paradoxical view of culture is still confused. Believers constantly discuss what the culture does that stands on the other side of the boundary lines of biblical living. It asks at what point one should separate from culture.

At the end of the day the paradox model is kinder, but still running from culture. Believers go into an area with love in their hearts, share the gospel, and then get out of there as fast as they can.

Evangelism in a paradoxical model looks less confrontational at home and more confrontational when away from home. The paradoxical believer occasionally travels to a different culture, confronts nonbelievers with the gospel, and goes home to be non-confrontational with his neighbors. He thinks his solid marriage and good work ethic will cause his neighbors to ask him about Jesus. Very rarely does he start a conversation in his neighborhood or workplace intentionally looking for the moment when he will encounter the difficult life questions that only Christ can answer. His only experience with evangelism is confrontation—a necessary pill to be swallowed out of town. In this model evangelism becomes a highly abnormal exercise. It is again something one does if one must. It is not a representative outflow of one's recreated personhood in Christ.

Believers living in paradox are not living missionally, but they are mission-friendly. They support the mission work of others. They love to send missionaries away to live in a culture and they hope to go for a visit next time vacation rolls around. They hope and pray for new believers and new churches in the targeted culture. They even hope for a change in the culture, but do not typically have any personal stake in that culture. Harvie Conn observes that the believer in paradox, like the anti-culture view, owns no property in the culture, and therefore feels little need to persevere through all the stages of his mission efforts.[70] Believers in paradox go into a culture they want to redeem, but they leave at day's end. Missional believers *invest* in the culture and remain after dark.

Most North American evangelicals embrace the paradoxical model. Many churches have great mission hearts that support the Cooperative Program (thank you, please continue) and other biblical mission enterprises. When it comes to living within the culture intentionally to win people to Christ, however, there is still that paradox of separation. Believers in paradox do not hate the culture, postmodernism, foreigners, or hippies—they do not really hate anyone. They consume what they like about the culture (movies, art, restaurants), but do not often plant gospel seeds in the prevailing non-believing culture.

[70] Conn, 201.

When they do plant gospel seeds, they certainly do not hang around to water them and see them grow. Perhaps the willingness to invest in others in their culture (not requiring them to cross over to the church culture first) is the most easily observable difference between mission-minded believers (paradoxical believers) and missional believers who want to transform the culture for Christ.

Believers Transforming Culture

Missional believers want to transform the culture for Christ one person at a time. It seems that believers wanting to transform culture do not think of culture as either sanctified or evil, but merely as the result of the gathered habits of people living within that particular culture. Missional believers think more positively about their prevailing culture because they focus on the redemption Christ brings to a people who, in turn, reform their culture to glorify Him in new ways. Missional believers know that Jesus can change everything.

The word *holistic* offers a good modifier to explain Christ's all-encompassing transformation. Holistic transformation helps us understand a missional attitude. Holistic transformation offers Christ's recreation to a person's heart, soul, mind, and strength, therefore, missional people address a person's emotional, spiritual, intellectual, and physical needs. Missional believers include all four spheres in evangelism. Missional people reach for emotional health by understanding that people need friends, and they need to be loved precisely where they live. Sure, people in the culture need to clean up their misbehaviors, but they need to be loved within those misbehaviors first.

Missional Christians touch the minds of yet-to-be-believers by relating the depths of human experience to the deep truths of the Bible. Surface answers will not do for people concerned with environmental politics, racism, job discrimination, teacher shortages, AIDS, overpriced housing, legalization of marijuana, homosexual marriage, single-parent families, or a cost-benefit analysis of war. Transformation demands intellectual rigor—surface scratching answers will not go unchallenged. Mental exercise dives deep to understand how God works and how people tick. The difficulties of classical disciplines such as theology, philosophy, or ethics do not deter transformational believers. Before the culture will accept the Bible as the perfect book, believers will need to engage peoples' minds more deeply. Missional believers realize that mental assent to biblical inerrancy is not the point of evangelism! Evangelism's goal is making disciples, which includes Christ's redemption of the whole person: mind, heart, soul, and physical body.

Missional believers understand that life often comes apart because of one's physical needs. The Gospel includes physical help. Because Christ died a physical death, his death leads to a physical change, meaning that when a believer dies, he or she receives a new physical body that will not decay, but will live forever (see 1 Cor. 15:35-44). That is not all, however, for the Gospel is also good news to those who suffer physical ills in this life. While we can not predict His physical healings, one is foolish to deny that Jesus sometimes heals the physical ailment of persons with faith. Moreover, Christ gives all of His followers the ability and task to bring physical healing wherever we are able. Someone who is thirsty, hungry, suffering in prison, or too cold at night needs food, clean water, a visit, or some more clothes. Missional believers provide for such physical needs, and in so doing, they offer common grace and good news.

The previous two behavioral models (Believers Against Culture, and Believers and Culture in Paradox) do not offer an effective method for evangelism in North America. Based on the current deplorable response of people in North America to the Gospel, combined with the fact that most evangelicals either stand against prevailing culture or confused alongside their prevailing culture, one easily concludes that the two perspectives are highly ineffective. Since two ineffective models dominate evangelical churches in twenty-first century North America, we may have found a significant reason why so little disciple-making happens here.

To be missional is to be evangelistically effective. Missional living means evangelism is not so much something to be done (an action to be taken) as it is a part of one's being as a new creation in Christ. Missional evangelism will imitate Christ and the early church by its willingness to take time and stay within a culture until people come completely to Christ. As such, missional evangelism may take longer to make converts, but it will not stop at conversion—missional evangelism makes disciples.

Niebuhr called his final model "Christ the Transformer of Culture." He observed a model that counts on Christ to work through people to transform culture completely. Niebuhr sees the model worked out most clearly in the Gospel of John. With Christ, believers can so love the world that we cannot condemn it but look to Him to save it (see Jn. 3:16-17). Without Christ, believers can do nothing (see Jn.15:5). Paul also wrote extensively about Christ's redemptive transformation of the whole person (see Col. 3:1-17), as did Augustine and John Calvin.[71]

To transform the prevailing culture demands that believers first transform the Christian subculture into one that lives missionally. Believers might start by measuring that which pleases God: mercy, justice, and humility (see Mic. 6:8). Missional Christianity will mark its territory with love, and Jesus guarantees that the world apart from Him will take notice of missional love. Some will join the family of God and others will hate believers more than they do now, but the church will get noticed (see Jn. 13:35, 15:18-19). Few persons who have dealt with the culture think that believers will see transformation anytime soon, but that's not the point. The transformer model does not expect humanity to actively transform much of anything. It is rather, faith in Christ the Transformer, in Christ the Creator in whom a missional believer trusts.

There is no running in this model. Evangelism is done by personal, steady, consistent lifestyle and words of grace. Rather than stay in his comfortable Christian sub-culture, transformers spend most of their time with their non-Christian neighbors. In that sense, the transformation is thoroughly missional.

The missional believer invests her life in the lives of non-believers—she trades her needs for theirs. When she goes to dinner, she listens more. She never forces the topic of

[71] H. Richard Niebuhr, *Christ and Culture* (New York: Harper and Row, 1951; Harper Torchbooks, 1975), 196, 206, 217. Used with permission.

conversation onto spiritual matters, but gently guides peoples' natural curiosity about how God does things. She remains constantly and intentionally aware of her neighbor's spiritual need and is always prepared to discuss faith in Christ (see 1 Pet. 3:15).

A missional believer recognizes pain in his neighbor's life and he learns to speak the language that demonstrates God's grace. Even when his neighbor makes a terrible mess of her life, he will express Christ's ability to transform her condition. The transformer offers love that does not require or consume anything.

Transformational behavior is messy, and this is the point at which it becomes synonymous with missional behavior. Missional living leads to a messy life. It leads to phone calls at the wrong times. Missional living will cost believers sleep when conversation goes into the wee hours. A missional home puts order behind time spent with non-believing friends. It opens a room to one in need of a place to stay. It puts up with children who do not know how to handle one's dishes carefully. Missional evangelism is confrontational at times, but is more often marked by wisdom, kindness and an almost irrational trust in God to transform people.

Missional believers will not intentionally cross moral or legal boundaries, but know that the immediate need for Christ in a culture demands that one holds his tongue in spite of many sins observed. Christ comes first. They cannot focus on outward appearances. The abuse of alcohol, tobacco, drugs, and sex are specific points at which missional believers must willingly engage messy lives in order that some might be saved. A missional believer must somehow actually separate the sin from the sinner, and not merely talk about doing so. Instead of sinful behavior, he focuses on God who has sent him to the people in need of grace. He looks past many things so he may see the person. He will look past an individual that curses every other word, and that will purposely offend a Christian either curiously seeking a reaction or to see if he can be driven away. He understands that the enemy will try to make him angry, afraid, and impatient so that he will run back to a safer environment and away from the culture that so desperately needs Good News.

For the redeemed man or woman of God, missional evangelism is the normal state of following Christ. The most important mark of missional evangelism is its normalcy. Rather than something that one puts on like a uniform for peculiar occasions, missional believers embrace evangelism as one of the most normal things they do. Missional people choose secular employment intentionally to have more contact with people who need Christ. Church planters, when missional, choose intentional (not bivocational) employment in a secular environment. Missional people give up some salary by making coffee drinks instead of occupying a large church's pastoral office because they cannot stand to trade the lost world in need for the safety of their study. Will it not be a wonderful day when a church supplements its pastor's salary to serve coffee at the local shop so he can be more effective for the kingdom? Missional believers will turn such wild dreams into reality with extra foam on top.

The model demonstrates a life that imitates the apostle Paul, who went into an area, found a job, developed relationships with lost people, neighbors, and coworkers; and led them to Christ. Since tents do not sell too well in twenty-first century North America, missional believers will start service businesses that connect with nonbelievers in different ways. Lawn services meet the same people every few days for years on end. Hair stylists, financial consultants, lawyers, apartments managers, nannies, painters, and yes, artists all have opportunities to demonstrate Christ to a secular culture.

Transformers make friends with the parents of their children's friends because that is a normal thing that one does. Through the power of the Spirit, they pray diligently and wait expectantly for the opportunity to lead their new friends to Christ.

They serve in their community so they can gain credibility with people and tell them about Jesus. Missional churches fill with people who expect opportunities to specifically, clearly, and lovingly demonstrate the love of Christ and offer a verbal witness of the Good News of Jesus Christ.

Summary

Three prevailing elements emerge for effective evangelism. First, the Holy Spirit must be completely in charge for one to effectively cut through the prevailing cultural morass to reach people with the Gospel. Only the Holy Spirit can give us the boldness to love people beyond our comfortable barriers. He gives us the right words to say in love that avoids our tendencies to sound condemning. The Holy Spirit provides us with insight and direction when we do not know what to do. Most importantly, it is the Spirit who opens the hearts of non-believers to the missional message (see Acts 16:14).

Second, missional men and women must enjoy a passionate love for people. They feel a magnetic calling, an inexplicable drawing to a particular people group or sub-culture. Missional believers possess the Father's love for all people and yet acknowledge a sense of His calling to reach these people.

Third, missional belief needs time and a place to demonstrate its love. Missional living and effective evangelism require space for casual, sustained interaction with non-believers. Typically, the only spaces deemed safe enough for non-believers to drop their guard are public environments within the community. A coffee shop, park, soup kitchen, art gallery, shoe store, or health club come to mind first. A sanctuary might fit the need, but only after decades of hard work.

To develop the kinds of places needed to engage the prevailing culture requires financial investment from the larger Christian community. To avoid the need and not support missional believers now will inevitably result in the same complete collapse of Christianity in North America as has occurred in Western Europe.

A movement of missional believers seems to be in its incipient phase in every city in the U.S. Perhaps the Holy Spirit will usher in the next phase of Christianity in North America as an era when evangelism becomes *normal* for Christ-followers. This is my prayer.

Part 2

CHAPTER SIX

Sending… Same Activity… Same Mission…

"As You sent Me into the world, I also have sent them into the world." John 17:18

Sending! If there is an activity that provides us with a glimpse of the heart of God, it is *sending*. God loved His people so much that He *sent* His Son to earth. He became flesh and dwelt among us to seek and save the lost. Driven by a love for His people, by a passion to see the disconnected connected, God *sent* His Son. Jesus then *sent* the twelve. He *sent* the seventy with the same activity, same mission: God's mission to form one people from all peoples. In John 17:18, Jesus acknowledges that He was *sent* by the Father and that He now sends the church—same activity, same mission, God's mission. In the Book of Acts, we see that God then *sent* the Holy Spirit to empower His disciples, to allow God Himself to reside in the lives of believers. This same Spirit compels, *sends*, us into the harvest to proclaim the gospel of Christ, to seek and save the lost—same activity, same mission—driven by a love for people, by a passion to see the disconnected connected to God and His people.

Sending! If there is an activity that captures, that stirs the hearts of Southern Baptists, it might be *sending*. When a group of ministers met in Augusta, Georgia in 1845, to establish the Southern Baptist Convention (SBC), they simultaneously created two separate boards to oversee the domestic and foreign missionary work of the Convention. One of the three main purposes of the Board of Domestic Missions was the *sending* of missionaries to frontier settlements. Today, the North American Mission Board *sends* more than 5,000 missionaries into North America to proclaim the gospel and plant new churches. The Foreign Mission Board held its first commissioning service in 1846. Since then more than 15,000 missionaries have been *sent* to proclaim the gospel around the world. Today, a third of that number still serve through the International Mission Board. Same activity, same mission—driven by a love for people, by a passion to see the disconnected connected to God and to His people.

Since 1845 Southern Baptists have been *sending* missionaries through our agencies, literally around the world to proclaim the gospel. Today, across North America there is a renewed emphasis upon *sending*. It too has resulted in the sending of Christ's disciples into the world. But this time it is the local church who is sending missionaries, often without crossing geographical barriers or going through SBC missions agencies. And not necessarily sending them around the world, but rather commissioning them as missionaries or witnesses to serve across town, into their communities, workplaces, apartment buildings, and organizations. *Sending*. Same activity… same mission… driven by a love for people, by a passion to see the disconnected connected to God and to His people.

Are these churches *missional*? Would it be better to describe them as indigenous? Culturally engaged? Incarnational? Missionary sending? Missionary producing? Immersed in culture? First century? Biblical? Acts 1:8? Normal? All of these terms, including missional, "could" describe a church with a passion for sending disciples into the harvest to intentionally engage the lost, the disconnected, from all people groups in their heart language. Some disciples, called of God, will be sent as missionaries, crossing cultural barriers to reach the lost and establish New Testament churches. Others, out of a love for God and people, will be sent into their sphere of relationships and proclaim the good news of Jesus Christ. Sending—same activity, same mission—God's mission.

In the following pages, we will explore the activities of churches across North America that share four common characteristics:

- A passion to reach the lost with the gospel of Jesus Christ
- An appropriate connection or adaptation to the culture (contextualization) in which they serve
- A faithfulness to God's Word
- A desire to see new churches planted throughout North America and around the world

My intent as the compiler of this work is not to hold them up as *the model* for reaching North America. Many great churches with these four characteristics exist in Southern Baptist life. Yet, within each of these churches, are values worthy of exploring. Enjoy their stories. Learn from them. Send me additional churches from which we can learn, and we will share them with you in the future.

John M. Bailey
Director of Enlistment and Missional Networks Team
Church Planting Group
North American Mission Board

CHAPTER SEVEN

The Father's House:

Sailing into Uncharted Waters

Think of the missional church as a ship. Ships have many purposes, but mainly, ships sail. A ship would not be a ship if it stayed in one place anchored down. Nor would a ship be a ship if it sat safely at the dock.

The purpose of a ship is to sail, to go, to move, to find adventure. In a similar way, that is the purpose of the missional church. As it was said before, God is a sending God, and thus, His church should be a sending movement of disciples to all corners of the earth. One such corner is a coastal city called Corpus Christi, located in the southern part of Texas. Corpus Christi, a city that is 60 percent Hispanic, is called "the Sparkling City by the Sea," because of its beauty and many tourist attractions. In 2003, Corpus Christi was given the award for All-American City.

More than beauty, awards, and attractions, Corpus Christi is home to The Father's House, a missional church in the heart of the city. The Father's House is about movement —a discipleship movement with the desire to reach Corpus Christi (Jerusalem), the surrounding suburbs and towns (Judea), Texas (Samaria), and all over North America and the world (the ends of the earth). This is why the mission statement of The Father's House says: "To mobilize a Christ-centered movement of multiplying leaders who change the course of human history."

On The Father's House Web page (*www.tfhcorpus.com*), there is a statement, originally penned by the famous Brazilian writer, Paulo Coelho, which really captures the essence of The Father's House. It says: "The dock is the safest place for a ship, but that's not what ships are made for." Intrigued by this, I asked Bob Gomez, pastor and creative architect of The Father's House, to shed some light on this. "Christians need to get off the pew and sweat and bleed," Gomez told me. "Christianity is not safe and predictable. It's on the edge; it's a risk, it's getting out of your comfort zone. And I want to help more and more Christians leave the dock and go into the deep, blue ocean of faith."[72]

A Passion for the Disconnected

Gomez is passionate about helping believers become all-out disciples of Jesus who will *sail* to wherever God will lead them. But his passion goes beyond the four walls of the church to where people are living. (In all reality, The Father's House does not have four walls at all. They use no buildings and meet, mostly, in homes throughout the area.) As a missional leader, Gomez believes that we are to interact with the unchurched and the disconnected by engaging with them on their turf. "I heard Alan Hirsch and Michael Frost, authors of *The Shaping of Things to Come*, speak at a conference about the American church,"

[72] Bob Gomez, phone interview with author, October 2006.

explained Gomez. "They said, 'If you invite people to church, 30 percent of them may come at some point or another. But 70 percent will never attend a church.'"

The traditional model of church tends to go after that 30 percent, although there are some that do reach out to the 70 percent, and do so effectively. Missional churches, however, tend to focus on that 70 percent through building relationships intentionally, oftentimes apart from church buildings and church programs. This is what The Father's House is all about. Many of the people they minister to are those that have been hurt by "the church" in the past or feel that it is irrelevant. Churches, Bob mentioned, tend to be more competitive because they are all going after that 30 percent; and in doing so, are trying to outdo each other by making it bigger or brighter.

Originally from the Corpus Christi area, Bob Gomez started ministry in his home town in Sinton, Texas, where, early on, he started preaching at a local Hispanic church. After he graduated with his undergraduate degree, he started working for Wal-Mart and was transferred to Kingsville, a town to the south of Corpus Christi. After some time, Gomez left Wal-Mart and started serving part-time in a Hispanic church doing youth ministry while working toward his Master's degree.

Eventually, he was asked to start an English service in addition to serving as a youth pastor. He agreed and the service did very well… so well, in fact, that it began to out-grow the main, Spanish-speaking service. Shortly after this, Gomez received a call to come be a full-time pastor at a different church in Kingsville. He agreed and resigned his position, in spite of tension and pressure from his previous church. Nevertheless, he knew God was calling him to make the move, and it was at this church that God really began to reshape Bob's thinking about *church* and what it meant to live missionally as a disciple of Jesus.

A Holy Dissatisfaction

Missional leaders are constantly moving forward, unlearning things they have learned; learning new things and so on. To be missional one must begin to think missionally —which means thinking like a missionary, *going* as a passion-filled witness of Christ, with the purpose of reaching all people groups. And this is what happened to Bob Gomez. He began to see some fundamental flaws with the church he was a part of. This led to what he calls a "holy dissatisfaction" with how the church was expressing itself.

He watched, week after week, month after month, more and more people come to church, sit down, sing songs, listen to an inspirational message, then leave. It was the come-to-us mentality. The church where Gomez was serving became too inwardly-focused and was not reaching the community or the world. He knew that there had to be more. Jesus, after all, went out to where the people lived; He ate with them, spent time with them, and loved on them. "My whole world was Christian… I didn't know any lost people. I was taught, 'come out from among them and be separate,'" Gomez said. Although we are called to be set apart for the Lord we cannot hibernate in our Christian subcultures and "bubbles" and think that is missional. We have to go out, driven by the mission of God, and be where the people are.

His "dissatisfaction" turned into a season of researching and investigating. And so Gomez left his full-time pastorate and ventured out into the uncharted waters of the missional church. This move, however, was not easy and brought about more tension. "The challenge has been the church—the institution, you know, the building with the cross and steeple," Gomez stated. "They (the church) tend to lash out against things they are unfamiliar with. In too many cases, they simply assume we are compromising the gospel just because we don't fit into their existing box of methodology." The reality is, however, Gomez did not compromise the gospel; he began to think missionally about the gospel. "I felt like Joseph," Gomez said. "I had these dreams and visions and people in the church were like 'who do you think you are?' People thought I was nuts."

Church planters that think this way tend to go against the flow of the institutional, traditional church that has dominated our country for years now. They typically move away from programs, attractional services, and how-to sermons. Because of this, it can create some tension with others who think differently.

When Gomez first started the church plant, he created an evangelistic group (what he calls a Huddle) in a town 30 miles from Corpus Christi. Soon after he arrived, he got a call from a local pastor that was very upset that Gomez did not ask "his permission." This pastor did not understand why he was in his territory, and therefore, felt threatened by him. That was the beginning of many more hurtful experiences for Gomez, a young, enthusiastic church planter who was just getting started and feeling misunderstood. When you move out of familiar waters, you can almost expect opposition from religious structures. Jesus sure did.

The Father's House is a grassroots movement that came about as a result of Bob's holy dissatisfaction with the traditional church. Gomez, because of his heart for the lost and disconnected, took what he learned from his previous church experiences and created a discipleship movement from the ground up. This was not so much a reaction for him, but a burning passion to see Christ formed in the lives of people outside the traditional church. Out of this passion, the idea of the Huddle was birthed.

A Huddle is very simple, requiring the selection of a verse or two, and then a discussion following. It's something where lost people can feel comfortable asking questions, where they can see authentic faith lived out, and where they can develop into disciples. The aim is to make Huddles simple, not just teach and preach the Bible. They are about connecting people to God and to other people, reaching people who would never step into a church.

Welcome to Motel Transformation

Just north of Corpus Christi, there is a small, low-income community called Taft. Taft has a reputation for being a rough town with a high percentage of murders and drug abuse. Gomez happened to know a man that worked at a little motel there. One day, he explained to this guy and his girlfriend what a Huddle is. They seemed interested and decided they wanted to have the Huddle right in the motel.

This motel, however, was known for its wild drinking parties. Every other day there was a party, and Bob's friend, feeling guilty for his drinking, dropped out of the Huddle shortly after it started. In time, however, he came back and said he wanted to be a part of the group again and promised Gomez he would not drink.

Gomez told him, "I don't care if you or your buddies want to drink. Just give one hour of your week to learn about spiritual things, that's all I ask." The couple agreed and started up the Huddle again. In fact, they began to grow in their faith and, eventually, the girlfriend became the facilitator of the group.

The Motel Huddle has reached the disconnected people that many would call "outcasts." One particular person—a gang-banging, tattooed-looking guy—caught wind of the Huddle and became curious about it. At first he did not want to come and made sure everyone in the group knew that he did not want to come. But in time, he began to soften up and eventually came. At the end of the Huddle, one last question is asked. The question is, "Who is one person you'd like to see come closer to God?" Then the opportunity is given for people to pray a one-sentence prayer for that particular person.

At the first Huddle this guy came to, he told the group about his son, who was on drugs, and desperately needed God. So, the person next to him prayed for his son. The next week the guys' son showed up! In time, he hosted a Huddle in his home right before he died of liver damage from years of heavy drinking. Gomez mentioned that he and the group were able to engage him in spiritual conversations up to the very end. "Whether he realized it or not," Gomez said, "he was seeking, and I just prayed that before he died he gave his life to Christ." The Motel Huddle is an example of incarnational ministry because it is taking *church* to where people live (or in this case, work and party). Most of those folks would not come in off the street to attend a traditional church—so The Father's House brings church to them.

The Beauty of Community

Huddles are small groups which are open to everyone regardless of age, race, socio-economic bracket, churched, or unchurched. The objective is not to get people to come to church but to invite them into a relationship with Jesus through inviting them to be part of an authentic community. The Father's House is not about growing numerically, necessarily; they are about growing deeper and equipping disciples that can go out and change their world. That is the point of a missional church: to develop and equip disciples and then send them as a witness into their world, with the eyes of a missionary.

This happens best in community, and that is what Huddles are all about. The environment is one where people, no matter where they are in their spiritual journey, can feel loved and valued for who they are. The key is relationships, which take time and wisdom. The wisdom comes in knowing where people are spiritually, what types of needs they have, how much they can handle, and where to lead them next. That is the equipping part of discipleship.

That said, Huddles, in order to be effective in equipping disciples, operate in different stages. Says Gomez, "We move people along in discipleship, which can take a long time. At some point, we need to get past a light-hearted discussion and get deeper in teaching the Word and what it really means to be disciple." So Gomez and his team came up with a standard: After a person's been a part of a Huddle for 10 weeks, they move on to the next level.

The first type of Huddle is your standard small group with the purpose of promoting discussion. The second type of group is called a half-court Huddle, which gets more into Scripture—with a short, expository sermon and some application. After 10 weeks of the half-court Huddle, a person then moves to the last type of group: a full-court Huddle.

A full-court Huddle goes deeper into Scripture, focusing more on expository teaching and application questions on how God speaks into people's lives. There is no particular formula for how Huddles work. It depends on where the person is on their spiritual journey. Some are ready for a full-time Huddle right away. Others, however, may have some baggage and hurts from religion, or just a lot of questions, and need to start with a basic Huddle.

The key is to know where a person is spiritually and then lead him or her to the next level. The ultimate goal, however, is to equip people to become disciples themselves who are making other disciples. Gomez does not see time as a factor in discipleship; he and his leaders equip people to facilitate Huddles right away, not requiring them to jump through hoops. When people come to Christ in Huddles, they are encouraged to find people in their own networks, sharing with their families and friends, and begin a Huddle with them. Gomez uses the word *oikos*, the Greek word for "households," as his strategy for Huddles.

People's households (and other networks) are natural places for people to start making disciples. Again, this takes time, but the point is to start with the people you know and to go from there. One example of this is a lady who received Christ in her Huddle and the following week asked if she could lead that Huddle. "We are re-injecting disciples back into their world to disciple others from day one," Gomez mentioned.

Throughout his years of ministry, Bob Gomez has learned to listen to people and their needs to find out where they fit in this discipleship process. "You need to be able to breathe with people, which takes time," he says. "You can't expect them to go at the pace you'd like them to go." Discipleship is a process that involves community, vulnerability, and patience. It's not a quick-fix, seven-step program, or a six-week class that is taught. We in America have a tendency to rely on formulas and how-to's. But discipleship is not like that; it is all about meeting people where they are and then moving them along the journey one step at a time, removing obstacles that keep them from Jesus. Like a ship out on the high seas, there will be times of great storms and times of great peace. The point is that the ship keeps moving forward, facing whatever it needs to face.

A Disciple-Making Movement

What does a church planting movement look like? What does a disciple-making movement look like? At some point we have to ask ourselves that question. It has been said already that a missional church is a movement away from the traditional, attractional model of church where people come to us, to an incarnational approach in which disciples are sent into the harvest.

The Father's House is a movement-minded church with the purpose of making disciples who will transform the world, and, as their mission states, *change the course of human history*. Last year, The Father's House made an important decision to go back to ground zero and re-think their mission. They decided to stop their public worship services so that it would not compete with the Huddles. They believed strongly in going to where the people are rather than the people having to come to them. Although this paradigm shift has been difficult at times, Gomez and his leaders have embraced this change with great enthusiasm.

As a church, The Father's House has moved away from the come-to-us mentality to an incarnational mentality—that is, going as missionaries to where the people are. Their vision is to saturate their region with reproducing churches, and spread throughout Texas, North America, and the world. To do that, Gomez and his team began to hash out their vision of what a missional movement looks like, and how to mobilize more leaders who want to be a part of it.

The Father's House is made up of leaders who are called and committed to the vision of making disciples by authentically living among the people in Corpus Christi and the Coastal Bend Region. It may appear that The Father's House is a small church, made up of 30 to 35 people; but these people are highly missional and are spread throughout a 70 mile radius. The leaders are missionaries located strategically in five different cities around their region. Gomez says, "Every leader is a seed planted in the middle of their *oikos*, intent on leading people to Christ, and thereby planting a new church in the process." Jesus said that His followers are to be salt and light (see Matt. 5:13-14)—and that is what these leaders are doing—living as salt and light among the people.

The missional movement of The Father's House is based on Deuteronomy 1:13-15 (NIV), "Choose some wise, understanding and respected men from each of your tribes, and I will set them over you . . . So I took the leading men of your tribes, wise and respected men, and appointed them to have authority over you—as commanders of thousands, hundreds, of fifties and of tens." Gomez disciples and shepherds leaders, who in return disciple and shepherd other people (in their Huddles). These leaders, then, come together on a monthly basis—a private meeting not open to the public—to pray, sing, and hear an expository message. The message is recorded and made into a DVD. These DVD-talks are then used as tools for the Huddles. The Father's House is a ministry that is passionate about mobilizing leaders who can reproduce themselves in others. Huddles are the medium in which this is done. Each one looks different, depending on the community in which it is located and the various needs of the group.

Another way that The Father's House attempts to mobilize Christ-followers, and a way to see this movement become more widespread, is through partnership with other local churches in the area. The Father's House is passionate about creating unity among the churches as well as equipping people who have a desire to be missional in their communities but do not know how, or do not have the opportunity. Gomez says, "Our purpose is to mobilize leaders. Why reinvent the wheel? We have been on a long journey of experiments, moving forward and backwards, embracing change and dealing with ensuring pain. Having gone through the desert, we feel prepared and ready to call out the special forces in churches . . . to see a missional movement take place." He has recently started talking with different churches to see if they are interested in this movement. Some churches gave him strange looks and said, "What are you talking about?" Others were more open to him and willing to listen.

Three churches, in fact, have expressed interest in partnering with The Father's House. One church, for example, that is located on the south side of Corpus Christi, seems very interested. Gomez told the pastor that he is not interested in *taking* people from their church, but rather he is looking to raise up missionary-leaders and equip them to plant churches. It is partnership with a purpose. And the purpose is to find, then equip, leaders who are interested in building the kingdom of God in Corpus Christi and beyond. "Even if it is only 10 people," Gomez said, "that would be great. We measures success by how many disciples we can find." Bob Gomez is an example of an apostolic leader who understands the importance of training up people to passionately live out God's mission to reach all peoples.

From Dream to Vision

Apostolic leadership is vital for the health and sustenance of the missional church. Without this leadership, God's mission will be hindered. We must re-think our training and experiences in ministry from the modern, attractional way of church to the incarnational, missional way. Apostolic leaders, like Bob Gomez, are the ones that are (and must!) lead the church in new and fresh ways.

One thing that apostolic leaders do is create an environment that allows people to dream for God. The Father's House does this well. The leaders are constantly asking questions, seeking the heart of God, and dreaming big. In fact, they have put together a few basic values that make up the DNA of The Father's House.

First, is simplicity. As mentioned earlier in this book, simplicity is an essential characteristic to the missional church. For too long the church has been bogged down by lots of programs, building campaigns, finances, and staff issues. "We want to keep things simple, uncluttered, and easily reproducible," Gomez stated. The Father's House is all about loving people as Jesus did and then teaching them to love people the same way. That is it, pure and simple.

Second, The Father's House is focused on moving forward with the vision and a willingness to adapt as necessary. They believe strongly in the importance of appropriate contextualization to effectively reach and disciple indigenous people. Because of this,

Gomez and the leaders have had to embrace various changes in ministry, and at times, difficult changes. But they have adapted well because they know they are called. These leaders understand that being missional is a journey, a journey to learn, re-learn, unlearn, and adapt to the ever-changing culture around them. They know it is a journey because they believe they are *called* to this journey, and are therefore, committed. Gomez does not recruit volunteers; he prays, sets the vision, and watches who God brings along the journey.

Third, The Father's House believes in the importance of accepting people where they are. Rather than judging people, they walk with people and love them for who they are, where they are, and point them to Jesus who can help them become who He wants them to be. "You can't depend on seminary-trained men and woman to make a movement," Gomez said. "What you need are people who love Jesus with all their hearts! That's how a movement takes place. We've begun to see glimpses of that happening."

In addition to these values, The Father's House sees a bigger picture of God's mission in the world. They have a commitment to carry out God's mission to reach all peoples, beyond Corpus Christi and its surrounding areas. This mission starts at home (in their Jerusalem) and then moves out from there. Although a large percentage of those involved in the Father's House are Hispanic, they see beyond their own people group and are reaching out to other people groups as well, with the goal of making disciples of "all nations."

The first goal is to see every leader of The Father's House (those that are committed to the vision and meet monthly) develop a team of 10 disciples. This team of 10 could take a lifetime. But, we must remember that Jesus' command for us was to make disciples first (see Matt. 28:19-20), not necessarily plant churches. Planting churches is a natural by-product of disciple making. The modern church often makes the mistake of making disciples after they come into the church. The Father's House, on the other hand, understands the importance of making disciples incarnationally, although it can be challenging and can take longer.

Second, The Father's House is committed to seeing this movement spread from Texas to California. They are aware that this could take 20 years, yet believe nothing is impossible with God. Movements, after all, do just that: they move, they multiply. When we make disciples who make disciples, it will spread; it will be reproducible. Bob Gomez believes that if each leader makes a team of 10 disciples, and then those 10 reproduce that and make disciples, it will be a discipleship movement that will spread out to the coast, seeping into every city, suburb, and town along the way.

Third, The Father's House is committed to seeing a similar movement of discipleship established in the Middle East. The Middle Eastern culture is in some ways similar to the Hispanic culture. Gomez would argue that because Hispanics look similar to Arabs, and have similar lifestyles (such as the importance of the family structure), they could be very effective in starting an underground discipleship movement. He believes that a movement of the gospel can (and must) seep into Islamic countries that have tended to view Christianity as weak and a "Western" religion. The way it seeps in is through making disciples who will be missionaries to their families and other networks.

Fourth and finally, The Father's House has a desire to have a retreat center where missional leaders from America and around the world can come, learn, and be refreshed. Because Corpus Christi is known for being a tourist destination, this would be the perfect place to create a retreat center. It is so important that we surround ourselves with others who can inspire us to continue looking at Christianity as a radical and passionate movement that can transform the world and reach all peoples. This is exactly what The Father's House is intending to do.

Sailing Onward

A previous chapter of this book defined the missional church as a *biblically faithful, culturally appropriate, reproducing community of Christ-followers who abandon themselves to passionately pursue the living out of God's mission to reach all peoples.* The Father's House is doing just that. They are an inspiration of what a missional church looks like and acts like. Bob Gomez reminds me of Caleb in Numbers 14. If you remember, Moses sent the 12 spies to check out the new "Promised Land"—the place where God was leading them as His people. The 12 went out to survey the land, and after 40 days, came back and gave their report.

After the Israelites had their little pity party and cried out that they wanted to go back to Egypt and die (see Num. 14:1-2), Caleb stood up (along with Joshua) and said: "The land we passed through and explored is an extremely good land… don't be afraid of the people of the land, for we will devour them. Their protection has been removed from them, and the Lord is with us" (Num. 14:7; 9, HCSB). Caleb saw what the others did not see; he saw what they thought was impossible. He saw so clearly because he knew the Lord was with him and with the Israelites. Bob Gomez and the leaders of The Father's House see more clearly than most people see. They refuse to allow any "giant" to push them around. We, too, must be Calebs who stand up against any obstacle, trusting our God who is on a mission—a mission that is worldwide and unstoppable.

Therefore, The Father's House is more than a church in Corpus Christi; it is a movement in Texas and beyond. In fact, The Father's House is thinking about changing their name to the X movement. This new name has a dual-meaning. X represents the Roman numeral 10 as well as Christ in Greek. In a lifetime, their challenge is to make 10 disciples' of Christ who will love Him passionately and share Him with others.

This X movement really captures the essence of what The Father's House is all about, and what we, too, should be about. Simply put, we are to be the church, not go to church or do church. This is what we are made for. A ship may be safe at the dock, but it is not made for the dock. Ships need to move, to get out and explore uncharted areas, taking risks, constantly going forward. The church needs to be a ship that refuses to stay at the dock or even in the shallow waters. That said, let us put up our sails and move forward, led by our Great Captain who calls out, "All aboard!"

CHAPTER EIGHT

The Journey Church:

Missional Juggernaut in St. Louis

If you've ever been to St. Louis, you probably remember the huge arch that spans the Mississippi River, making it look like a gateway to a giant McDonald's® restaurant. Not far from that arch, more than 1,300 people will be worshiping on two campuses in a church called The Journey Church. Their worship will be different from what you find in most places in the city. Many of the congregants come from local colleges. A high percentage have Ph.D.'s. They're not the kind of people to put up with nonsense, fakery, or pretense. In fact, the one thing most of them come for is reality, the reality of worship, love, community, beauty, and other values, which in their eyes seem to have been forgotten or left behind by the mainstream church.

The first thing you'll note is the hymns at the start of the service. They're "real" hymns, the good, old-time, gospel, God-honoring, God-centered poetry of old that inflamed the churches of revivals in England and the United States. The hymns of Charles Wesley, Isaac Watts, and Fanny Crosby.

You'll find many of these favorites sung in churches the world over. But not like this. Not with this enthusiasm and sense of... worship! Yes, a supreme sense that God is there, listening and enjoying His people, and His people enjoying Him back.

There's something else, the reading of numerous scriptures and passages from the Bible. Not just one or two. Not just a verse here and there, but whole passages. All of it pointing the worshipers to God and Jesus. All of it reminding those present how great, good, wise, and perfect God is. All of it moving the congregation to a profound sense of worship and adoration toward their Creator.

Following this august time, a lone preacher stands to give a message. It's expository, straight from a book of the Bible, continuing from where he left off last week, and to be continued next week from where he ends today. His name is Darrin Patrick, a bit young, only 35 years old, for leading such a large congregation. His voice is not too deep, but it's friendly and persuasive. As a person sitting in one of the seats in this center which had once been a Catholic convent, you are drawn to this man. You sense immediately that he believes what he's saying down to his very toes. He speaks with passion, even fire, and he does something else: he calls his listeners to deep and abiding repentance. He points out real sins and tells each person to consider what he might have done this past week that displeased God. Patrick takes what is said in the passage of Scripture, applies it to today in words everyone can understand and identify with, and then he calls you to honest and heart-searching repentance.

Where can you hear messages like that these days? Not in many churches in St. Louis. That's why so many visitors come to the church. They believe they will get the truth here.

They are sure their differing opinions will be acknowledged and heard. They also know they will be respected. So they give the whole presentation and service a great deal of their respect.

Following the message, comes a time of real repentance in which they share Communion. They do this every Sunday. This is their time of "calling people back to the gospel, back to repentance, and back to the acknowledgement that they can't do this without God,"[73] Patrick says. People bow their heads, confess their sins silently, and seek God's forgiveness and grace.

That done, a celebration follows. Now the hymns become joyous, uplifting, full of hope and worship of the God who has granted them all they need to practice what they have learned.

At the end, everyone leaves with a sense of jubilation. Once again, God has broken through their stress-filled, sometimes angry, sometimes hurting world, and made them feel loved, befriended, supported, and like they matter.

During the week, more than three-quarters of these believers will again meet in small groups in homes. There the teaching will be reinforced, more worship will follow, and sometimes the small-group members will share a startling story or two of God's goodness. People in these groups will become close friends, closer than many others in their worlds. They will love and help one another. They will be there when someone becomes sick or dies. They'll give their money, time, words, and prayers for each other, because they believe intensely that community is what the church is all about. They are the community of God. God is in their midst every moment of the week, working around them and through them to penetrate and influence the broken and hurting people of the world, who have not yet met their awesome Lord.

Who Is this Missional Leader?

Darrin Patrick and his wife Amie, have three children, ranging in age from six months to six years. They live not far from the church, even though the neighborhood has some crime and jumps from half-million-dollar homes to gang-infested tenements. Patrick attended Southwest Baptist University where he received a B.A. in Bible and Biblical Languages. He then obtained an M.Div. from Midwestern Baptist Theological Seminary in Kansas City in 1997, with an emphasis in church planting. He is currently pursuing a D.Min. at Covenant Seminary in St. Louis.

He conceived The Journey Church while in seminary, and had his chance to begin it in 2002. The church now has two campuses, and they're getting ready to begin a third. Their building is right in the middle of the city, five minutes from downtown. The second campus is in Clayton/University City, and the third will be in West County. Patrick preaches at each of them.

[73] Darrin Patrick, phone interview with author, 3 November, 2006.

St. Louis recently discovered it had the highest crime rate of any large city in the United States. That hasn't daunted Patrick from serving where he is. Church members have "a huge desire to serve the poor and be part of the solutions in the public schools," he says. "We're trying to do after-school programs for the kids and helping stop the disintegration of the family in the inner city. It's an urban area, being re-urbanized. Within one block there will be crime-infested homes, in the next, million-dollar homes. You see a lot of cars and people all around us. It's an old Catholic Church complex that we purchased several years ago."

The area features mostly transient people. Many are pursuing graduate degrees and they're in St. Louis to get an education. Patrick says, "Our congregation is very young, very urban. The people are of a postmodern mind-set. They're highly mobile, and sexually diverse in their practices. These people don't have much Christian memory of their growing up years. I call them post-Christian."

Most of Journey Church's growth has come from word of mouth. "People bringing people," Patrick says, "Our community really draws people. We emphasize truth in our worship services. We believe God is very direct and specific about what He requires of us morally and spiritually. So we don't sugarcoat things, even the really tough stuff in the Bible like what it says about the gay lifestyle, abortion, as well as things like stealing, lying, adultery, and so on. We try to be honest on every level and people respond to that. I just go straight through books of the Bible. We'll write a commentary on the material so people can follow along in a study book. I use Greek and Hebrew when it's necessary, point out how the Bible applies to life today, and give original meaning if it's not clear from the text."

Planting the Church

The Journey Church started in September of 2002. Patrick moved to St. Louis in 2001, and started meeting people from the parish. He knew St. Louis from past experiences and felt God's leading that it was the right place for him.

"Meeting people wasn't hard," he says. "I went to a lot of 'third-place' locations for people. You know, they have their home and work, the first two places, and then they have a third place where they go to relax, read, get a latte, or whatever. I would go into places where music was being played, coffee shops, cafes, places like that. I'd talk to people, hang out, and start conversations. I would really pray while sitting there and looking around, that God would give me discernment. I didn't want to be obnoxious, but I would notice what people were reading. I was really looking for 'divine appointments.' I'd notice a guy with a wedding ring on or studying a book. So I'd ask him how long he had been married, or what school he attended. I'd try to build a relationship. I rarely talked about the fact that I was a pastor. Sometimes I'd throw out that I was planting a church and ask people if they'd be interested. I'd give them my card and hook up with them the next time I found them at the place. I built some good friendships before ever mentioning God or Christ."

Finally, in 2002, Patrick felt he had a signal from God to go for it, so he contacted many of the people he'd gotten to know and built friendships with, inviting them to the first service. About 30 people came. Seeing those people there made Patrick realize he was in the right place at the right time. He says, "When we finally started we met for corporate worship. I knew we were in the right place by who showed up, who stayed. I knew this was what I was made to do. The people who came really affirmed what I wanted to do by their enthusiasm and eagerness to worship God in spirit and truth. I saw that I was having a real impact and God was moving. This church had been in my mind for years and finally I got to see it out there, in reality."

It was an immense lift and it bolstered his belief that God would be with them in this work.

Five Distinct Missional Values

The First Value: Mission

As for the values of this missional church plant, Patrick says there are five distinctives. He says, "First is mission, we believe we are sent. The church is just like being a missionary, sent. Everything we do is missional. We're a church not for ourselves, but for the world. This grounds and organizes us in everything we do. Just as God the Father sent the Son, the Son sent the Spirit, and the Spirit sent the disciples, so they have sent us. Our mission is to go out there and bring people into the church, so that they can go out and bring in others. We're a family."

One of the ways Patrick sees The Journey doing this kind of missional work is through something they call "Midrash," from the old rabbinic texts and commentaries on the Bible. They sponsor debates in the community about subjects the community is interested in discussing.

"For instance," Patrick says, "there's the embryonic stem cell issue that's on the ballot in Missouri. We offered an event where we brought people together on both sides of the issue, several experts, and an ethicist from St. Louis University. There we engaged people in an open debate between the people on the stage. Then we opened it up for questions and opinions from the audience. It was really good. More than 300 people showed up."

The Journey Church specifically tries to engage people in the community about subjects they're already talking about. They bring in people on various sides of an issue and let it rip, so to speak. A lot of people respect their integrity in letting others speak, not just the Christians.

A big issue in the community some time ago was about legalizing marijuana. They put on another debate.

Where do they stage this? Not at the church campus, because some people would turn away because it looked too religious. Rather, they sponsor the debates in a local micro-brewery, which has a large gathering room that seats hundreds of people. The beauty of this plan is that the micro-brewery advertises the events for the church. "You know," Patrick says, "people come out of the restaurant and come to the discussion." As a result, they speak to a very eclectic and different mix of people. Not your standard Christians, but people from all walks of life, backgrounds, races, and beliefs.

Other discussions they have sponsored have been such things as:

- "Bush, Faith, and War" where they talked about the Iraq war, President Bush, Christianity, and pacifism.
- The *DaVinci Code* where they brought in people from Opus Dei (the "bad guy" organization in the book), a Catholic priest, a neo-pagan believer, and a Ph.D. Protestant who was an expert in church history.
- "Poverty and Crime in St. Louis."

At these meetings, an elder from the church moderates. Patrick says, "We don't present gospel, but we have built this reputation in the community where you can be honest about what your view is with us. People come to the church because they perceive us as tolerant and not judgmental or anything like that. When they come to church, they then hear the gospel. These meetings are kind of a pre-evangelism thing we use."

There are also times at these meetings when they simply throw the topic out to those in the room. Whatever anyone wants to talk about. "We really stress 1 Peter 3:15," Patrick says, "stating our hope with 'gentleness and respect' to people who disagree with us. There are many issues out there that really are gray, not black and white. So we wrestle with the tension and paradox in the topic. This is the only place in our city where you can go and have a discussion like that and not be lambasted. Thus, a lot of people like it, and more come to each one."

The Second Value: Truth

Truth is the second missional value Patrick emphasizes. He says, "We believe God has revealed Himself specifically in Jesus and the Scriptures, generally in nature and in conscience. We know God's character, will, and ways from Scripture. We try to be both objective about the truth in terms of its plain meaning and sense, and subjective in the sense that it's experiential. We proclaim this truth in the context and culture where we live. Like 1 Corinthians 9 says, we want to 'be all things to all people.'"

One way this works in the church context is through something like the series that Patrick was preaching at the time of this interview. He says, "We're doing a series from the book of Proverbs on sex. How do I approach it from a truth perspective, but also from an experiential standpoint? Well, instead of leading with something like just saying, 'sex outside marriage is wrong,' I approach it a little more subtly and positively. I talk about the beauty of sex in covenant, in marriage, and the idea of oneness that comes with that. What this kind of beauty and oneness means sexually, physically, socially, and so on, in the mingling of souls. I really describe it in as positive a light as I can, showing the real power and loveliness of sex in a marital context. Then I come back to the question, 'Now do you see why God says sex must be in marriage? That's the only place this level of intimacy and unity can occur.' So I lead with the beauty of oneness, and I bring in more of the story of why this is true. This seems to be far more effective in getting the truth about sex to the people, instead of getting them all rebellious and negative about it from the beginning with a negative approach. That's how we believe the truth should be presented, in a positive way and in a way that glorifies God, rather than a way that gets people feeling rebellious and angry."

The Third Value: Worship

Patrick talks about worshiping God as a Trinity. He says, "Basically, we worship a triune God. We're big on the Trinity. God is community… seeking worshipers after Himself. Worship is not just a public thing, but a private thing. We try to guard against worship as just being at church. Your thoughts, motives, words, and actions all matter to God every day, every minute. Worship is a lifestyle. You are obeying and worshiping God every single day in everything that you do. Not just on Sundays, or while doing your quiet time. We're to worship Him in everything we do. When we're eating, interacting with our kids. Everything is worship. Everything is spiritual."

This effects the way Patrick prepares to preach on Sunday. "For me," he says, "it really shows up in the preaching. I meditate on the text that I'm preaching on that week. I try to repent in what I'm finding in the text all week before I deliver the message. So I'm encountering God and worshiping in that process. For instance, this past week, this whole Ted Haggard thing broke in the news about him having sexual relations with a gay prostitute. We don't know the truth of this at this point, but the news gave me pause as I studied for my sermon. I don't think I'm in a situation where I'd mess up like he supposedly did. But I see a real need to repent and think about my sexuality and what I have found in Proverbs. This happens every week as I plan my messages."

It's a powerful thought about the missional values that The Journey Church projects. Truth should lead us not only to worship, but also to repentance. Worship should result not only in repentance, but celebration of God's forgiveness and love. Those kinds of values are what Journey is all about.

The Fourth Value: Community

A missional church like Journey believes intensely that they are a community, part of God's living family, a picture of the community that will exist one day in heaven. Patrick says, "The idea here is that we're a church that doesn't live in isolation. We worship together, serve together, witness together. God is a community. He is other-affirming. The Father gave all judgment to Son. The Son honors the Father. The Spirit honors the Son."

Patrick believes that's the way the church is supposed to work. The church and its members exist as part of one another. They can't think of themselves just as individuals doing what they want. What each one does affects other believers, affects their community. That's why repentance and teaching about sin is so important to them. So that in community, they can build up one another, train each other as disciples, and become more like Christ in every way.

How does this work out in Journey? Patrick says the primary means is the community of small groups. He says, "This is where people share life together. That's our main time where people do things together. We have meals together. About 70 percent of the church is in such a group. They don't just come on Sunday, but in the middle of the week. They share and do community. There's a lot of conflict because of it. People realize things wrong about their lives. People find out they're not a consumer, but a participant. Through community, they have totally changed mind-sets of how they operate in church. People become accountable to one another, responsible. They have a lot of ongoing church discipline."

Church discipline is a biggie in the Journey community. Patrick says, "We value membership highly. You can't be a member of our church and live a godless life. So we have to do church discipline fairly often."

"For instance," Patrick says, "there was a young woman who was a member of the church. She was deceived by a man who wasn't a believer. She wanted to marry him, but he wasn't a Christian. We felt compelled to confront her about it. We followed the principles in Matthew 18:15-17 about church discipline. First, one person, then several and finally the whole church spoke to her about her need to change her mind. However, she wouldn't repent. In the end, we had to dis-fellowship her because of it."

Another case happened when one of the worship team members stopped treating his wife with respect. Patrick says, "He was very rude to her and hard on her. They ended up divorcing. We met with him and took him through the same Matthew 18 process. Again, he wouldn't repent, and we ended up dis-fellowshipping him."

Or course, many of these situations end at the first or second step, because the person in question does repent. Part of the purity and success of The Journey Church is that they take sin seriously and really work to help its members live godly lives. This is what community is all about—promoting spiritual growth, turning away from sin, and committing to Christ.

The Fifth Value: Beauty

This value is a little harder to pin down, but in the postmodern church it's becoming more prevalent and impactful. It's really a return to the arts in church. For centuries, Christians have avoided interest and investment in art: painting, sculpture, high-brow forms of music, literature, and so on. Some said these things were worldly and not to be part of the church. Some churches, like The Journey Church, remind people that God is a God of creativity, of inventiveness, and of beauty. Take a look at the world around you, and you can't help but notice the variety, the perfection, the wondrous detail and elegance of God's handiwork. These things need to be reveled in, enjoyed, and shared. In fact, to Patrick this is the primary impetus behind the value of beauty. God is a person who loves beauty and wants His people to express it on all kinds of levels, in and out of the church, to show Him off to the world and glorify His greatness and grandeur.

Patrick says, "God has created everything including humans. They're made in His image. They have gifts and talents, and are to use those for God's glory. When they use those abilities, they display and demonstrate the beauty of God. We really encourage people to use their artistic gifts. We have a big outreach to artists in our area."

How do they use these artists? Through paintings, in worship services, through music, dance, and sculpture. Patrick says, "We're getting ready to turn this old convent, which is part of this Catholic facility we meet in, into an art house. In one room, you can paint, in another sculpt, in another work on and compose music. We're designing the whole building to be used by artists. They also do videos, movies, audio things, drama, all those kinds of things. I want to teach our people to enjoy the beauty in our world and use it to draw them closer to God."

Planting New Churches

A big part of a missional church vision is to plant new churches. The Journey Church is part of planting new churches, while maintaining the campuses where Patrick preaches. These plants are completely autonomous, separate churches, not connected to The Journey Church after they get started. However, they are all missional churches of the Southern Baptist Convention.

The method Journey uses in church planting is through first raising up and training church planters through an intentional internship program. Patrick says, "We give them money and some people. The goal is to plant the church, and then for them to send out more planters to plant even more churches. The sending idea again."

All of Journey's church plants are thriving. Patrick says, "You need about three years to see if it'll make it. But it's looking good right now." These churches are all around St. Louis. Some are on the Illinois side, too.

How much money does it take to do this? "It varies," Patrick says, "and depends on a lot of things. Typically, it takes at least $100,000. Depending on the area, though, it may take as much as $300,000. We don't want the pastor to work or the wife to work, if they have small children. We don't want them to feel under pressure to start the church so they can get people to give the money to run it. So we pay his salary for a couple of years."

Journey helps the church planter build a good core group toward a start. This normally takes finding about 50 people willing to be part of this, although that number can be less.

What kind of person do they look for as a church planter? Patrick says, "He has to be highly entrepreneurial. Not a person who's afraid to take risks. We want him to be solid theologically, and culturally solid, in that he knows how to get the gospel out in his given culture. We also want him to have a good marriage and be a good father because the people in the church will be looking to him as the primary example of Christ."

One of the young men Patrick brought into the church has recently gone out and planted a new congregation in St. Charles, a nearby community. Patrick says that they trained him for a year or so and taught him what he needed to know about how to work with people in the culture and out of it, how to approach possible members, build relationships, and ultimately start a new church. Patrick takes personal interest in working with these men and sending them out. He uses his training from Midwestern Baptist Theological Seminary in church planting to teach these men. More importantly, he invites them into his own experiences and helps them see the exact steps and plans one must put in place to make a successful plant.

This planter finally went out (was "sent") and began developing the relationships much the same way Patrick had when he initially started The Journey Church. In time, with the financial and spiritual support of the sending church, Patrick says, "He started with about 40 people. That number doubled in a couple of months. He now has a couple of staff members and they're getting ready to engage their culture. He's doing great." This young planter went to Southwest Baptist College and Southwestern Baptist Theological Seminary.

It should be clear by now that The Journey Church under the leadership of Darrin Patrick is on the cutting edge. They're influencing their culture, engaging it in conversation, and leading people out of lost lifestyles into embracing God and Christ with passion and joy.

Ultimately, this is the primary mark of a missional church, one that penetrates and transforms the culture and community around it.

CHAPTER NINE

Western Alberta:

Reaching the Multitudes with the Gospel of Christ

The wind-swept prairies of Western Alberta may conjure images of tumbleweed and ghost towns for out-of-towners, but for area residents, home is a place of skyscrapers, construction, and brand-new subdivisions. Alberta's population has surged in recent years, due primarily to shifts in migration from other provinces, but also influenced by Canada's continued boom in foreign immigration. In fact, of all the Canadian provinces, Alberta showed the highest rate of growth in Canada's 2001 census. The national trend toward urbanization is evident in the region, as both Calgary and Edmonton, Alberta's two largest cities, have recently exceeded 1 million people.[74]

For pastors in this area, the challenge is keeping up with the continued growth of this region, where nearly one quarter of the population claims no religious affiliation.[75] Here, church leaders are like the disciples, staring at a hungry crowd of 5,000 wondering how on earth to feed all of the people. According to Calgary church planter, Nick Melazzo, watching God work in the Calgary area is like watching Him divide the fishes and loaves. "The best part is the missional adventure," said Melazzo. "God is present with us. We're like those driven by the wind. We don't always have a plan, but we always have a purpose, and it takes us in some really unexpected places."[76]

The city of Calgary boasts the highest population in Alberta. Located in the foothills of the Rocky Mountains, Calgary stole the international spotlight in 1988 when it became the first Canadian city to host the Olympic Winter Games. It remains a popular destination for winter sports enthusiasts, and is part of the growing urban region dubbed the Calgary-Edmonton corridor. Other large cities in the area include Red Deer, (population 82,971), which is located to the north of Calgary, and Lethbridge, (population 78,713), which is located to the south, near the Alberta/Montana border.

While the number of foreign-born immigrants living in the Calgary area is not as high as the number living in cities in the province of Ontario, where the immigrant population soars to over 3 million, about 15 percent of Alberta's population is comprised of foreign immigrants. Most of Canada's immigrants come from Asian countries, including the Middle East. Others come from Europe, the Caribbean, Central and South America, Africa, and the United States. In Calgary, visible minorities account for 17 percent of the population, so believers do not have to go far to "proclaim His deeds among the peoples"

[74] Statistics Canada. *A Profile of the Canadian Population: where we live.* 2001 Census Analysis Ser. Catalogue No.: 96F0030XIE2001001. 2(Ottawa, Ontario: Statistics Canada, 2003), Available: *http://geodepot.statcan.ca/Diss/Highlights/Highlights_e.cfm.*

[75] Statistics Canada. *Religions in Canada.* 2001 Census Analysis Ser. Catalogue No.: 96F0030XIE2001015. (Ottawa, Ontario: Statistics Canada, 2003), Available: *http://www12.statcan.ca/english/census01/Products/Analytic/companion/rel/canada.cfm.*

[76] Nick Melazzo, phone interview with author, 31 October, 2006.

(Ps. 9:11, HCSB). Representatives from dozens of tribes and tongues and nations can be found in a single neighborhood.[77]

But how receptive are the people of southern Alberta to the good news? Although Canada is a predominantly Roman Catholic country, Protestants outnumber Roman Catholics in Alberta and represent the religious majority. However, the province is showing an alarming increase in secularization. Nearly one quarter of Alberta's population reported that they had no religious affiliation. That figure represents about 700,000 people and a 39 percent increase in secularization over a 10-year period.[78] In Calgary, 25 percent of the people claim no religious affiliation.[79]

This shift away from religious affiliation is part of a nationwide trend that has especially affected British Columbia, Alberta's neighbor to the west. In a 2006 article in Statistics Canada's *Canadian Social Trends*, Warren Clark and Grant Schellenberg report that between 1985 and 2004, "The proportion of adult Canadians who either have no religious affiliation or do have a religion but don't attend regular services increased from 31 percent to 43 percent…."

This trend is most severe in British Columbia, where 60 percent of the people either reported no religious affiliation or did not attend any religious services.[80] Data from the National Church Planting Congress concurs, showing that just six percent of Canadians fill the pews at evangelical churches on a given Sunday.[81] However, polls that inquire after people's feelings toward such things as the centrality of Christ and the cross, the Bible, values, and morality show that despite the low church attendance, evangelicalism is gaining ground in Canada.[82] As Clark and Schellenberg note, "declining attendance may overstate the extent to which Canada is becoming secularized, since a considerable proportion of Canadians do not attend religious services but do engage in religious practices on their own." Their study found that almost half of those Canadian adults who do not regularly attend services placed a high degree of importance on their religion.[83]

In addition to the challenge of reaching the nonreligious and unchurched of Alberta, Christians in the area are encountering a growing mission field among adherents of Islam, Buddhism, Hinduism, and Sikhism. Between 1991 and 2001, the number of Muslims in Alberta rose 58 percent, and in Calgary the number increased by 86.5 percent. There are over 25,000 Muslims in Calgary. The numbers of Buddhists and Hindus in Calgary also

[77] Statistics Canada. *Ethnocultural portrait: Provinces and territories.* 2001 Census Analysis Ser. Catalogue No.: 96F0030XIE2001015. (Ottawa, Ontario: Statistics Canada, 2003), Available: *www.12.statcan/english/census01/products/analytic/companion/etoimm/provs.cfm*

[78] Statistics Canada. *Religions in Canada.* 2001 Census Analysis Ser. Catalogue No.: 96F0030XIE2001015. (Ottawa, Ontario: Statistics Canada, 2003), Available: *http://www12.statcan.ca/english/census01/Products/Analytic/companion/rel/canada.cfm.*

[79] Murray Moerman editor, *Discipling Our Nation: Equipping The Canadian Church For Its Mission* (Delta, BC Canada: Church Leadership Library, 2005), 267

[80] Warren Clark and Grant Schellenberg, *"Who's Religious?" Canadian Social Trends* summer 2006, 2.

[81] Moerman, ed., *Discipling Our Nation,* 2.

[82] Ibid., 3

[83] Clark and Schellenberg, *"Who's Religious?"* 6-7.

rose substantially and the number of Sikhs more than doubled.[84] Immigration accounts for much of the dramatic influx of these Eastern religions.

With its recent surge in population, diversity of people groups, and large number of unchurched, southern Alberta is a prime location for missional churches to make an impact. As Jesus told His disciples, "Open your eyes and look at the fields, for they are ready for harvest" (John 4:35, HCSB). While the harvest is plentiful, the workers are few. For example, in Red Deer, a city of over 82,000 people, there are just two Southern Baptist churches present. In order for there to be one evangelical church for every 1,000 people, Red Deer would need 35 new churches. Lethbridge would need 31 new churches, and Calgary would need a staggering 628 new churches.

Church planters working out of the Canadian Convention of Southern Baptists (CCSB), headquartered in Cochrane, Alberta, have their work cut out for them. Tim Williams is the CCSB's church planting strategist for Western Canada. He says that the lack of evangelical presence in the region makes it difficult to establish a core group of like-minded individuals in a given community. Canada isn't like the Bible Belt of the Southern United States, where people are familiar with the Southern Baptist church and evangelicalism, so growing a congregation takes patience and creativity.

"One of the things you learn when working in an area without a strong evangelical presence is that the best way to reach people is to really get involved in the community,"[85] said Williams. "That doesn't mean simply planning church-sponsored activities. It means participating in and supporting the activities that are already ongoing. This is how you begin to build relationships with people right where they are." For example, members of Big Rock Baptist Fellowship, Williams' church plant in Okotoks Alberta, participated in a river cleanup in their community. Whether it's reading a book to children for story time at the local library or helping with a community picnic, the key is "letting people know that you care, without making them feel like you expect something in return," Williams said. In this way, missional churches can reflect the values of having an intentional, unconditional love for all people with cultural adaptability.

The CCSB's strategy for reaching the lost of Alberta involves identifying key leaders in communities, mobilizing laypeople to pray for and participate in the community-centered ministries that these key leaders develop. It involves expanding the influence of these ministries by planting more and more missional churches across the region. One of the most effective tools in accomplishing this has been through a seven-year-old CCSB church planting initiative for college and seminary students called Current.[86] Every summer between 30 to 50 students from Canada and the United States spend six weeks working with key leaders in Canadian communities, learning about church planting and assisting church leaders with their community ministries. In addition to Alberta, students have served in British Columbia, Yukon, Northwest Territories, Saskatchewan, Manitoba, and Ontario.

84 Statistics Canada. *Religions in Canada. 2001* Census Analysis Ser. Catalogue No.: 96F0030XIE2001015, (Ottawa, Ontario: Statistics Canada, 2003), Available: *http://www12.statcan.ca/english/census01/Products/Analytic/companion/rel/canada.cfm.*

85 Tim Williams, phone interview with author, 30 October, 1 November, 2006.

86 *http://www.currentcanada.com*

Some of the more mature teams are placed where there is no existing work and no strategic contacts. These students, part of Extreme Current, are equipped to take initiative, build relationships, and explore where God is at work in certain locations. Over 150 students have participated in Current since its inception, and 30 former Current participants are now back in Canada and involved in ministry there. One is even pastoring a church. Certainly these young people have taken Paul's advice to Timothy, "No one should despise your youth; instead, you should be an example to the believers in speech, in conduct, in love, in faith, in purity" (1 Timothy 4:12, HCSB).

"Current was one of the most uplifting, encouraging experiences of my life," said Holly Meeks, a 2006 participant of the program. "The time spent in training gave me the confidence needed to make genuine connections with nonbelievers and really be able to share the love of God with them… I can't express the joy I felt as we witnessed people's hardened hearts be opened to our message. Many lives were changed this summer, including my own."[87]

Current gives young people like Meeks an opportunity to develop a more missional attitude about the role of the church in the world. By working in areas with a limited evangelical presence, participants develop a passion for spreading the gospel and planting churches. After working with Christian leaders who are serving on the front lines, students learn practical ways to effectively connect with the culture of the community and infuse the truth of God's Word into ministry. While Williams rejoices over the number of students who have decided to return to ministry in Canada, he says it is just as exciting to think about the impact the other students will have in missional churches around the world.

Current is just one way in which the CCSB is "planting all kinds of churches using all kinds of people," said Williams. As of September 2006, the CCSB reports that 45 congregations exist in Alberta. The one thing that all of these churches seem to have in common is that they are all unique. According to the CCSB, when working in such a diverse and un-charted mission field, strategic leaders must reject the one-model approach to church planting and church growing. If leaders want to be missional in their approach, they must be like Paul, who learned to "become all things to all people, so that [he] may by all means save some" (1 Cor. 9:22, HCSB). The following churches in Western Alberta can be described as missional in their approach. They show a passion to reach the lost with the gospel, an appropriate connection and adaptation to the culture, a faithfulness to God's Word, and a desire not only to grow, but to see new churches planted throughout their land and throughout the world.

Blogging the Truth in Love: Tapestry, Rocky Ridge

Nick Melazzo, leader of a church plant in Calgary called Tapestry, Rocky Ridge, doesn't talk like a preacher. His online blog reads more like a casual conversation, and includes an eclectic mix of Bible study notes, humor, pop culture references, systematic theology, and poetic musings. Visitors to the site can sense the excitement of this seminary student as he reports on a recent Sunday morning study of the book of Romans. He writes, "Beginning

[87] Holly Meeks, e-mail, 1 November, 2006.

to 'get' Romans for the first time is pretty stinkin' cool, and boy does it mess with your theology. Yesterday was as good a study as we've ever had. Questions, struggle, sharing, conversation, laughter, and everything we want to be about on Sunday morning. Between that and the cinnamon sticky rolls, a good time was had by all."

Melazzo said that the Web site at *www.tapestrycalgary.com* is an important strategy for maintaining a presence in a community where his church "lacks any substantial real estate," but where most people are Internet savvy. This is just one way in which Tapestry combines contextualization with a commitment to God's Word, two of the characteristics of missional churches.

Tapestry, Rocky Ridge, is a daughter church of Tapestry, Tuscany, a church led by pastor Jim Boyd and his family, who have a vision for creating a network of churches in the Calgary area. Melazzo and a small group of believers meet in coffee shops and living rooms across the community. Melazzo emphasizes the importance of building relationships, so that the church is more of a movement than an institution.

Both Tapestry churches like to use the term "symbiosis" to describe the nature of their ministries. "Symbiosis" is a term usually associated with biological organisms that live in close physical association with one another. The term can also apply to mutually beneficial relationships between different people or groups, and for members of Tapestry signifies the importance of community. "We get together on Sundays for coffee and conversation," Melazzo said. "No show, just real people trying to live like Jesus. If you're a real person, you'll fit right in. If you're a fake person, we can help you be real. If you're not a person, you probably shouldn't come." Clearly, members of Tapestry share the missional value of authenticity.

Melazzo said that when people ask about Tapestry, he tells them, "We're a church, but not like you're used to." At Tapestry, Rocky Ridge, they don't count attendance. They don't hold regularly scheduled Sunday morning services; they don't have a building. They don't invite people to a lot of church-sponsored events, and, well, they don't really want to. Melazzo feels that Jesus called believers to be the church in the world, not to simply invite the world into the church.

Key to winning the trust and interest of the people of Calgary, according to Melazzo, is getting involved in the community and reaching out in authentic, Christ-like ways. Members regularly volunteer in the community, doing everything from painting faces to serving sausage, from mowing lawns to supporting the local children's hospital. Tapestry hosts sports camps in the summer and movie nights in the fall, and every four to six weeks, participants enjoy a dinner party together. Through activities such as these, Melazzo and his church have connected with Muslims from Pakistan, Hindus from India, Catholics from the Philippines, atheists from England, and Caucasians from all kinds of backgrounds. In this way, Tapestry fulfills the missional characteristic of seeking to take the message of hope to the entire world, one people group at a time.

But according to Melazzo, being "missional" is not for the faint of heart. He writes in his blog:

> For some reason, we really want to liken God to certainty. But faith is so much more a calculated risk. It's not knowing how things will turn out; it's knowing that Jesus is worth whatever you might risk. The only certainty we're given is in the person of God Himself, because if we were given the details of our life, we wouldn't need faith. And if we knew exactly what was going to happen, we would not need to dream. But God calls us to dream with Him, and to love Him enough to believe that those dreams are worth the risk. Dreams of beauty and justice and newness, dreams of the future kingdom of God come into the here and now.

Walking with God and Hanging out with People: Riverside Baptist Church, Red Deer

Even though the congregation of his church in Red Deer, Alberta, has grown to about 50 people in just three years, pastor Ashley Olinger isn't satisfied with simply filling the pews. Red Deer and the surrounding area, which is located in the booming Calgary-Edmonton Corridor, is home to approximately 300,000 people, and is growing rapidly. According to Olinger, a native of Canada, all 300,000 of these people are loved by God and deserve the chance to hear the good news. Riverside Baptist Church and its Korean church plant are the only Southern Baptist ministries in the city, making the challenge of reaching each person difficult, but not impossible.

As God reminded Jeremiah, "Look, I am the Lord, the God of all flesh. Is anything to hard for me" (Jer. 32:27, HCSB)? With this verse in mind, Olinger has identified several communities in the area that need church plants and has worked tirelessly to begin sowing seeds. "The purpose of the church is to grow the kingdom of God, not to grow one massive congregation in one location," said Olinger. "Too many churches direct all of their energy inward. While fellowship and church health is very important, I believe it is secondary to fulfilling the missionary mandate."[88]

There is no doubt that Olinger has a passion for the mission of God and is prepared to respond to God's call for the formation of one people from all peoples. Despite a large number of ministries and activities, Riverside Baptist reflects the missional value of simplicity in purpose, process, and programming. Olinger's goal is clear—to launch an association of churches in Central Alberta. His strategy is defined—to apply these eight steps to each community: (1) saturate the community with prayer, (2) scout out the community, (3) continue ongoing ministry outreach, (4) discover a watchman, (5) start Bible studies, (6) form a core group, (7) launch a church service, and (8) start churches elsewhere.

"Canadians are good people," said Olinger. "They are kind and courteous, and like to be involved in value-based activities that strengthen their communities. However, they tend to see churches as parasites. They see a church as an organization that is only out there for

[88] Ashley Olinger, phone interview with author, 31 October, 2006.

itself, looking to raise money and increase in number. What we want to do is change that perception and let these people know that a church can really benefit the community."

Through activities such as Backyard Bible Clubs, neighborhood barbecues, sports camps, Vacation Bible Schools, community carnivals, and other unique family oriented events, the people of Riverside Baptist Church are working to transform Central Alberta into a community of believers, one relationship at a time. Members of Riverside organize prayerwalks in which they journey together through communities, pray specifically for each individual neighborhood, street, and home, and leave flyers in mailboxes, letting people know that they were prayed for. They also work closely with members of their Korean church plant, teaching English-as-a-Second Language classes and assisting them with outreach. In fact, the church's witness has been so influential in the area, that non-Christians in the community of Springbrook have actually requested a church plant. According to Olinger, this couldn't have happened without the faithful work of believers in the congregation.

Take, for example, Dale Constantine. Constantine is a mechanic who works in the oil and gas industry in Red Deer. His special ministry through Riverside Baptist Church is called Team G-Force, which provides families in the area with the opportunity to enjoy the experience of operating and repairing remote controlled cars and trucks. With the help of corporate sponsorship, the ministry provides technical and supportive instruction to anyone who owns or would like to own a remote-controlled truck or car at no cost. Anyone is welcome to participate, but before becoming an official member of the team, participants must demonstrate basic proficiency in the maintenance of their trucks and must memorize John 3:16 and Colossians 3:23.

In addition to these ministries, the church recently launched a young adult group called DIVE that meets at Red Deer College for Bible study and community activities. Riverside is also taking advantage of mission-minded youth through IMPACT, or **I**nvolving young people to **M**ake a difference **P**lanting an **A**ssociation of **C**hurches **T**hroughout central Alberta. For seven weeks every summer IMPACT strategically places teams of young people from the United States and Canada in communities where Riverside church is ministering. This gives students the opportunity to use their gifts and talents to share God's love in practical ways to the people of Red Deer. The goal of IMPACT is simple: "to walk with God and hang out with people."

Olinger said he encourages members of his church to develop their own ideas for outreach and take initiative in fulfilling the Great Commission on a daily basis. However, the missional nature of his church has frightened some away. "Sometimes we encounter people who come from church backgrounds where they were never expected to participate, except, of course on Sunday mornings," he said. "Very little of what we do as a church focuses on ourselves. We focus on obeying Christ's command to 'go,' and so we've actually lost some people in the process. Not everyone wants to be part of a church that is constantly on the move."

Reaching Out, No Strings Attached:
A Place Called Hope, Lethbridge

One of the values of a missional church is expressing unconditional love for all people. For Scott Dollar, pastor of A Place Called Hope, Lethbridge, Southern Alberta, this proves to be both a daunting and exciting challenge. A Place Called Hope, which in just one year has grown to a core group of about 25, represents the only Southern Baptist ministry in Lethbridge. Only a few other evangelical churches exist in the region. In addition to the many unchurched and agnostic members of the community, Mormons make up a large percentage of the population, as Lethbridge is an historical settlement for members of the Church of Jesus Christ of Latter-day Saints. This is a community where many hearts are hardened toward the gospel. When Dollar first arrived in Lethbridge, he went door to door asking people what they would like to see in a local church. An overwhelming number responded that they would like to see a church that is committed to helping build the community.

"The people here are cautious," Dollar said. "They would rather observe and watch something from a distance before getting involved."[89] With that in mind, A Place Called Hope has directed its energy toward community involvement, "with no strings attached," Dollar said. Prayerwalks help foster a passion for reaching the lost within the hearts of members of the congregation; sports camps attract children from the community and expose them to caring believers; block parties draw families who might normally be wary of going to church; and Vacation Bible Schools are often the first place children in this community hear the gospel message. Dollar and other church leaders regularly pass out flyers around town, encouraging members of the community to log on to their Web site at *www.aplacecalledhope.ca* and fill out a prayer request form or a community survey. Through community events such as these, Dollar and his congregation have touched over 500 people in the Lethbridge area, an area that the CCSB targeted as one of its most significant church plant needs in Alberta.

A Place Called Hope created another Web site specifically designed to reach the Mormon community both in Lethbridge and across North America. The site *123mormon.com* encourages Mormons to test their religion and helps them reconsider their faith in the privacy of their own homes, where they do not have to fear repercussions from fellow Mormons. On this site, Mormons can learn about the prophetic claims of Founder Joseph Smith that were never fulfilled and study the inconsistencies between the Book of Mormon and the Bible and within the Book of Mormon itself. Dollar's hope is that the Web site will simply get Mormons to think; he leaves the rest up to the Holy Spirit. In this way, A Place Called Hope reflects the missional value of cultural adaptability.

"Our goal is to be involved in the community, help build community, and love people like Jesus loved, regardless of whether they become followers of Christ or not," said Dollar. "As we build on this, we will continue to plant seeds, cultivate those seeds, and see a harvest in the future." Dollar's advice to pastors who wish to make their churches more missional is to "seek to model everything you do around the example of Jesus in the Gospels.

[89] Scott Dollar, phone interview with author, 30 October, 2006.

Jesus loved people even if they did not follow Him. He went to all people. When the opportunity presented itself, He shared about the kingdom of God."

Engaging in Dialogue: Arabic Baptist Church of Calgary

After the Pentecost, foreigners living in Jerusalem expressed both delight and curiosity when they heard Peter and the apostles "declaring the wonders of God in [their] own tongues." (See Acts 2.) In a country like Canada, where over 5 million people speak a language other than English or French at home, the missional church must learn to meet the needs of a variety of people groups, and make an effort to share the gospel in a cultural context.[90] In Calgary, over 7,500 citizens speak Arabic. Many of them are immigrants from countries such as Pakistan, Sudan, and Iran, and many are Muslims.[91] When Wagdi Iskander immigrated to Alberta from Sudan 20 years ago, he made a commitment to bring the gospel to this specific demographic, and since then, he has planted three thriving Arabic churches in Canada.

Iskander oversees Arabic churches in Calgary, Edmonton, and Regina, Saskatchewan. The first church to take off was Arabic Baptist Church of Calgary, which got started after Iskander hosted an Arabic concert in the community. It now has a congregation of about 60 people. According to Iskander, it is important that these churches preserve the traditions of the Arabic community, so services are conducted in Arabic, the music is traditional, cultural family values are encouraged, and fellowship flourishes. "We do a lot of eating," says Iskander in his thick Sudanese accent. "I don't know if we got that from the Baptists or if the Baptists got that from us, but we love food and fellowship!"[92] Members reach out to other Arabs in the community by spotting Arabic names in the phone book and then sending letters or stopping by people's homes to make contact. Iskander works with other Baptist churches in the area to help grow a stronger children's ministry at the church, as many young people in the congregation who have grown up in Canada do not speak Arabic. Like many pastors around the world, he is also working on a building campaign.

Because so many of the Arabic people in Calgary are Muslims, Arabic Baptist Church has been instrumental in fostering positive relationships between Muslims and Christians in the area. The church regularly sponsors forums in which a Christian scholar and a Muslim scholar address a specific topic, such as 'peace' or 'justice.' The speakers begin by sharing thoughts on the topic, the Christian speaking from the Bible and the Muslim speaking from the Koran. They then each have an opportunity to critique one another's ideas. This is followed by questions from the audience. Maintaining an attitude of dialogue rather than debate is key to keeping things harmonious and fruitful, so all of the statements and questions are pre-written to avoid confrontation. Besides providing a great opportunity for Muslims to hear the gospel, these forums have given Iskander and other church leaders the opportunity to build positive relationships with Muslim leaders in the community. "Our goal is not to win a debate," said Iskander. "Our goal is to share the gospel. The idea is to promote friendship and to build bridges. We want to keep in contact with our Muslim

[90] Statistics Canada. *Language Composition of Canada.* 2001 Census Analysis Ser. (Ottawa, Ontario: Statistics Canada, 2003), Available: *http://www.12statcan.ca/english/census01/products/highlights/LanguageComposition*
[91] Moerman, ed., *Discipling Our Nation,* 283.
[92] Wagdi Iskander, phone interview with author, 1 November, 2006.

friends so that we can invite them to some of our activities and continue to show them God's love."

Planting Seeds: Trinity Baptist Church, Calgary

With a congregation of about 160 people, complete with a youth group, children's ministry, and senior pastor of over 10 years, Trinity Baptist Church in Calgary resembles a lot of other strong, growing Southern Baptist churches. But according to pastor Rob Blackaby, his goal is not to simply raise a congregation of people who are committed to attending church, but to raise a congregation of missionaries who are committed to leaving it. Trinity Baptist Church reflects several values of a missional church, but perhaps most profound is its commitment to church planting and missional leadership development.

Blackaby has led Trinity to broaden its scope of ministry to include several communities across the Calgary area including, most recently, church plants in Parkland, Cranston, Lake Chaparral, Pincher Creek, Okotoks, Nanton, and Lethbridge. (A Place Called Hope is a daughter church of Trinity Baptist Church.) By September 2007, Trinity will launch a network of churches that will range throughout the region.

As a more established church, Trinity can help support these church plants, both financially and spiritually. According to Blackaby, Trinity's help ranges from raising money for new buildings, to mentoring leaders, to keeping the young churches financially accountable, to sending out teams from the congregation to assist in ministry. No wonder Trinity Baptist Church has adopted a vision statement: "Joining God to do more than we could ask or imagine, for His glory!"

When it comes to outreach ministries, Blackaby and his congregation do not gauge success based on the number of people who attend a given event. Instead, they want to see three things happen as a result of their interaction with the lost of Calgary. Members of Trinity want to (1) give the lost a reason to ask about the hope that is within believers, (2) show them what the kingdom looks like, and (3) prove that this church is not a gimmick, but that it exists for the benefit of others. Members seek out opportunities to communicate this message not only through more conventional, church-sponsored ministries such as block parties, sports camps, and scrapbooking clubs, but also through simple acts of community support. This can range from building gazebos and bandstands in neighborhoods that request it to taking up special offerings for those in need, and serving barbecue at the annual Calgary Stampede.

When Trinity Baptist Church initiated a fund-raising drive for Katrina victims, the response was overwhelming. Blackaby suspects that Calgarians responded because "the people around here don't want a church, but they sure want the kingdom."[93] When they see a group of people who supports the community and is centered on others, they want to get involved.

Being missional takes patience; it isn't for pastors who like to see really big numbers really fast. Blackaby said that it can take years to even gain a foothole in towns such as

[93] Rob Blackaby, 1 November, 2006.

Lethbridge, where many people's hearts are hardened toward religion and the gospel. "You can't just expect to recite the Four Spiritual Laws and then see massive conversions," said Blackaby. "You have to have patience. You have to be creative. Sometimes you just have to trust that the seeds you are planting will one day be harvested, even if you are not around to see it happen."

Some believe Canada's ethnic diversity and secularization are an indication of where the United States is headed. If so, we need to learn from our partners in Canada. First, see your community as a mosaic of people, not as a melting pot. Seek to identify people groups and understand their worldviews. Second, note the hunger in Canada for community. People feel isolated and hunger for relationships. Connect people with people, then move them toward Christ. Third, have a passion to plant churches. They understand that their environment requires the planting of a wide variety of churches if they are going to reach the lost with the gospel of Jesus Christ. Finally, depend on God to achieve His mission to gather, for His glory, a people from all peoples. Prayer is not a part of their strategy. It is their strategy.

CHAPTER TEN

Japanese International Baptist Church:

A Mission without a Model

For Japanese International Baptist Church (JIBC) in Tigard, Oregon, eight miles south of Portland, carrying out the mission of God has meant not abandoning the Japanese culture so integral to its origin and identity, but leveraging it for the sake of the gospel.

Seven years ago the church transitioned from being a Japanese-speaking congregation to one that conducts worship services in Japanese and English. It was a move intended to meet the needs of Japanese-American people. It became one that required the church to truly live up to its name: First it was Japanese, and now it is international.

"We are becoming multicultural, kind of a mosaic church," said Pastor Mike Yokoy, who has served the church for the past 24 years. "It has been a transformation that both excites and somewhat perplexes its 60-year-old leader, a surprising, if rewarding, byproduct of being a missional church situated in Portland's urban fringe.

"I don't know why they're coming to Japanese International Baptist Church," said Yokoy of the Anglos who make up about a third of the congregation, previously comprised mostly of Asians, predominantly Japanese. "But God is calling me to minister to the people that are here."[94]

Desperately Seeking a Savior

Japanese International Baptist Church got its start in 1979, some four years before Yokoy relocated to the states from Japan. His explanation for why he left Japan, where he served as a bivocational associate pastor while working for a trading company, is stark in its simplicity: "God called."

Yokoy was a college student contemplating launching his career when he became a Christian. He already had a job lined up after graduation and was eagerly anticipating the next stage of his life. All that forward-thinking commanding his attention left its impact. He found himself mulling over another upcoming certainty: his eventual death. He yearned for a solution to that impending crisis, and he went looking for one. First, he visited a Buddhist temple to try to "learn how to overcome the future." He came up empty in his quest.

"I started looking for the answer, but no answer came to me." The future, which had looked so positive and appealing when he was considering his career, now looked grim and foreboding when he considered his death. Contemplating this, he spiraled downwards into a state of depression. "I tried to suicide myself," Yokoy admitted. "But it failed."

[94] Mike Yokoy, phone interview by author, 21, 28 September and 18, October 2006.

Meanwhile, his parents had become Christians, and Yokoy, and after returning to his home in Tokyo following graduation, saw the change in them. After receiving a visit from their pastor, he started attending their Southern Baptist church. "I realized the Word, the Bible, was really speaking to me in my heart." He learned the words that Jesus spoke from the cross; words to the Father of forgiveness, and he found them powerful and compelling; words "that stuck in my head." When he connected those words to his own life, coming to terms with the realization that Jesus also spoke them to him personally, they changed his future and his eternity. "I realized that was for me. I wasn't discouraged any more with my life."

A Missional Leader in the Making

Taking up residence in the states happened as a coincidence of God's design, the kind that served to define Yokoy's style of missional leadership and his calling. He was enroute to Brazil for a mission trip when he stopped over in San Francisco to attend Nineteenth Avenue Baptist Church, one of the few Japanese-speaking congregations in existence in the U.S. at that time. There he met a couple, a Japanese woman and her American military husband. He watched the woman dissolve into tears during the worship service, so obviously and profoundly moved she could not contain herself—and he could not prevent himself from asking questions:

"'I was wondering what happened? Why are you so touched by the service?'" She responded that it was the first time they had listened to the gospel of Jesus Christ in her own language. Her heartfelt response to this new experience was enlightening for Yokoy—and something of a discovery.

"The heart language is very important for us to listen to the gospel," Yokoy realized. He had grasped a key concept, one that he would never forget as a leader and which he would instill in the church he would soon plant: the need to communicate the gospel in the heart language of the listener. In that awakening was born a desire to go to the United States to tell the Japanese living there about Jesus in the language they understood best.

Back in his native Japan, people questioned why he felt led to America when there were so many Japanese who needed to hear right where he was—less than one percent of the Japanese in that country are professing Christians—but Yokoy did not question what he felt called to do. "'I don't know, but God called us,'" he responded.[95]

Realizing he needed an official reason to enter the U.S., he enrolled in Luther Rice Seminary (LRS), packed up his wife Yumiko and three sons, and settled into a life in Jacksonville, Florida.

Yokoy, who was then in his early 30s, was a full-time student at LRS enjoying the warm subtropical climate when he received a call from Tigard a year later. He had already gotten acquainted with this Japanese congregation, and it was losing its pastor, who was returning

[95] Michitsugu Yokoi, "A New Paradigm in Japanese Ministry: God at Work through Southern Baptists in the Pacific Northwest," *Baptist History and Heritage,* Summer-Fall, 2004, *Http://findarticles.com/p/articles/mi_mONXG/is_3_39/ai_n8685614* (accessed October 9, 2006).

to Japan. Although the congregation consisted of only about 10 people, they could financially support a pastor. Would Yokoy consider the position?

He wanted to turn it down. "I didn't feel that was the direction I should go. I wanted to stay in our area in Florida." Furthermore, he knew not only were there very few Japanese-speaking congregations anywhere in the U.S.—so the field was wide open right where he was—there also were very few churches of any kind in the Northwest. It was a factor that both repelled and intrigued him. He did not want to give up either the comfortable climate of warm weather or the warm support of other churches and Christians.

The pull of the mission overwhelmed him, however, and he found his focus. "God struck my heart to come in this direction. I could not resist." Having already crossed one culture in the leap across the ocean from Japan to America, he made another. He moved to the Pacific Northwest. "God changed my life."

A Church and a Movement Take Root

JIBC had barely established a permanent presence in Portland when Yokoy led the church to begin the process of multiplication. When Yokoy agreed to serve the Japanese congregation as its pastor in 1983, it had not yet assumed the formal structure of a church. He followed two previous pastors, including founding pastor John T. Kamiyama, who moved from Portland to start a Japanese church in Salt Lake City, and Shiro "Jimmy" Sasake, who moved back to Japan to minister to the Japanese there. Kamiyama had visited several Portland churches without letting them know that he was a Japanese pastor to determine receptivity to Japanese in the Christian community. He got a single return visit from Metropolitan Baptist Church, which later agreed to sponsor the mission. After Yokoy arrived on the scene, Metropolitan was still funding half of his modest $500 monthly salary.[96]

Yokoy served as mission pastor until JIBC was formally organized as a church in 1988 with 44 charter members. A year later the congregation purchased four acres of land with a loan from the Home Mission Board, now the North American Mission Board (NAMB). By 1995 the church was finally ready to build and constructed a 7,000-square-foot facility. Meanwhile, a congregation that began with only a handful of people was growing steadily in the years that followed, setting precedents and breaking records along the way.[97]

JIBC became the first Southern Baptist Japanese church organized in the Pacific Northwest, and the first Japanese Southern Baptist congregation since World War II to build its own facility. With an average attendance of 180 today, it ranks as one of the largest Japanese churches of any kind in the United States.[98]

The church has not been content with those accomplishments. One of the most outstanding characteristics distinguishing JIBC as a missional church is its expansive church planting efforts. Since its inception, the church has assisted in planting 10 other Japanese churches, beginning with an initial church plant in Tacoma, Washington. Yokoy

[96] Yokoi, "A New Paradigm in Japanese Ministry," 1.
[97] Yokoi, "A New Paradigm in Japanese Ministry," 1.
[98] Ibid., 1.

commuted weekly to Tacoma to preach in a Bible study to help get that congregation established. He later also commuted weekly to Phoenix, Arizona, for a year to assist with the development of a congregation there. Both churches were dubbed after their namesake, JIBC, becoming Japanese International Baptist Church of Tacoma and Phoenix, respectively. "I didn't intend that," said a modest Yokoy. His weekly commutes to their communities, funded by JIBC, evidently made an impression, although Yokoy shrugs off his personal contribution with self-deprecating humor. "I was still young at the time."

Members of JIBC also made regular treks to Tacoma and Phoenix to encourage the fledgling congregations, but by the time the Phoenix church was in its second-year stretch, Yokoy, who was flying to Phoenix and spending two or three nights a week in Arizona, also was growing concerned about how much time he was sacrificing from his family. He started sending staff members there in his place but with a new tactic. They went in three- to four-month stretches at a time until a pastor came from Japan to take over the church the third year.

Working in partnership with NAMB as a church planter, Yokoy also helped start Japanese churches in Boston, Denver, Los Angeles, San Jose, Indianapolis, Chicago, and Vancouver. He traveled to each of these cities to conduct preliminary survey work to determine whether a congregation would be viable there. Although a return visit to the city was "rare," according to Yokoy, he has mentored these other church planters through phone calls and e-mail. In addition, JIBC took up special offerings for each new church plant.

Meanwhile, under Yokoy's leadership, JIBC in Tigard was becoming training ground for other church planters. Yokoy also joined with two other Japanese pastors and their churches to form the Japanese Church Planting Network for the purpose of planting Japanese churches in all 50 states. "The vision is at least one church in one state," Yokoy said. Twelve churches now belong to the network, each contributing one to two percent of its budget to the network to support new church planters. For example, the Japanese Church Planting Network recently trained a couple through JIBC now taking up residence in St. Louis to plant a church there. Training for church planters often occurs at JIBC, which also provides training through its association and the Northwest Baptist Convention.

JIBC recruits pastors from Japan to come to the states as church planters, offering those six months of training. It is not an easy task because the small Christian population in Japan means churches there struggle to find their own pastors. Despite this, Yokoy finds, through prayer, they keep coming.

"They need to be trained here before we send them out because they need to know the culture," Yokoy said. Yet Japanese church planting in America differs from church planting in Japan primarily because in Japan church planters can "fish from all the rivers," according to Yokoy, but in the states "we have to find a good river to fish."
To aid in cultivating prospective church planters, JIBC has started its own Bible school. The church enlists teachers from Japan to teach weekend courses and seminars, which it also has begun offering to online students. Although it is not yet accredited, the church

has entered discussions with Golden Gate Southern Baptist Theological Seminary on cooperative education.

JIBC's activity in church planting means that Yokoy, a father of six, including two daughters and a son born since he moved to the states, traces a family tree of another kind because of JIBC's influence as a missional church committed to planting churches. JIBC helped start the church in Tacoma—the same year it purchased its land—commissioning one of its members as the church planter. That church in turn planted a church in Lynwood. "We say we're the grandfather," Yokoy chuckled. Now the grandson is considering giving birth to yet another church and is in the process of developing a church plant between North Seattle and Vancouver, Washington, making four generations of churches that JIBC will be able to claim in its lineage. "The next one will be the great-grandson or daughter."

It Takes a Relationship

As a missional church, JIBC understands that the context for most unbelievers to consider a relationship with Jesus Christ is in a relationship. Therefore, small group ministry is vital at JIBC as an environment for connecting Christians with people outside the church. Utilizing small groups as connectors to their community makes room for incarnational living, or embodying Christ, outside the church walls.

There is a practical side to this as well. Like many other language churches, JIBC's borders are fluid and reach beyond the confines of Tigard city limits. "This is not a typical community church," Yokoy said. "Our members are scattered throughout the city (Portland)."

So are their small groups, where newcomers typically go first to home Bible studies before they ever attend a worship service on the church campus, the JIBC ideal. Indeed, Yokoy identifies "the joy of salvation" as what church members embody so well that it leads unbelievers to desire their own relationship with Jesus Christ. "The Christian himself or herself has joy in their daily lives," Yokoy said. "They will see the joy in him or her and then the power to draw the people into a small group. So we want them to come to small group and have fellowship before they come to the church. So relationship will be first, then worship."

One Church Bridging Two Cultures

Finding the river with fish and the right bait to catch them requires Yokoy to stay intimately involved in the Japanese community in Portland. Many are business people or employees in what Yokoy dubbed Portland's "Silicon Forest." Others own family businesses or are professionals, like doctors and lawyers.

Missional churches like JIBC strive to establish themselves so that from the outset they can penetrate the culture they serve. At the beginning for JIBC that meant speaking Japanese, utilizing Japanese music, and serving up Japanese meals. Although an ethnic language church like JIBC, established to meet the needs of a specific people group, might be excused then for assuming it had correctly defined its cultural box for its duration, JIBC has learned that for it to carry out its mission it must pay attention to the culture within the culture and seek to cross it accordingly.

Perhaps the most significant cultural phenomenon JIBC has been intentional about trying to reflect is diversity. Communication and understanding of competing and complementing cultures within an increasingly diverse congregation is a primary way the church crosses cultures. Not only does JIBC offer worship services in two languages, an English-speaking early Sunday service and a Japanese service later that morning, meetings and churchwide activities, like the church's harvest carnival or Christmas family night, are conducted in two languages, an important but arduous enterprise. "We have time limitations," Yokoy noted. "Translation takes lots of time to do."

While the two worship services strive to be identical musically, they differ in most other ways. Not only is the language different, they have different pastors, different messages, and a different focus, according to Yokoy.

Back-to-back Sunday Schools also serve both language needs of adults in the church. Youth and children—one out of three people in the congregation is under age 18—who usually speak English only, are served by English classes. Even the church's Web site, *jibconline.com*, accommodates both Japanese and English readers.

Making the jump to becoming a bilingual church was "a big struggle at the time," Yokoy admitted. While the church was trying to find a pastor to take leadership of the English services, Yokoy conducted them himself. A year passed in the search process before the church enlisted the services of a Korean pastor to lead the English services. In time, however, the young Korean pastor launched out on his own, and part of the English-speaking congregation, which had been growing, followed. It was, as Yokoy describes with wry humor, "unintentional church planting."

He has accepted the loss with good grace. "God blessed a whole congregation. He started another Asian Baptist church. Praise the Lord for that."

It also, however, highlighted the church's continuing need to minister across cultures rather than focusing only on one. Meanwhile, needing a replacement to lead the English service, the church went through 50 resumes with no true candidate in sight. "We wanted to have unity in the search," Yokoy said. Ten months later, however, the search committee had not agreed on anyone.

With no more potential candidates, someone suggested Yokoy's son, who was then a seminary student. "I didn't even want him to become a pastor because he was young and inexperienced," Yokoy recalled. It appeared, however, the committee had finally found common ground, and they tapped Kenji to become the church's English pastor.

A qualifying characteristic in Kenji's favor was his mixed marriage, also a characteristic of many of those attending the English-speaking worship service. Like so many others in the congregation, Kenji has a Caucasian spouse. In addition to such couples, that worship service also is peopled by second- and third-generation Japanese-Americans who speak only English, an estimated 60 percent of the congregation, according to Yokoy.

"Conversation does not work to fill the spiritual hunger," said Yokoy, who recognized in the English-speaking people attending the church the same desire as the Japanese's to hear the gospel in their heart language. "We needed ownership of an English congregation."

The creation of an English-speaking worship service in 1999 opened up a harvest field that surpassed Yokoy's original expectations. "We are effectively reaching the Japanese-speaking people," he said, "but they are effectively reaching English-speaking people." What was once a very focused and limited target audience for the gospel—Yokoy estimates that there are some 4,000 Japanese in Portland—is no longer limited by language. Relationships that move beyond language and ethnicity put other cultures within JIBC's reach. "English speaking (worship services) can reach anybody who speaks English," he pointed out. "The target is very wide." Caucasians in the church already number 29, according to Yokoy, and in addition to them there are a number of Japanese who speak English only. The church also employs an Anglo as its administrator, a choice made because of his gift mix, but reflective of the emerging face of the congregation.

Prayer, Not Programs to Guide Them

JIBC identifies itself as a purpose-driven church, a paradigm Yokoy embraced in 2000 after attending a Purpose-Driven Church conference with Rick Warren, pastor of Saddleback Baptist Church. Following that conference, Yokoy led JIBC to adopt core values, a vision statement, and mission statement. One of the characteristics of a missional church is seeking the heart of God, and pastors and staff spent concerted time praying about these, hammering them out in discussion before presenting them to the church body:

JIBC Core Values

1. Ministering to people of Japanese ancestry and others who may be directly or indirectly related to them in some way.
2. Accepting each other's differences yet expanding JIBC's confession of faith in unity.
3. Using both English and Japanese.
4. Providing a church unified in love that can reach out to the wholefamily.
5. Seeking the infilling and presence of the Holy Spirit in every meeting.
6. Giving importance to the prayer ministry.

JIBC Vision Statement

We exist as a church in Portland, Oregon, to be blessed and to joyfully:

1. Provide high quality Spirit-filled worship.
2. Have fellowship filled church with the love of Christ.
3. Use every opportunity to spread the gospel.
4. Send well trained people to Japan and all areas of the world.

JIBC Mission Statement

1. Worship in Spirit and Truth.
2. Teach God's Word consistently and let people apply it for daily life.

3. Receive the Holy Spirit's power through people to advance spiritual warfare.
4. Demonstrate His love and expand the Kingdom of God by ABF (Agape Bible Fellowship) Ministries.

Of its six core values, which the church drew up and adopted while assuming the purpose-driven paradigm, many embrace a missional church stance. Prayer takes a vital role in the church's ministry. The church meets regularly for prayer Wednesday mornings and evenings. Prayerwalks, intercessory prayer, and a healing ministry, which consists of praying for the sick, also are practiced.

Beyond that, however, JIBC tries to make seeking the heart of God, a missional church distinctive, not only drive its ministries but be the source from which any such ministry is derived. For example, prayer is the process by which the vision for any new ministry is approved. Not only do initiating parties seek God's guidance, but they encourage others to join them in prayer, too. While JIBC utilizes a practical formula to start the process—they determine interest with a small survey through the church bulletin—they seek the empowerment of the Holy Spirit as a signal that this is right for the church before any ministry is implemented.

Keeping it Simple

Yokoy has taken to heart the missional church principle of simplifying church, making changes over the past few years with the goal of streamlining church operations—to the point of cutting ministries and ministry leaders, a move which at first glance may seem at odds with the demands of a growing church. He has also curtailed bureaucracy to maintain focus on purpose and not process. "We have learned to have a meeting-less ministry," he said. "Baptists have a lot of meetings. We are so tired of meetings."

The less-is-more philosophy shows up as the church limits what it undertakes in ministry. Indeed, starting ministries is a careful, prayerful process rather than impulsive or whimsical. "Staff members do not encourage people to start ministries," Yokoy noted. Nor do staffers organize or run ministries themselves. "We do not control anything." Instead, they try to determine if God is beginning new ministries in their midst.

In that process, church staffers take a back seat to laity. "We will observe the ministry, whether it is going well or not, and will help," but staff remain hands-off on day-to-day operation. Such an operational philosophy espouses the principles of missional leadership, releasing the church at large to do the ministry God created them to do, encouraging people to discover their own dreams for ministry, and develop their gifts to make them happen. In addition to Yokoy, JIBC has a staff of seven, four of whom are part-time, including support staff. Yokoy's son, Michi, serves as worship pastor, and the church administrator is Anglo, another cultural bridge.

Church members also are encouraged to prioritize their involvement as necessary to keep church life simple and focused. "We ask them to first commit to worship," said Yokoy. Small group is the next desired priority, and third is prayer meeting.

Although leaders receive training, home Bible studies are conducted with the goal of not requiring leaders to engage in rigorous weekly preparation. "They are encouraged to be coordinators of the meeting," Yokoy said. Leaders are provided materials, daily devotions, which are available in Japanese and have small-group resources. "They don't have to prepare."

The church is further broken down into more small groups—children, youth, young adults, seniors—to encourage efficiency in outreach. "We encourage small-group ministry in every area of the church."

Even evangelism and missions are conducted with simplicity in mind. Yokoy trains church leaders that there are three types of people groups awaiting their evangelistic efforts. Group A is composed of the people who have exhibited signs of wanting to know Jesus Christ. Christians, Yokoy said, led by the Spirit will know who these people are by their interest.

Group B is composed of people who are not obviously seeking Him, but they have not rejected Christ outright either. Group C are people who outwardly reject Christ as Lord and Savior.

Yokoy encourages small group leaders to mentally categorize every newcomer in one of these three groups. Then he goes a step farther. "I encourage leaders to stick to Class A. Of course, we need to focus on B and C—we're trying to reach B and C." So small-group leaders will not get discouraged, Yokoy tries to keep their focus on Group A for a purpose. "They see people saved. Then they'll have the power to focus on B and C."

The results have been rewarding. JIBC has baptized more than 10 people a year for the past five years and have had as many as 25 baptisms in a single year. To discover prospects, church members work with parachurch ministries and leaders to find and reach seekers.

Eyes on the World

The need for evangelism and mission where they are located in Portland is critical, according to Yokoy, who noted that only one out of four people attended a church of any kind in their area the previous year—and that included the Easter- and Christmas-only attendees. Oregon ranks as one of the least churched states in the country, he said.

Being a missional church, however, means assuming responsibility not only for one's Jerusalem, Judea, and Samaria, but also the ends of the earth. Yokoy, therefore, is training the church to see the global picture, too. JIBC supports the Cooperative Program to partner with other churches in deploying missionaries all over the world. It also sends its own people to take part in the mission of proclaiming Jesus Christ. In addition to sending mission teams back to Japan on a regular basis, JIBC has had members take mission trips to Africa, for example, and other parts of Asia. Teams also have been involved in rebuilding work going on in New Orleans.

"The goal for us is to open our eyes overseas," Yokoy said. ". . . focus our eyes on the world rather than this area."

The Cultural Chameleon

Although JIBC has been instrumental in establishing several of the existing Japanese churches in the United States, staying alert to cultural changes and adapting to them in the manner of a missional church has meant actually moving away from its focus on the Japanese, according to Yokoy.

For example, the church serves a weekly ethnic lunch, limited to 75 people, on a first-come, first-served basis. What was once an opportunity for Japanese people to sample their native foods again has evolved into ethnically mixed fare. "The menu is changing all the time," Yokoy noted—because the people who are preparing the meals are no longer Japanese nationals only but people of other nationalities who introduce their own dishes.

"Culture is really changing in our church," Yokoy said. "I'm changing, too. The longer I live here in the states, the more I'm getting Americanized. The more we have diverse people the less we're interested in Japanese culture."

What remains of interest to them, however, is unity, one of their core values, which recognizes diversity for what it is, a culture that is never so stagnant that the missional church should not be looking for evidences of its evolution and adapting to them as such changes take place.

For example, on a recent Sunday, JIBC baptized five people, four in the English service and one in the Japanese worship service. Of the five, two were Anglos and one was of mixed racial heritage (Native American and Scottish). The fourth was Asian, and the fifth was Japanese-American. Four of those five had little understanding of Japanese culture, according to Yokoy, but they have been baptized into a church established for Japanese. As of now, about a third of the congregation is of other ethnic backgrounds.

The church is not relinquishing claims to its Japanese culture or intending to abandon its heritage because it desires to leverage it for the sake of the gospel. It is still JIBC's understanding of the Japanese culture that acts as the bait that initially attracts the attention of most newcomers, according to Yokoy. But it is Christ, radiant in the lives of the people, who draws them in.

"Otherwise they don't stay. They become members because of our culture initially but because of our faith, they join with us." It is another missional church characteristic, this authenticity in the Christian life that becomes apparent to the unbeliever.

This shift in focus is not to the exclusion of the culture in which JIBC finds itself, but an acknowledgement of it. Their understanding of their culture allows them to mix regularly with unbelievers, but their focus on faith is what draws the unbeliever to them. "They are being blessed by their faith in Jesus. Our church is Christ-centered, not culture-centered any more." In that respect, JIBC also exhibits an all-important characteristic of the missional church: an unconditional love for people. Instead of letting their doors close around the Japanese culture upon which it was based, JIBC has assumed a missional stance by extending acceptance and love for all people, regardless of their ethnicity. Indeed, Kenji

Yokoy, English pastor, has identified a group that is growing in the church, people with a history of substance abuse—presumably drawn to the congregation, not because of its expertise in dealing with such problems, but because of the love and acceptance the church shows for people of all types.

"Originally when we first started this congregation we did not think we would be able to reach people who are not interested in the Japanese culture or are not connected to Japanese, but out heart has always been to reach everyone for Christ—everyone that we possibly can," Kenji said.[99]

Yokoy admitted that they are poised on the brink of something he does not quite know how to navigate. "That's why I don't know in the future how to do it. There's no model." Although he has seen Korean churches take a similar path, "Japanese and Koreans are really different, culturally different."

In other words, it is a walk of faith—a journey that is propelling Yokoy and JIBC into uncharted territory as they live out their mission of proclaiming Christ to their community and the world.

[99] Kenji Yokoy, phone interview by author, 23 October, 2006.

CHAPTER ELEVEN

Cuyahoga Valley Church:

Planting Churches Inside and Out

Although he's worn the title of pastor for some 20 years, Rick Duncan readily identifies himself in broader, and yet more precise, terms. "I'm a missionary," he said. It follows then that the church he planted, Cuyahoga Valley Church (CVC) in Broadview Heights, Ohio, a suburb of Cleveland, can be defined that way, too. Not only has it found a way to live out the mission of God by planting churches all over the world, it has identified and developed the church within.

Duncan was 33 years old when he moved to Cleveland to plant a church. A graduate of Vanderbilt University in Nashville, he played college baseball and was drafted by the Minnesota Twins. He spent about five years playing minor league baseball before he went to work for the Fellowship of Christian Athletes in Florida. At age 30 he made his way to Mid-America Baptist Theological Seminary in Memphis, a school that emphasized missions and evangelism, "where everybody would end up in foreign missions"[100]if the president had his way, according to Duncan.

Duncan's next move following seminary, therefore, was to sign up to become a church planter through the Church Planter Apprentice program offered through the Home Mission Board, now the North American Mission Board (NAMB). Duncan's uncle, Don Davidson, was serving as state missions director in Ohio and suggested he consider planting a church there. He also had another opportunity present itself in Florida. He sought the counsel of the president of Mid-America, Gray Allison, whose direction Duncan recalls as this: "'Rick, anybody can go to Orlando. Who will go to Cleveland?'" In those words Duncan heard an Isaiah 6 call to Ohio.

He contacted a friend, the chaplain for Cleveland area sports teams, including the Cleveland Browns, to inquire about the spiritual climate in Cleveland. The response he received would not be considered encouraging by many. His friend painted a bleak picture, noting that area pastors and churches were discouraged and depressed over the spiritual condition of the area. It was, however, the right motivator for a missionary like Duncan. In 1987 he and his wife Maryanne moved to Cleveland to plant a church sponsored by Far Hills Community Church in Dayton.

Although he previously had served as a youth pastor at a church in Memphis and an intern at Bellevue Baptist Church pastored by Adrian Rogers, it would be his first experience starting a church from scratch and serving as its lead pastor. "That was kind of a culture shock for me, coming from Bellevue Baptist Church."

[100] Rick Duncan, interview by author, 28 October, 2006 and 7 November, 2006.

Duncan had soon established three Bible studies, but he was discovering that in those days there was not a lot out there on how to plant a church. He got some tapes from Rick Warren, founding pastor of Saddleback Community Church in Saddleback, California, and listened to them "over and over again." He attended a church planting seminar offered by Fuller Theological Seminary. "We made a lot of mistakes early on," he said. Six months into the experience, teams came from churches down South, including Bellevue, to give support.

Eventually, on the heels of a mass mailing to some 13,000 households, Cuyahoga Valley Church launched in 1987 with some 120 people gathering for its first service. By the next Sunday, however, attendance was down to 75—and dropping.

How CVC halted its downward spiral and has grown steadily since into a congregation of nearly 1,500 people (not including attendance at its Sevenoseven worship services) is the outcome of an ardent pursuit of its mission.

The Prayer That Changed CVC History

Although no one can predict how things might have turned out if the church had adapted to a different scenario, Duncan points to a prayer as the initiator of things to come. CVC spent years meeting in rented schools, first in an elementary school and then a middle school, before it came into its own in terms of property and buildings. Operating "church in a truck," the body spent a laborious 14 years setting up and taking down everything needed for Sunday service: sound equipment, tables, children's materials, coffeepots, etc. It was backbreaking work, and the desire to be housed in a permanent place resulted in the formation of a property search team to look for 10 acres upon which to build.[101]

Meanwhile, the church had plateaued at about 450 to 500 in attendance—with no property in sight. "We had a hard time in that area," Duncan admitted. Eventually the property search team itself resigned. This setback turned out to be a watershed event.

When a property search team regrouped they realized they were pursuing a goal from their perspective rather than from God's. They no longer looked for property in the same way. They no longer prayed in the same spirit. They sought God's direction. "We stopped asking, 'Where are there 10 acres?' to, 'Where does God want us to be?'" When they put that question to God, they found an answer: the corner of Wallings Road and I-77, a highly visible location in suburban Cleveland.

The church approached owners of six parcels of land not already up for sale. Soon five of them agreed—all about the same time—to sell their property. "We really feel like that was God prompting all these people to sell their property." The church acquired 16.5 acres with three houses.

It wasn't, however, a smooth process from that point on. Finding a building plan that was acceptable and affordable remained a challenge. Construction finally began in 1999, and the church was able to occupy the building in 2001. The congregation erected

[101] "Our History," *http://www.cuyahogavalleychurch.com/history/history/html* (accessed October 26, 2006).

a cornerstone, not allocated to a corner of the facility or hidden by shrubbery, but deliberately placed in a prime spot above its doorway: "To God Alone Be the Glory." Moving into its own facility immediately spiked attendance and the church broke the 500 barrier. As the church reached more people—services went from two to three then four, including a Saturday night worship service and three morning worship services—the buildings multiplied, too. Phase II and III included developing and completing classrooms in the unfinished lower level. Most recently the church reconfigured existing space by removing offices and classrooms to enlarge the worship center. It also added a balcony, parking and trailers.[102]

Making a Mission of Young Adults

CVC, which had sought from inception to be culturally relevant through the use of contemporary music, appropriate Bible teaching and dramas, determined a few years ago to take further steps to stay relevant to a new generation and attuned to its culture. By 1998 the vision to create a mission to young adults was also forming. Duncan said a friend at McLean Bible Church in Washington, D.C., which founded a similar ministry, Frontline, to appeal to young adults, sparked the idea. "He planted some seeds with me."

Duncan recognized that to appeal to Cleveland's population of some 300,000 young adults, part of the most unchurched generation in U.S. history, would require crossing cultural barriers created by the passage of time and a church that was beginning, like its pastor, to show some age. Although Duncan had been a 30-something when he planted CVC, he was now middle-aged, and his congregation was aging along with him. "It helped educate us to reach some people in the community that we weren't reaching." They recognized barriers that were not simply generational in nature but included elements from the postmodern worldview of this younger generation. "So the communication style that works for that audience is different," Duncan said, noting that it is "more relational, more story-driven, more raw and more authentic."

Thus, Sevenoseven Ministries was created almost four years ago to reach adults age 18-30. Although 707 worship services are conducted on campus under the CVC umbrella of ministry, they brand themselves for a younger audience through the use of five screens which project the audience rather than the now traditional Power Point, humorous video clips and a U2-style worship band, updating CVC's worship style for a generation of young adults raised in an age of multi-media and technology.[103]

In addition, 707 has its own pastor, worship leader and community groups, making it truly a church within a church. "We felt like if we're going to reach that audience they don't need to be hearing from a 53-year-old guy," said Duncan. He noted that he only occasionally addresses the 707 crowd. "If we're going to win that crowd we need to empower leaders in that age bracket to have the freedom to reach their peers." According to Duncan, it constitutes delegation with authority, but it's got to be done. "You need to treat it like it's a foreign mission" and find a spokesman who understands the pluralism, tolerance and truth-is-relative philosophies of that generation." Thinking that a 50-year-

[102] "Our History." *http://cuyahogavalleychurch.com/history/history.html* (accessed October 26, 2006).

[103] Kima Jude, "One Size Doesn't Fit All: Planting Missional Churches," *On Mission* (Fall 2006), 36.

old can do it because he's "a cool 50-year-old" won't work. Thinking that you can reach them through "big church" won't either, Duncan said. Instead, you've got to find someone who can speak their language.

Although CVC considers 707 a church in its own right, it does feed back into the parent church. "As people kind of grow out of that they come into the Sunday morning experience." The difference between the Sunday morning and Sunday night worship services is, in a word, "polish," according to Duncan. On Sunday nights there is "no pretense of watering anything down. They're a little bit more, 'Hey, just give me the straight stuff." It's: 'Here is what the Bible says—just deal with it.'"

Sevenoseven apparently inherited the DNA of its parent church. Included in seven statements listed on its website are core values that CVC has modeled:

- Sevenoseven believes that our source of authority and guidance is the Bible, not man's wisdom.
- The focus of our ministry is God's love for people, not programs.
- The message of Sevenoseven is found in the person of Jesus Christ.
- We believe that people grow best in an authentic, caring community.
- The goal of Sevenoseven is to produce passionate followers of Jesus.
- People are very important to us, and we believe that every Christian has a
- God-given ministry to serve.
- We believe strongly that the process of our ministry is spiritual reproduction, not just addition.[104]

Just as finding the right property had to be steered by the right kind of prayer, the formation of 707 required it, too, according to Nancy Still, age 27 and a student at Moody Bible Institute. Still was a student at Cleveland State University and part of the 707 core group when she walked the campus and prayed "asking the Lord to bring them in."

The name 707 Ministries itself is derived from Matthew 7:7: "Ask and it will be given to you; seek and you will find; knock and the door will be opened to you" (NIV). Since knocking on that door, 707 Ministries has exploded with growth. It has expanded to three Sunday evening worship services and a Tuesday service. Another campus was established, 707 West, reaching up to 1,700 young adults, many of whom drive long distances to attend, making the 707 congregation more regional than CVC. That congregation is more multi-cultural, too, according to Duncan, because that generation is better at crossing racial barriers than were their parents. "We baby boomers talk like we are, but we don't really live it out." Sevenoseven West was expected to transfer into another ministry, but at the time of this writing, 707 was planning yet another campus.[105]

Multiplying the Mission

Beyond the church-within-a-church model as an extension of itself, Cuyahoga Valley identifies church planting in its city, state and around the world as central to its mission.

[104] "What Is Sevenoseven?" *http://www.sevenoseven.com/bet/what/* (accessed November 1, 2006).
[105] Jude, *On Mission,* 36-37.

One way it has done this is to encourage members and leaders to make the leap from CVC to a new church plant, transforming themselves into church planters. For example, a former church missions director, Tom Wright, launched a multi-cultural church, Mosaic, in Cleveland's Chinatown last year. Wright had been involved in a ministry to international students, attempting to reach them with the gospel so that it would be exported to their home countries, when his focus shifted to the internationals that remain here, according to Randy Chestnut, director of missions for Greater Cleveland Association of Baptists, who lauds such against-the-grain innovation. "Some people have churches that start an international ministry. Here we have an international ministry that starts a church." The 40 people attending represent seven or so people groups. "Tom's passion is to see a church that's going to look a lot like heaven." In addition to providing financial and spiritual support—and the church planter—CVC has encouraged its members to "go down and be a part of that."[106]

Likewise, a bass guitarist for 707 Ministries planted a church, The Village Chapel, in Cleveland's urban Slavic Village. A Ukrainian intern started a church for Ukrainian young adults, Mercy Hill Chapel, offering English and Ukrainian services to share Christ with that people group. "These are guys that are leaders," Duncan said. Chestnut attributes what amounts to a sacrifice by CVC to the greater mission to Duncan's willingness to spend the church in multiplication. "He actually released some people to go as God led them."

CVC also is sponsoring a suburban church start, NorthPointe Community Church, in West Lake, and will be involved in a church start slated for 2007, Church of the Hills in the Sycamore Hills/Macedonia area. Out of nine new church plants begun over the past year in Cleveland, CVC has been involved in more than half, according to Chestnut, offering financial and prayer support and by mobilizing people for the mission effort.

In addition to responding to the unreached people groups in their own proximity, CVC extends their church planting efforts globally. "One of our passions also is planting churches overseas," Duncan noted. The congregation's church-planting efforts have included Thailand, Ghana, Ukraine and El Salvador. To date CVC, working with the International Mission Board (IMB), has planted 15 churches in Ghana, where it adopted the unreached people group, Nzema. Mission teams have been going regularly to Ghana since 1998 to conduct crusades, do personal evangelism and, working through the Ghana Baptist Convention, to train pastors.

Just as the church has managed to communicate a passion for church planting internalized by its leaders and members for local endeavors, individuals also are carrying it with them—or are being compelled by it—into the rest of the world. For example, the daughter of one of the church's ministers married an El Salvadoran and helped start an orphanage, Love and Hope Ministries, in that country. Planted along with the orphanage was a church, which has already established a preaching point beyond itself. "The dream is to start more orphanages (and more churches)," Duncan said. "That's the global piece." Moreover, former CVCers are faithfully serving on the mission field, supported by the IMB in India and Ukraine.

[106] Randy Chestnut, phone interview by author, 3 November, 2006.

Because Cleveland is, compared to other large cities, a very homogenous environment, Cuyahoga Valley Church mirrors that makeup, a fact that Duncan accepts. Forcing itself to cross cultures by "jumping over the heads" of the people group before them is not CVC's style, he said. He's concluded that even in a multi-cultural setting, the people involved are attracted to a homogenous factor that unifies them. Meanwhile, the church is intentionally crossing cultures by crossing oceans or, sometimes, the railroad tracks.

Developing a passion for such mission endeavors is a self-fueled movement, according to Duncan. "What we've found is that when people go on mission they experience a transformation that's hard to duplicate any other way."

Yet formal training has its place—especially if Duncan is able to mentor others and help them avoid mistakes. CVC works to provide training for potential and prospective church planters. It has recently joined with Glocalnet, a ministry organized by NorthWood Church in Dallas, Texas, which trains church planters in an intensive nine-month to year long apprentice program. Churches involved in Glocalnet partner together to pool resources, knowledge and a passion for church planting.

CVC is also helping bring someone on staff in their association to help launch new churches as a church planter strategist working for Cleveland Hope and CVC. Cleveland has been designated a Strategic Focus City, meaning that it has been targeted for a massive church planting effort by NAMB. Part of the strategist's job will be to start a church-planting school at CVC in 2007. "When training takes place, this (CVC) is where it happens," Duncan said.

Duncan also supports the association's Church Planting Network, which meets several times a year for fellowship, encouragement and practical resourcing. Duncan often teaches during the meetings, according to Chestnut.

The goal for Cleveland Hope is to start 20 new churches in the two-year period ending in 2007. Simply by being designated a Strategic Focus City, Cleveland's churches will grow even more over the next few years. But Chestnut is looking much farther ahead to measure its success. "The most important thing, as I tell people, we will know we're successful not when we plant churches but when the churches we plant plant churches." Chestnut also looks forward to an indigenous church planter movement that will end the tedious process of importing church planters to expedite Kingdom work.

Until then CVC and Duncan's leadership have been integral to the strides that Cleveland has already made, Chestnut said. He noted that Duncan, a native of Tennessee, while not indigenous, has helped create the kind of church environment that will initiate and sustain that kind of movement. "You've got to find that church that has the passion for it. There's a lot about climate and culture that you want to put people into. It's more caught than taught."

Finding God's Direction

While it seems church planting is rippling out in almost every direction, Duncan assured that CVC's church-planting efforts are deliberately channeled through the conduit of prayer. For example, he said CVC is praying about involvement in the Middle East. Interestingly, it is in the church's mission efforts that Duncan sees the most focus and intensity of prayer. "We don't have what I classify as a dynamic prayer meeting every week," he admitted. "But we're seeing prayer beginning to permeate our ministries more and more, particularly in the area of missions." He made a correlation between those who pray and those who do missions, noting that some of those most committed to prayer also are those most committed to missions.

One of the aspects of prayer that CVC has tried to make a focus is confession, according to Duncan, so that the church can then be guided by God and discern His leadership. With that in mind, Duncan has preached message series on confession. Church staffers hold solemn assemblies, setting aside periods of time together for the simple, humble act of confessing their sins. "We believe if we can become a broken people that will help a lot."

The Context for a Transformed Life

Like other churches determined to remain missional, CVC looks to its small groups as the means by which they stay on mission in the world. "The win for us is really a transformed life," said Duncan. "We say we think the best place that happens is in a Community Group."

CVC offers 123 groups and has 1,322 people in them, some 60 percent of its membership, according to Duncan. These groups typically meet in homes. According to Duncan, "some of it is a building issue for us." "Our building kind of forced us to this." While separate worship services are offered for children and adults, there is not enough space for small groups to meet on campus. The children's high-energy worship featuring drama and videos may be attended by more than 400 (youth and children worship services are not counted in attendance figures).

It is not a dilemma that has caused Duncan concern. "I think it helps build community better, too. If you're sitting around someone's kitchen table or living room or den, you're going to build a better bond than if you're sitting in a church building." Moreover, breaking out of the church box helps the congregation stay missional, according to Duncan. "It gets us out of church into the world in a better way."

To encourage participation off site, the church offers what it calls *Group Connect* three times a year to assimilate newcomers into a small group. A group's purpose is to "come together to care for one another, worship and learn," according to Duncan. "But you also come together to do missions."

As each small group finds ways to do missions they keep the church at large missional. For example, small groups have taken meals to a fire station in an attempt to develop relationships with the firefighters. "Who knows what God will do then?"

The church's mission team aids in this by providing small groups with serving options. Duncan explains, "so part of the experience is to be on mission in some way."

Free to be on Mission

Although the church has not formally adopted simplicity as one of its primary goals next year, Duncan said the church continually strives to make church life simple. (2007 goals include helping people grow toward spiritual maturity through participation within the life and ministries of the church, reaching an ever increasing percentage of Northeast Ohio with the gospel, and improving administrative/organizational/management operations of the church.) "One of our phrases that we're using for ourselves in '07 is *slow down*," he said. "It doesn't mean we're not going to be on mission anymore." In fact, it means that CVCers will be more efficiently on mission, according to Duncan.

A sign in an assistant's office expresses it well: "*Clarify, simplify, unify*." "We're in the process of trying to simplify things." Although the church has already streamlined business meetings to discussion of major items—"we adopt a budget"—Duncan believes simplicity liberates people to serve in more important ways. "We let people do what they want to do within the confines of that budget."

The missions committee, which inherits the biggest portion of the budget with 18 percent going to mission causes, operates with some accountability—but also a tremendous amount of freedom. "My attitude is get out of the way of the people," Duncan said. "I try to stay as a senior pastor up at 30,000 feet. We really try to empower people to do what God has called them to do."

The resulting vision and creativity is inspiring, he said. For example, after serving a stint in Iraq, one serviceman wanted to send supplies to soldiers there. CVC collected 30,000 shoeboxes stuffed with items for the troops, including copies of *The Purpose Driven Life* by Rick Warren. "Not that we always give thumbs up to everything someone wants to do," he said. "But if we can make it happen, we're going to make it happen."

Duncan said he experienced something of a defining moment some time ago when the writer of some material he was reading posed these thought-provoking questions: "'If your church disappeared from your community would the community notice? Would your community care?'" Aside from being relieved that some of the community's traffic problems would dissipate, Duncan wasn't sure the community would miss CVC.

That revelation changed the way he does ministry. Now he keeps community in focus. For example, the church regularly operates food drives. Grocery bags are printed with a list of desired items and handed out to members who fill the bags and bring them back to church with groceries inside. They then place the bags behind their cars in the church parking lot, where they are picked up by a truck, sorted and delivered to local city agencies that handle food distribution.

Where Duncan once suspected indifference from the city fathers he now finds gratitude, tangible in the letters he receives thanking the church for its help. "Our attitude is they're doing something really positive, and if it's a religious-neutral organization, we want to help them."

Despite registering increased approval from city agencies, Duncan confessed to harboring even higher hopes for CVC. "I'm still not satisfied with where we are. If we left, would the community care? I think we've made some inroads."

Opening Doors for the Gospel

Just as CVC tries to keep its church operations simple, its evangelistic strategy embraces a simple concept, too. Two words: *Invest* and *invite.* Church members are encouraged to invest their lives in someone who needs Christ, according to Duncan. "The reason they're coming is because somebody befriends them. We really feel like that's a strategy that seems to be working."

The second step, however, is to invite them to church. With that in mind, the church works to keep what it terms its *foyer* environment, or worship services—the place where newcomers go first—accessible, according to Duncan. "We try to use words that communicate to the uninitiated while at the same time trying to provide meat for the believer."

Duncan develops and communicates messages with the 35-year-old dad in mind, knowing that if he can reach that person, he'll reach most of the rest of the audience, too. "It's got to process through him first."

Likewise, during the children's Blast worship, leaders try to engage the fourth grade boy. "If you keep a fourth grade boy interested, the kindergarten kid's going to be okay, too." Blast, for example, is designed specifically to engage the irreligious. "Every Sunday is VBS. It's a program you want to bring your unchurched to."

Duncan applies that kind of standard to adult fare, too. After every Saturday night worship, the first service of the weekend, the creative planning team meets to evaluate the service's effectiveness and impact and do any needed tweaking before worship on Sunday. "We don't want a cringe factor going on," Duncan explained. "We really pay close attention to the environment that we're creating because we feel that people can meet God." Because of that, Duncan doesn't try to accommodate the demands of believers who want "sermons to be like a seminary lecture.

"I'm going to try to teach the Bible and give the saints something," he explained, "But I'm not going to forget the lost." Salvation generally requires, according to Duncan, many hearings, a cumulative effect rather than a single, swift blow. To keep his messages relevant, Duncan said he uses Adrian Rogers' formula of asking: *What? So what? Now what?* "The heavy emphasis is on the whole issue of application." To drive the so what question home, Duncan said he tries to imagine scenarios listeners may be facing, keeping that 35-year-old lost man in mind. "I try to get in that guy's life somehow."

"There's a missionary motive for why we're doing church the way we're doing it here." Being culturally relevant is important because "the cross is barrier enough," according to Duncan. For example, when Duncan first came to Cleveland 24 years ago the results of a survey conducted by Wright State University in Dayton convinced him that it would be beneficial to not use Baptist in the church's name. The survey indicated that Ohioans associated the word Baptist with legalism.

Converting the Act of Baptism

Outside of its invest-and-invite strategy, the church also utilizes mass evangelism tactics. For example, it attempted to leverage interest in the Da Vinci Code by sending out more than 23,000 pieces of material inviting people to learn more about the subjects it addressed—"not so much because we think it's all that effective," Duncan admitted, "but it gives people an opportunity to get out and do something. It plows up the fields in the community."

Although during worship services CVC invites people to fill out cards to indicate their desire to receive Christ "we don't believe that equals conversion," Duncan said. Follow-up is one-on-one to ensure that the person truly understands the gospel. If that has not happened, then someone will attempt to lead the person to Christ at that time or re-confirm the decision, according to Duncan. A baptism class gives others an opportunity to confirm the salvation experience. "We really work hard on qualifying the experience."

CVC discovered that a lot of people had never seen immersion baptism, and that the ritual itself can be poignant and inspiring to a novice generation. Therefore, to maximize the experience, the church videotapes the testimonies of those being baptized and plays them on screen during musical worship prior to the baptisms. "It's real intimate kind of experience, and I think it's an attractive experience."

Highlighting baptism in this way has resulted in numerous more baptisms. "One of the things that has happened around here is baptism has become a contagious thing." CVC and 707 baptized more than 160 people one Sunday last August with the 707 evening service lasting until midnight.

Joy and Grace Factors

At the heart of Duncan's missional leadership is a very simple motive, but one that fully embodies Christ: "I want to help contribute to an increase in the level of joy in my circle of influence," he explained. "The way you get to joy is faith in Christ." He cited Psalm 100 as his inspiration, a passage whose fulfillment depends on a missional church movement. "What I'm about is hopefully bringing joy to the world."

Meanwhile, Duncan takes no credit for what He's seen God do through CVC over the past 20 years. "God has just for whatever reason seen fit to show grace here." He's watched other church planters come and go—gifted men whose churches failed while CVC flourished. "Grace. It's just sheer grace—because we've done awful stupid things. "The only way you can explain the good things that have gone on here—God's inscrutable reasons. He gets the applause."

CHAPTER TWELVE

Peace Baptist Church:

Breaking the Cultural Barrier of Church Planting

If it never occurred to you that church planting may be a victim of its culture, it may be because you have not met pastor Tyrone Barnette, founder of Peace Baptist Church in Decatur, Georgia. Even then you may not know unless Barnette enlightens you—because you would not draw this conclusion from studying his church. The African-American church he planted has broken the cultural barrier of church planting. It has been directly involved in planting several churches across the globe—and Peace has just begun, according to Barnette. "We're just hitting the tip of the iceberg in church planting."[107]

Barnette started Peace Baptist in Decatur, Georgia almost 15 years ago with a vision not to just begin a single congregation but a church that would plant other churches. "The Lord put in my heart when we first started the church that we would change the way African-Americans do church," Barnette said. "There are not a lot of African-American churches that plant churches."

Barnette, who was raised in North Carolina, credits his family's influence, including parents and grandparents, with implanting a desire in him to make church plants the catalyst for changing the world. "It was that early exposure that they gave me to the concept of church planting." For example, on a recent trip home to conduct a funeral, Barnette stayed at his mother's house—but she was not there. Instead, she was ministering at a women's shelter where she stayed overnight.

Barnette attended North Carolina State University in Raleigh and got involved in United Student Fellowship, a campus ministry including a worship service attended by 300 students and faculty and 150 in Bible study. "We really tried to reach the African-Americans on campus."

That experience prepared him for what would come next. His wife accepted a scholarship at Georgia Tech to pursue her degree in mechanical engineering, and the couple ended up in Decatur. "We basically followed the money," Barnette said with wry humor. "It was Georgia Tech and their wonderful offer. But it was God's sovereign plan to bring us here." Then age 27, Barnette determined to bloom where he had been planted and started doing some planting of his own. It did not matter that he had no mentor and at that time was not yet connected to the Southern Baptist Convention (SBC). He began a church in 1993 with 14 people and a dream. His very first message outlined the shape of things to come: a church committed to discipleship, outreach—and church planting. Less than 15 years later, Peace Baptist has an average worship attendance of 1,750 and still dreams of things to come, particularly in the area of church planting.

---

[107] Rev. Tyrone E. Barnette, phone interview by author, 1, 7 November, 2006.

The Heart for a City

Situated in the heart of Decatur, some seven miles outside of Atlanta's city limits, Peace Baptist takes its place in the urban inner city, an area dotted with apartment complexes and small gas stations. Although Peace has met in 11 places over the years, including using the space of another church, it is committed to urban ministry. Because of that, Peace has developed several key ministries to meet the community needs.

David's Den consists of six apartments located across from the church facility where men, recovering drug addicts, can live following time spent in rehab. It operates in conjunction with Recovery at Work, a program developed to help put such men back to work. Peace on the Move, a separate program set up to receive government grants, houses the Recovery at Work program. Meanwhile, Celebrate Recovery, a 12-step rehabilitation program, meets every Friday night at the church, joined by inhabitants of Rosie's House, the church's shelter for women.

"To me this is the greatest program that I have ever seen in my life for doing ministry,"[108] said Brian Bullard, assistant pastor. The practical help of walking men through the tasks like getting a driver's license or a job, difficult for the person just released from prison, often becomes spiritually life changing. "We see these guys come in with no teeth, no driver's license, in and out of jail. Their whole appearance changes; their whole attitude changes." Many find regular employment after their experience at David's Den. "If you want to see transformation, it's actually amazing."

The community has witnessed the transformation, too, according to Barnette, and now views Peace as a community resource. When he first settled in Decatur, Barnette recognized it for what it was: a drug-infested, crime-ridden inner city. "It was just a terrible community." The church soon began hosting community meetings with the police. Conditions improved. "We work with all the families. We believe we've been a light."

For example, instead of sending offenders to jail, judges routinely mandate them to David's Den for rehabilitation. It is a win-win situation because while the success rate against recidivism is a mere 20 percent for most secular programs, for Peace it is a whopping 60 to 70 percent, according to Barnette. The church's community involvement extends well beyond the justice system, too. If, for example, the local school has a problem with gangs, it calls the church.

Barnette's philosophy is that the church should be a resource for every part of public life. "You've got to be involved in every aspect of your community." That means that Peace intentionally seeks out civic and business leaders to develop relationships with them. "You always have to be in the community,' Barnette said. "It makes a big difference when the church is made up of people in the community." For example, 10 percent of the local elementary school teachers attend Peace. The church knows what's going on in the school. "We always have our hand on the pulse of the community." Community involvement also entails partnering with secular agencies with an understanding of the church's role: "We'll take the spiritual component of what you're doing."

[108] Brian Bullard, phone interview by author, 31 October, 2006.

If this sounds like a rosy picture of church/community relations Barnette also takes pains to disabuse the naïve. "It's difficult. All of that is challenging. It sounds really good, but you make a lot of mistakes." In short, the church does not win them all. "They take what you give them and don't use it the way you intended them to use it. But you have to take the good with the bad."

Indeed, even if the church is preventing some 70 percent of the men who go to David's Den from becoming repeat offenders, that also means they are unsuccessful 30 percent of the time. "That 30 percent that won't conform gives us fits," Barnette pointed out.

The Peace distinction is that the church will not quit. "A lot of churches shrink back when they hit a wall," Barnette noted. "You can't do that. You have to have a resilient, tenacious spirit." Indeed, he encourages his congregation to understand—then accept—the associated risks because they will yield the greatest rewards. "I tell them the juiciest fruit is often up high out on the limb."

The church operates some 47 ministries, a number that is comparatively low by Peace standards. At one time the church was operating more than 70. "We're establishing more," Barnette said. "Most all of these ministries are run by lay people. God has done something in their hearts." For example, Peace received an award for being the church that gives out the most groceries in a several county area. It received a $100,000 grant from the governor's office to expand its foster care/adoption ministry. Barnette, with his wife Tabitha, adopted his oldest son, now 20, out of foster care at about the same time he was founding Peace Baptist. He and his wife also have two natural children.

What They Will Leave Behind

Peace Baptist Church is a growing presence in Decatur, near the I-285/I-20 corridor, but one that needs more space to accommodate its congregation. The church recently purchased 40 acres four miles away. "We're still in an area where a lot of people don't want to minister," Barnette said.

The acquisition of the new property is what Bullard described as "an act of God, a miracle." While searching for property, the church heard about land that already had been under contract and was able to secure it for $2.6 million. Until it purchased the 18,000 square-foot building it now occupies, Peace met in homes, schools, and shared space with another church, Indian Creek Baptist Church. An Anglo congregation also situated in Decatur's urban area, Indian Creek was in decline when Barnette asked the church if it would be willing to let Peace use its facilities. "We were supposed to be there three weeks," Barnette said. "We ended up being there three years."

The partnership was a testimony to two churches' ability to cross racial lines through Christ. "We were able to really come together at a time when it was difficult in that part of town," Barnette said. While Indian Creek blessed Peace with the use of its facilities, a church that had been declining also found new life. "It was really a blessing. It was a time when their ministry was going down somewhat. We were able to encourage each other. They're doing fine now."

The Stone Mountain Baptist Association offered its encouragement to Peace when it purchased its first building by giving the church $15,000. "We are so appreciative of our association," Bullard said. "It has been an awesome resource for us." Four months later, Peace returned the $15,000 to the association, a gesture of faith in God's provision among a people of limited economic resources. "Everything we've done, our church members have done," Barnette said. "It's just the faithful giving of our members." Although the church recently accepted a grant to develop its ministries, it was a move that came after years of building its faith in God's provision through the church. "We've proved that we're going to do it, regardless," Barnette said, "because God called, and He provides." Barnette has served as moderator of Stone Mountain Association, becoming the first African-American and youngest person to serve in that role.[109]

The eventual move to their new property will not take them out of the heart of the city, but even if it did, they have already planned a way to maintain their ministry there: they are leaving themselves behind. Instead of selling their old church building Peace intends to make it a "church planting mecca," according to Bullard.

While the church's worship center will move to the new property, and the congregation plans to develop a Ministry Village there, the old building will become the church's Urban Ministry Center and will be used to maintain its transitional housing and house other ministries as well as several other churches simultaneously. "As these missions grow and are able to move out on their own, this building will continue to be used for new missions."

Churches currently meeting at Peace Baptist include a Caribbean Pacific Indian church, a new congregation comprised of Fiji nationals—the "only congregation that we know of in the state of Georgia and potentially the U.S. with a church with that descent." As they learned the history of this people group, they discovered their common bond with African-Americans. Descended from India, this people group was enslaved and ended up in the Caribbean, where the two cultures merged. In addition to giving them space in their fellowship hall to meet on Sundays, Peace provides the congregation financial support and makes all the resources of their church, such as access to bulletins, cards, and so on available to the other church.

Another church, a French-African congregation, also worships in their fellowship hall earlier on Sundays. This church normally conducts services in French, but if someone comes in who leaders do not recognize, they will immediately switch to English to make sure there is no language barrier, according to Bullard. Meanwhile, Peace also is in discussions with an Ethiopian church to see if it can be added to its storehouse. "We didn't want to wait until we left the building."

Although the church will maintain two facilities, Barnette has no aspirations to pastor in both vicinities. Instead, he wants each congregation to be autonomous. "I have no desire to be multi-site," he explained, noting that should not be construed as criticism of the churches that are doing it. "I'm not wired up that way. I'm highly relational. I'd rather send men who have the DNA for church planting in them." And sending them is part of

[109] "Rev. Tyrone E. Barnette," *http://www.peacebaptistchurch/org/index.cfm/pageid/982 accessed* (Nov. 6, 2006)

the Peace plan because Barnette wants churches with DNA for planting more churches infiltrating communities. "We've got to have that in other areas of our city."

Oh, The Places They Will Go

Although Peace is planning to foster a church-planting hub, not all the churches it sponsors will come to them. Peace already has a track record for sacrificing pastors and people to plant churches in other places. For example, one assistant pastor, Robert Miller, planted a church, Trinity Baptist, in Ellenwood, Georgia, sponsored through the association. Peace financially supported the church for three years.

It also sponsored Harvest House Baptist Church in Covington, Georgia, planted by another former assistant pastor. Although that church no longer exists, Peace helped it make a down payment on a building. It also provided support to church starts in Stone Mountain and Tucker, Georgia. "It's not about getting a whole lot of members at Peace," Bullard explained. "It's about spreading the gospel."

Bullard speaks from first-hand understanding because he, too, is about to make the leap from Peace assistant pastor to church planter. A new church plant, Community Fellowship Baptist Church, is slated to launch in 2007 with Bullard, who has been on staff at Peace for five years, leading it. The church's minister of worship, Vincent Watson, also will plant New Christian Center in Loganville, Georgia. Barnette's willingness to lead a church to encourage such new church plants, despite the sacrifice of people and resources by the parent church, is "why I have the greatest pastor in the world," according to Bullard.

In addition to these church plants, Peace has been involved in starting several churches overseas, sending resources and funding to accomplish them. Barnette helped build five churches in Africa. Peace also has worked to establish churches in South Africa's Zululand, organizing two or three mission trips a year to go there. It has provided those congregations with direct monthly support, not included in its Cooperative Program giving. Peace also brings the South African pastors to its church as part of their ongoing relationship. Church members also get involved in other mission trips through a ministry called Simon's Branch, an international missions organization.

Peace also is in the beginning stages of a two-year project with Leadership Network, based in Dallas, Texas, through which information and resources will be poured into 12 churches nationwide to spur church planting. The possibilities of what can be accomplished excite Barnette, who points to the 3,211 churches that were planted over five years by 20 churches who were involved in the network. The focus will be on church planting among African-American churches, and Barnette, who is president of the African-American Fellowship of the Georgia Baptist Convention, has high hopes that he will get all 127 of those churches involved. Peace recently hosted a church planting conference attended by nearly 200 people representing 17 churches. "We're trying to build a group of African-American churches that will begin to plant and make a kingdom impact in a big way."

The result of this will be a Church Planting Institute at Peace under the larger umbrella of the Urban Ministry Center. The way Barnette sees it, church planting must be tied to meeting needs for community development. "I don't want to just have church that meets and kum-bah-yahs," he said. "We have to be missional."

Not Growing Too Fast

Despite doing ministry fueled by an urgency to spread the gospel, Peace has taken steps—some of which Barnette now characterizes as missteps—to make sure growth has been systematic and contained to manageable proportions.

"In the early years I saw that the church was going to grow very quickly," he said. Because 50 to 60 percent of the congregants were new Christians, Barnette worked to make church membership, instead of easy, the prize of the committed. For example, he offered an 8 a.m. service only for two and half years "so that we could really establish some best practices." It was a move intended as much for himself and his own growth as the church's, he admitted, because it gave him time to develop as a leader. "I could learn myself."

At one point to curtail growth Peace did not accept any new members for a six-month stretch. "So you could get saved at Peace, but you couldn't join Peace," Barnette said, noting that it was an experiment in curtailing uncontrolled growth that did not last long. "That was a mistake. That was really silly. But we were trying to safeguard the health of our church." Not until this past year did Peace decide to advertise its church services, and prospective church members are still required to take a five-week membership course before they are considered official members.

By 1998 the church was hitting its stride, however, because as Bullard explained it, "we are such an outreach-driven church." Their social ministries like Feed the Need, by which Peace feeds more than a 100 people every other week, are designed to provide an outlet for witnessing. Therefore, the church makes a practice of keeping track of the people they help. For example, block parties, featuring musical acts, rides, and giveaways, are organized so that the unchurched can be identified by colored dots on their name badges. Every unchurched person receives a prize, and, while they are waiting for their gift in a tent, an evangelism team member will make their acquaintance and attempt to witness to them.

The church finds ways to get out of the building into its community in other ways, too. For example, through Mayhem on the MARTA the church unleashes its evangelism team to ride MARTA, Atlanta's railway system, solely for the purpose of witnessing to people on the train. While congregants are at worship during the second service at 10 a.m. Sundays, the church's Evangelism Assault Team goes door-to-door to meet its neighbors.

Such evangelistic efforts are not limited to their own neighborhoods. The church also involves itself in annual Crossover events in the cities where the Southern Baptist Convention is held. Training courses like *Share Jesus without Fear*, offered regularly on Sunday afternoons, prepare members for witnessing.

The fruits of those efforts have been impressive. For example, a designated Month of Evangelism, an effort to win 30 souls in 30 days, yielded 50 confessions of faith, according to Bullard. The church has baptized more than 300 people over the past five years, although that is a number that does not come close to reflecting the actual number of conversions taking place.

That is a weakness that Barnette readily admits. "We do a really good job of getting people saved," he said. "For whatever reason, we have trouble getting them baptized." Barnette does not, however, doubt that the salvation experiences were genuine ones. "They're serving," he said of the 200 people on the list who have not yet received baptism. "They're here, loving the Lord." Yet they still need to be educated on the importance of this step of obedience.

Living authentic Christian lives is vital to every church, but paramount in urban areas, especially in leaders, according to Barnette, who has done the hard work of removing people from leadership whose lives do not match up to biblical standards. Therefore, the church fosters "tremendous accountability, first among our leaders," according to Barnette. "It's very, very important." That standard then applies to the rest of the congregation. "We preach, teach holiness, righteousness. We hold each other to that. We don't compromise it."

Worship services themselves are created to be seeker-driven, according to Bullard, featuring "high-octane" contemporary music services incorporating distinctives like dance ministry and sermon illustrations that connect with their audience. "We try to keep pace with the times, things that people today can relate to." Barnette uses simplicity and plain teaching—he "doesn't use big words," according to Bullard, to stay connected to his audience. The church's ministers also are trained that "simple is better than complex," Bullard said, noting that "bureaucracy is a poor substitute for ministry." Yet, knowing the value of it, keeping it simple is sometimes "easier said than being done." When it works the way Peace church likes it, "it's just simple. It's just doing ministry."

The Need For Disciples

If Peace has another weakness it is in discipleship, according to Bullard. "We're woefully inadequate in discipleship," he said. To improve this, the church is restructuring that area of responsibility and parceling it out to four different people.

Small groups are part of the church strategy to foster such growth. Peace instituted small groups that meet every fourth Sunday following worship for food, fun, and fellowship. Instead of leaders, they have facilitators who guide them through their studies. Small groups also do quarterly mission projects, such as volunteer at the school. The question they are trained to ask themselves is: What is our small group going to do for our community?

In addition, some small groups meet in homes, and the church offers a Sunday School for each of its three worship hours. Barnette said the church also plans to expand its small group ministry in 2007 by changing its Wednesday night format from a strictly pastor-led Bible study to a small-group format followed by a 40-minute corporate worship service.

Although the church is large, it has only six full-time staffers. For example, Peace only hired an administrator within the past year. Instead, it relies on lay people to lead, and all members are expected to serve, according to the church's Web site: "Every member of Peace Baptist Church is expected to get involved in at least one ministry of the church.[110]

"People often ask me, 'How do you do so much with so little?'" Bullard said. Eighty-five percent of its ministries are lay led. For example, ministries to singles, married, and benevolence function through the leadership of a layperson. Full-time staffers devote themselves to discipling people to take those leadership positions. "We grow leaders," Bullard said. "That is solely our job."

The church also tutors their leaders to be constantly selecting and training their successors so that there is always someone who can pick up where another person left off. "We teach them: You are the leader. Who is the co-leader?" If someone is called to another place of service, there should be another person ready to pick up the mantle. "There should always be a second in charge."

The Spirit-Driven Church

Just as prayer is central to the individual Christian life, Peace recognizes it as a vital component to staying missional. Therefore, being sensitive to the "movement of the Spirit" requires focus on prayer, according to Bullard. For example, if someone who has been burned out of their home shows up at their church "we're open to do what we can." But prayer is the incubator for that endless storehouse of compassion.

Therefore, the church enlists a prayer team and structures prayer right under pastoral leadership, placing this above the decision-making or ministry of elders and deacons, according to Barnette. "We need that protection."

Prayer precedes corporate Wednesday Bible studies, and the congregation is invited to join. Every other Saturday, there is a prayer meeting that starts early in the day "and can go on for hours and hours," Bullard said. The church uses an Internet prayer line to keep members informed of needs. It also schedules Saturday morning prayer breakfasts and calls the congregation to the altar to pray during worship. Church members also are encouraged to make prayerwalking a practice. "You'll drive up and see people looking like they are talking to themselves," said Barnette. They are actually talking to God.

The People They Are Not Reaching

Although a church for all people is a lofty goal, the pastors of Peace recognize that is not their church. Right now Peace is populated by people who share a common denominator: "We're all in the same class, from the same side of the tracks," according to Bullard. Classifying it as blue-collar African-American, Bullard said the greatest divisor—and, it stands to reason, the greatest cultural barrier—is the one between economic classes—in this case, middle and lower. For example, an entire worship service could be filled with people in recovery.

[110]"Membership," *http://www.peacebaptistchurch/org/index.cfm/pageid/616 accessed* (Nov. 6, 2006)

Moreover, Peace, despite being located in an area where more than 120 languages are spoken within a three-mile radius, is 95 percent African-American, a fact of life that keeps church planting central to the church's mission. "We can't do it all." Although it has some Anglos and 17 different nationalities within the congregation, Barnette acknowledged the church's limitations: "We're still not able to reach everybody." Instead, Barnette believes the way to cross cultures is not through Peace, the church, but the churches Peace plants.

CHAPTER THIRTEEN

The AnchorPoint:

Embracing Community and Making Disciples

Missional churches live outwardly. Not content to stay insulated against the rest of the world, a missional church is passionate and intentional about reaching into its community. Even more importantly, it is dedicated to *going* out into that community, meeting people where they are instead of waiting for people to come to the church.

In the bustling Seattle suburb of Newcastle, Washington, The AnchorPoint is a young, missional body ministering in a community that isn't looking for the church. In Seattle, fewer than four percent of people attend a Christian church.[111] And Heath Pressley, The AnchorPoint's pastor, says it's not because there aren't churches in the city and its suburbs, or because people simply aren't interested. Pressley says his community is a place where many people are interested in spiritual things, but few believe that there is only one way to a relationship with God.[112] It is in this environment that each Sunday morning, The AnchorPoint meets in a local school cafeteria, inviting their community to experience authentic, dynamic worship of the One True God. Over coffee and donuts and around tables set up to resemble a café, the church is reaching out to Newcastle and beyond, offering to others the love through which Christ has drawn them to Himself. It's a difficult task, reaching out with a singular Truth in a place where people value tolerance, open-mindedness and self-sufficiency above all else. But The AnchorPoint occupies a very specific, clear calling: Connecting people with the heart of God.[113] The church is committed, through any means possible, to see its community reached with the Gospel, to see each person in Newcastle begin a personal, life-changing relationship with Jesus Christ.

A Heart for the Pacific Northwest

The AnchorPoint is one part of a long history of Southern Baptists praying for and ministering in the Pacific Northwest. When Heath Pressley was a college student at the University of Georgia, he became part of that history. As a summer missionary in the region, he met Gary Irby, who invited Pressley to help plant a church in Clackamas, Oregon. Pressley relocated, began attending Portland State University, and worked on the team planting Life Fellowship in Clackamas, a community south of Portland. He and his wife Jennifer, whom he met while in Oregon, served with the church for five years.

After serving in churches in Illinois and Washington, the Pressleys moved to Georgia to work with a church dedicated to reaching the youth in their community. Pressley was hired to begin a new church within the church just for the area's teenagers. While the ministry saw tremendous success (700 youth regularly attended worship services), Pressley says God began to work in a new way in him, calling him to something he had never expected.

[111] Seattle Church Planting web site, "About Seattle," Puget Sound Baptist Association, *http://www.seattlechurchplanting.com*.
[112] Heath Pressley, interview by author, 6 November 2006, Newcastle, Washington, tape recording.
[113] The AnchorPoint web site, "About Us," The AnchorPoint, *http://www.theanchorchurch.net*.

"I just really didn't see myself as a lead pastor. Through those two years (his last two years serving in Georgia), God shook me loose from hanging on to what I wanted to do and opened my eyes to the reality of what He had created me to do. I realized that He was calling me out of youth ministry, and that I was going to lead a church."[114]

Pressley had kept in close touch with Gary Irby, who was serving as a church planting strategist with the Puget Sound Baptist Association in Washington. Throughout the years, Irby had encouraged the Pressleys to pray about moving to the Seattle area to plant a church. Although they were well aware of the challenges facing any church planter, especially in a largely unchurched area like Seattle, the Pressleys felt God calling them to begin a new work in the Pacific Northwest.

The opportunity came when Irby called Pressley about a church plant sponsored by The Anchor, a Seattle church Irby helped plant in the 1990s. The Anchor was part of a major church planting emphasis in the region that continued through Seattle's time as one of the North American Mission Board's Strategic Focus Cities, and remains a focus of the Puget Sound Baptist Association. (Today, there are more than 30 church plants ministering in the Seattle area, ranging from those that launched two or three years ago to some that are gearing up to start next year).[115] The Anchor had a vision to help start more missional churches in the Seattle area, sponsoring 12 church plants through the years, including Lakeside Community Church in nearby Newcastle.

At the time that the Pressleys were praying about their next step, Lakeside had recently been shaken by scandal, and attendance declined rapidly from 250 to 50. At the same time, The Anchor was developing a strategy to sell their church property and use the resources to start new churches (called "anchor points") in the surrounding communities. As Lakeside's leadership began making decisions about the church's future, Irby and Dave Foster, The Anchor's pastor, helped lead the transition. Lakeside's members decided they would become the first anchor point church, continuing to minister in Newcastle. The church called Pressley as their pastor and began a rebuilding process, aiming toward a re-launch as The AnchorPoint. Back in the region where he first experienced church planting first-hand, Pressley began to lead a local body of believers, just as God had prepared him to do.

Back to the Beginning

When Pressley began to lead The AnchorPoint, he realized there was a need for renewed vision casting in the church. "The reality was that they (the remaining Lakeside members) were in ongoing ministry, full-launch mode, but with what had happened, they really needed to be back in core group development mode."

Pressley discontinued the church's weekly worship service and began a weekly Bible study in his home for church members. The changes weren't appreciated by everyone: the church dwindled from 50 people to three families, each of whom was firmly committed to The AnchorPoint.

[114] Heath Pressley, interview by author, 9 October 2006, Newcastle, Washington, tape recording.
[115] Seattle Church Planting web site, "Current Plants," Puget Sound Baptist Association, *http://www.seattlechurchplanting.com.*

"Those three families said, 'If everyone else leaves, we're going to stay… ' That was a hard nine-month process of casting vision and being firm in the reality of that vision," Pressley said.

At their weekly meetings in the Pressleys' home, the group discussed what would become the core values of The AnchorPoint, which were influenced by Erwin McManus' *An Unstoppable Force: Daring to Become the Church God Had in Mind.*[116] Above all, they prayed God would give them hearts to reach their community with His Truth. They wanted to know how they could partner with Him to carry out His mission.

"Our vision began and ended with: 'The reason we exist as a church is to reach this community. We don't exist to build each other up; we exist to see this entire community transformed by Jesus."

The young church encountered several struggles as they moved toward their goal of reaching those around them with the Gospel. Shortly after the church's official launch in 2004, Pressley sustained an ankle injury and was stuck at home for several weeks. Then, the Pressley's adopted daughter Gracie tested positive for tuberculosis, and the couple and their three children were quarantined in their home for two weeks. For two months after the launch, the Pressleys had to rely solely on prayer and their trust in God's power to continue the work He had started in Newcastle.

"God taught me that the success of our church isn't about anything that I do, but it's all about what He does. The importance of prayer was really re-taught to me through that process," Pressley says. With their gazes firmly fixed on what God could do in Newcastle and beyond, the Pressleys and other families of The AnchorPoint moved forward with the vision of what their church could become in His power.

A Love for People, A Focus on Relationships

You read earlier in this book that missional churches demonstrate unconditional love for people while joining God in His mission of reaching people with the Gospel. From the beginning, The AnchorPoint sought to build solid, redemptive relationships in Newcastle, motivated by the desire to see people in their community come to Christ and the realization that the church's efforts would be meaningless without an unconditional love for those people. Without many resources or people attending the weekly meeting, each family began to reach out to those around them. Of the church's 100-125 current regular attenders, Pressley says every one of those people or families can be traced back to a connection with one of the three original families in The AnchorPoint's core group.

"During that time, we had to focus on relationships. We built into our DNA that our church was not going to grow because we sent out mailers; it was going to grow because we all bought into lifestyle evangelism… Our initial growth wasn't because we had a great Web page; it was because everyone really bought into the fact that we needed to reach our friends, families, and coworkers."

[116] Erwin McManus, *An Unstoppable Force: Daring to Become the Church God Had in Mind* (Loveland, Colorado: Group Publishing Inc., 2001).

The AnchorPoint is dedicated to taking every opportunity to build inroads into the community; one way they've found to serve, love, and build relationships in Newcastle is by participating in city-wide events that aren't necessarily church-driven. Pressley quickly began to reach out to the city's government, befriending the mayor, city council members and other city employees, and offering the church as a resource and an open door. During the summer after the church's Easter 2004 launch, the church asked to sponsor a face painting table at the city's summer concert series, which hosts 2,000-3,000 attendees each week.

When the time came for the 2005 concert series, Pressley attended a Chamber of Commerce meeting where he heard about the need for sponsors for each concert in the 8-week series. He offered for The AnchorPoint to fund every week; as the official sponsor, the church was introduced at each concert and was able to set up an information booth along with the face painting table. It was one way to show the community that the church is passionate about building relationships in Newcastle, and that its first priority is going out, rather than getting people to come in.

"We don't want to say, 'Hey, come check us out.' We want to go. We want to be in the community. We want to immerse ourselves in people's lives, so that when they are spiritually ready, we're the ones they come to," Pressley says.

Jason and Nancy Dannemiller attended the summer concert series in 2004 and saw The AnchorPoint's face painting table. They checked out the church's Web site and visited one Sunday morning. Pressley says the couple had very little experience with church, but, like many people in their community, had definite ideas about what they thought the church was like. Surprised at how comfortable they felt in the worship service, the Dannemillers signed up to help at an upcoming city-wide event and joined the Pressleys weekly small group. Two years later, they have both given their lives to Christ, entering into a personal relationship with Him and growing as members of The AnchorPoint. The Dannemillers are examples of how relationships motivated by love can be redemptive and life-altering.

The AnchorPoint also participates in Newcastle's other major annual event, Newcastle Days, which gathers the community for music, fireworks, and other family activities. As one of the event's participating sponsors, the church set up an information booth and again set out to build relationships from the natural contacts they made. One such contact was the Newcastle City Clerk, who met Pressley during Newcastle Days and told him he had been meaning to visit the church. Pressley invited him to come the next day, and soon, he also was involved in the Pressleys' small group. He had been searching for a church ever since a friend had shared the Gospel with him and he had accepted Christ. Before that, he had been involved in both the Jehovah's Witnesses and Mormon faiths. Pressley says the freedom that comes from a relational, loving approach has been especially important in reaching out to people whose context of church is that being a part of it requires adhering to a strict set of do's and don'ts. "He's amazed that we just want to be friends," Pressley says.

There are several other ways the church is reaching into the community, building relationships and demonstrating love for people. Last summer, the church sponsored two weeks of camp for kids in the area. Visiting mission teams helped out with the Backyard Bible Club-type camps, which hosted more than 200 kids during the two weeks.

Additionally, The AnchorPoint is planning a community Christmas event in conjunction with the City of Newcastle, its Chamber of Commerce, the fire department, and several other area businesses. A Newcastle Christmas gives families an opportunity to celebrate the season together, making Christmas ornaments, sampling food from local vendors, having pictures made with Santa, and listening to Pressley's reading of the legend of the candy cane, a story that points to Jesus as Savior of the world. It's the kind of event that Pressley says the church is becoming known for in Newcastle, and it's another opportunity to begin redemptive relationships.[117]

Loving Through Adapting: Tailoring Your Approach

Along with building relationships in the community, The AnchorPoint acknowledges that loving people and being dedicated to sharing the Gospel with them means being sensitive to their needs, and to their personal history with church. Because of the considerable antagonism towards church in their community, The AnchorPoint is committed to create an environment where people coming to the church for the first time feel welcomed and comfortable. So, instead of a pulpit and pews, the church uses café tables and chairs for its worship services. The music is band-driven, and every element of the service is committed to the excellence that the driven, professional community of Newcastle expects. Reflecting another characteristic of a missional church, The AnchorPoint's approach is tailored to and adapted for the specific culture in which they live. "We're going to make decisions based on the needs of outsiders versus the comfort level of insiders," Pressley says.

That commitment to creating a safe environment for first-time visitors plays out in a number of seemingly small ways. For example, instead of having a greeting time during the service, The AnchorPoint begins its services with two worship songs, which allows people to grab coffee and a pastry and say hello to friends. Instead of a regimented time of greeting where regular attenders often turn to each other, Pressley says the time at the beginning of the service gives newer people a chance to connect with others in an informal setting. He also writes a humorous "Top Ten List" each week; whether the list focuses on politics, pop culture, or other current events, the purpose is the same: to create common ground and begin to break down preconceived notions about the church.

"I think there's this general idea that the church is not relevant to my everyday life, that it's this weird thing that I don't understand, and I'm pretty sure I don't want to be a part of it … So many people, when they come to church, they flip the relevant switch off, and they zone out. We want people to stay engaged, and we want to let you know that church can be exciting and funny," Pressley says.

While the focus is on creating an environment where people are comfortable and can connect with one another, The AnchorPoint doesn't adhere to a strictly attractional method of church. Along with loving people unconditionally and adapting to the culture to demonstrate that love, the church is firmly founded on the Bible and dedicated to

[117] Heath Pressley interview, 6 November 2006.

teaching God's Word. The teaching style is also tailored to the culture. In his messages, Pressley encourages his people in the foundational elements of discipleship, like prayer and reading the Bible. The focus is still on portraying a relationship with God as something that is accessible, no matter your background. But there is a call to action, and Pressley describes prayer and Bible study in terms his audience can understand.

"We talk about how God doesn't speak in King James language; there are no special words. It's just you having a conversation with God, and being still and opening your heart to hear God," he says.

People at The AnchorPoint are taught that Scripture is the inerrant Word of God, the guideline for everything. One small way this is communicated is through Scripture reading during worship services. Instead of projecting the words on a screen, Pressley encourages people to follow along in their own Bibles as he reads the passage. If someone doesn't have a Bible, the church will provide one. It's a simple way to encourage people by showing them that they can read the Bible, that it's understandable, and that God speaks to His people through it. The AnchorPoint is actively adapting to its culture, seeking to create environments where relationships are built and people are likely to return because they are forging connections and learning about God in a new way that is sometimes unexpected.

A Focus on Living Authentically

When the church first began to meet in the Pressleys' home and to develop their passion to see people come to Christ, Pressley encouraged the families to adopt the "radical minimum standard" principle discussed in Erwin McManus' *An Unstoppable Force: Daring to Become the Church God Had in Mind.*[118] The principle, which is one of the church's core values, states: "As followers of Jesus, we know that there are not multiple levels of commitment. Jesus gives the same calling to all people—'Come follow me.' This level of commitment is nothing short of giving Him complete control of our lives. The invitation to 'come follow me' is given to everyone, not just pastors and missionaries. So, in everything we do, we strive to help people give their life to that level of commitment in following Jesus, knowing that when they do, Jesus will help them discover what real life is all about."[119]

In other words, members of The AnchorPoint are called to give their lives away. You read earlier that missional churches encourage people to lead authentic Christian lives; at The AnchorPoint, that means submitting to Christ's leadership in every area of one's life. The core value is based on Jesus' teaching in Matthew 10:39 (NIV), "Whoever finds his life will lose it, and whoever loses his life for my sake will find it." The important elements of living authentically come together in a simple process at The AnchorPoint. Pressley calls it "the disciple-making process:"

1. The process begins with making a disciple from someone who doesn't yet know God. Pressley calls this the Entry Point, and it consists of an environment where people have the opportunity to hear and respond to the Gospel.
2. Next is the Connection Point, where people build relationships within the church

[118] Erwin McManus, *An Unstoppable Force: Daring to Become the Church God Had in Mind.*
[119] The AnchorPoint web site, "About Us."

body. Pressley divides this point into two groups: disciples who "need to" connect and those who "want to" connect. The church provides environments for both, hosting a monthly newcomers lunch for those who need to connect, and inviting those who are ready to go deeper to join a weekly small group, called a Life Group.

3. Finally, there is a Life Point, when someone gets to the point where they're ready to give their life away to see others reached with the Gospel. Disciples who reach this point are pursuing opportunities to serve on a ministry team, go on a mission trip, or become involved in helping one of the church plants sponsored by The AnchorPoint.

Even now, while the church is still young, there are many at The AnchorPoint who have been moved to give their lives away. For example, there is the church member who made an anonymous donation of $5,000 so that the church would be able to sponsor Newcastle's summer concert series. Or, there's Debbi Jorgenson, who felt like the church could be doing more together in the way of fellowship. When she approached Pressley about her idea, he appointed her event coordinator. Now, once of month, she organizes outings to Seattle Mariners games or seasonal events in the area. Pressley says she has raised the relational level of the church, and is using her giftedness to provide opportunities for people from within the church and community to connect with one another. At the AnchorPoint, as people increase their involvement and investment in the church, they are called to move from being church members to church leaders, living authentically through serving the body.

Joe and Laurie Mendoza have been involved with the church from the beginning, attending the weekly Bible study in the Pressleys home and eventually being among the first people baptized at The AnchorPoint. Now, they are key leaders within the church. Although hesitant at first to spearhead such a major project, Laurie runs the church's children ministry, which includes a weekly children's worship experience. Because of the high number of young families in the community, Laurie's ministry is extremely important to the overall ministry of the church, and Pressley says she has stepped up to every leadership opportunity she's been given. Joe Mendoza is a behind-the-scenes specialist at The AnchorPoint, someone who Pressley says isn't usually seen up front, but makes a huge impact on the church's daily and weekly operations. Because The AnchorPoint is a portable church and must set up and tear down their equipment each week, Joe came up with a system to change that project from a 2-hour ordeal to a 30-minute process.

God is using The AnchorPoint to draw out positive, affirming attributes that people didn't even know they possessed. The church is committed to recruiting servant leaders from within the church, helping people who have connected to Jesus through a personal relationship with Him, connect to His church through serving it. "We don't hire people from without; we're going to grow people up from within. We really do have a passion for igniting people's dreams," Pressley says.

As they develop as disciples, the church also encourages its people to live incarnational lives, building redemptive relationships outside of the church. They look different than the rest of the world because of how Christ has transformed them, but they are motivated by His love to be outwardly-focused, seeing others' need for Him and looking for opportunities to share who He is. Because so many at The AnchorPoint are new to church, Pressley focuses on relational evangelism. He says people who have experienced the power of Christ in their lives know what it feels like to be reached with the Gospel. Like in the beginning, when the three families reached out to their friends, neighbors and coworkers, Pressley still encourages his church to look around them and see the many opportunities that exist to share God's Truth.

Mark and Kathy Thorpe are one of the original couples who attended The AnchorPoint's first gatherings. Kathy's first experience with small group Bible study was a Beth Moore study for women in the church. Heath Pressley says Kathy experienced such phenomenal spiritual growth that she wants to lead a similar study for her friends. Mark Thorpe is a local teacher and coach who was hesitant to share his faith when the Pressleys first met him. At a recent birthday party for his wife, Mark asked Heath Pressley to lead a prayer in front of their family and friends, many of whom don't know Christ. Now he invites co-workers and friends to church services and outreach events, and is growing in his desire to see people come to know God in personal way. The Thorpes are living incarnationally, taking the church to their own parts of the community.

The AnchorPoint is filled with examples of people whose lives are being transformed because they are living authentically and incarnationally. They are disciples who are learning to serve the church and share the Gospel outside of the church. Because they have encountered a missional church that gives them opportunities to see where they fit in the Kingdom, they are becoming missional Christians.

Planting Churches and Crossing Cultures

"Even though we're still really a plant ourselves, we decided that if we don't do it within the first three years, we're never going to do it. So, we're going to do it!"

That's Pressley's take on The AnchorPoint's decision to sponsor two church plants in the Seattle area over the next several years. The strategy came about after the sale of The Anchor Seattle's property. The two churches had merged when Pressley came on as pastor, meeting in two separate locations until the worship gatherings were later merged as well. When the Seattle property was sold, the church decided to use part of the funds from the sale to help two new churches begin their ministry.

"When we sponsor a church plant, we don't just write them a check. We say that we're going to pray, play and pay. We're going to be in prayer for your church plant, we're going to send ministry teams to help your church plant, and we're going to partner with you financially," Pressley says.

Helping the church plants is just part of The AnchorPoint's ongoing pursuit of going out into the community and making disciples. Realizing that many different churches are needed to join in God's mission, they are committed to using their resources to further the Kingdom.

"If we hoard our resources, that's not Christ-like. We're called to give our lives individually away, and I believe that as a church, we've got to be modeling that . . . We've got to get beyond ourselves. If we stay outward, we're going to be a viable, living, spiritual community. But if we turn inward, we're going to shrivel and die," Pressley says.

The quest to remain outwardly-focused begins in Spring 2007, when Lifepointe Community Church officially launches in Snoqualmie, Washington, a quickly-growing Seattle suburb. The church will reach out to the thousands of Seattle commuters who live in Snoqualmie and the surrounding communities. The AnchorPoint has committed to sponsor Lifepointe, and planter Chris Weldon spoke recently at the church, explaining his church plant's mission and vision. Members of The AnchorPoint had an opportunity to hear about the new church and affirm that their congregation will be involved in the ministry. Weldon is already planning events for the new church, and Pressley is working to mobilize people from The AnchorPoint to assist in those events.

The Seattle area is a mix of various cultures; from young professionals commuting from the suburbs to a large second-generation Asian population, it is a city marked by great differences. But Pressley says Seattle is unlike some other places in that cultures mesh together well, forming a sort of community identity that transcends some of the differences in background. The second church plant that The AnchorPoint will sponsor has as its mission to help people assimilate into Seattle's culture. Through church planting strategist Gary Irby, Pressley met Damian Emetuche, a church planter from Africa who will plant Agape Community Center in the Edmonds area of Seattle in February 2007. Edmonds is home to a large population of immigrants from various countries, and Agape will focus on ministries that help people adapt to their new community.[120]

When Pressley met Emetuche, the pastors found that their churches shared many of the same values, along with a vision to "see the church express itself in contextual and relevant ways in a particular community." Pressley says The AnchorPoint will work alongside Agape Community Center to fill any service roles the new church needs, like childcare for services and outreach events. The AnchorPoint will do what they can to ensure that Agape is free and able to build relationships in Edmonds and beyond.

The church also is looking outwardly even further. When Pressley preached on reaching the ends of the earth with the Gospel, he encouraged the church to select a city within the 10/40 window (the region in the world which contains the fewest Christians), and to take responsibility as a church for reaching that city. The AnchorPoint selected DeShung, China, which is where the Pressleys' daughter Gracie is from. Through the Grace and Hope Foundation in DeShung, the church is able to sponsor children in orphanages so that they can be placed in foster care. Pressley hopes that in Summer 2007, the church will be able to send its first mission team to China, ministering in the orphanages and exploring the possibility of beginning a new work in DeShung.

In an earlier chapter of this book, you read that a missional church seeks ways to plant new missional churches, and that some of those new works are planted across cultural lines. Through Lifepointe Community Church, Agape Community Center and their presence in

[120] Seattle Church Planting web site, "Agape Community Center," Puget Sound Baptist Association, *http://www.seattlechurchplanting.com.*

DeShung, China, The AnchorPoint will experience a new way of joining God in His work, through partnering with like-minded believers to extend the reach of the Gospel in their community and their world.

Continuing to Join in God's Mission

Throughout its short history, The AnchorPoint has made strategic decisions to serve its community as a missional church. Above all, Heath Pressley and his church have sought to follow the Holy Spirit's leading on their journey to joining God in His mission in Newcastle, the greater Seattle area, and beyond. By encouraging his congregation to lead authentic Christian lives, Pressley has impressed upon them the importance of lifestyle, relational evangelism. The families of The AnchorPoint are reaching out to their own families and friends, sharing about the powerful transformation that comes from a personal relationship with Jesus Christ. They are acting out of love for the people around them, a love that reflects the love they themselves have been shown. The AnchorPoint is a church committed to creating an inviting environment while focusing on the reason the church exists; to invite others to a life-changing encounter with Christ. They are partnering with other churches in this mission, and encouraging believers in Christ to find the place in which they can serve the church. The AnchorPoint is crossing cultures, and tailoring their approach to the place in which they minister. There are definite challenges, like the isolation of a place where few churches are ministering effectively, and the occasional lack of resources to fulfill ministry dreams, but the church is steadfast in its calling to be salt and light.

CHAPTER FOURTEEN

Hope Community Church:

A Church of Misfit Toys

In the 1990s, an action-packed TV drama called *E.R.* aired and became an instant hit. The show gives viewers an inside look at what takes place in a chaotic, busy Emergency Room in downtown Chicago. Emergency Rooms (ER) and trauma centers are needed in our society daily, because people get sick and injured. More than that, though, our society needs missional leaders and churches willing to reach out to those who are spiritually sick, needy, and hurting—to serve as *spiritual* trauma centers.

An ER or trauma center is a fitting picture for how the church should be. Think about the types of people Jesus hung out with: prostitutes, tax collectors, lepers, fishermen, and, as Matthew says, "sinners." Jesus was truly missional in that He went to the "sick" of His day—those considered outcasts by the traditional, religion system. He declared that He didn't come for the healthy (speaking specifically to the religious rulers of His day who questioned Him for eating with tax collectors and sinners) but for the sick (see Matt. 10:12). He was known for throwing parties for tax collectors and using stories about throwing banquets for the poor, the blind, the lame, the sick, and those who cannot pay you back (see Luke 14:12-14). Because of this, Jesus was accused of being a "glutton," a "drunkard," and "demon possessed."

N.T. Wright says:

> "Jesus was offering a counter-agenda an utterly risky way of being Israel, the way of turning the other cheek and going the second mile, the way of losing your life to gain it. This was the kingdom-invitation he was issuing. This was the play for which he was holding auditions. Along with this radical invitation went a radical welcome. Wherever Jesus went, there seemed to be a celebration; the tradition of festive meals at which Jesus welcomed all and sundry is one of tmost securely established features of almost all recent scholarly portraits."[121]

The religious leaders of Israel (the Pharisees, the Sadducees, the scribes) turned on Jesus because of the types of people He invited to be part of His kingdom, those He would throw a party for and welcome with open arms. It was truly a counter-agenda, unlike what anyone (especially in religious circles) would have expected or thought. Jesus was very clear in His intentions in healing the brokenhearted, and setting the captive free; and so is Hope Community Church. It is a vital trauma center in an unlikely place with unlikely people.

A Christ-Centered Trauma Unit

In the small rural town of Lawrenceburg, Kentucky, known for its world-famous Wild Turkey whisky, is a church full of misfits—people who many churches would feel uncomfortable around. But Hope Community Church is not like many churches; it's

[121] N.T. Wright, *The Challenge of Jesus* (Downers Grove, Ill.: InterVarsity Press, 1999), 44-45.

a trauma center, an ER for Christ. "Most churches get the snotty noses and the brokenankles," Jeff Eaton, lead pastor of Hope Community, said, "but we get those who have gunshot wounds."[122]

Eaton, who refers to himself as the "misfit preacher," calls Hope Community Church "an island of misfit toys and Rudolph the Red Nose Reindeers." The people who come to Hope Community are the type of people that most churches don't want. There are Harley bikers, burley hunters and outdoorsmen, and many who have come from a life of addictions and hurtful family lives. They are needy. Messy.

Steve Rose, associate pastor and the one who oversees the student ministries at Hope Community, tells about a so-called misfit who recently came to Christ. This person grew up as a pastor's kid and was around church all his life. However, his life took a turn as he got heavily involved in drugs and alcohol and was headed for a nasty divorce.

His supervisor at work shared with him about a group he leads at Hope Community called Encourage Hope, a group that deals with addiction issues and recovery. At the end of his rope, the man decided to try the group. Shortly after he came, he gave his life to Jesus and was baptized at the church. He and his wife are working on their marriage and have joined a couple's small group. "We have a lot of addicts here," said Rose. "They come to one of our groups, and the lie they've believed gets exposed and healing takes place."[123]

Hope Community Church is truly missional in that it embraces a total unconditional love for people by seeing them not just as they are, but what they can be in Christ. "Many churches say they're open to all people," Eaton stated, "but they're really not. They say, 'come as you are, but come like us.'" Eaton compares the contemporary, institutional church to a current television commercial. In this particular bank advertisement, a man walks into an office to receive counseling. The man speaks English, but the counselor speaks French. They can't communicate with one another. It is very awkward for both of them.

That is, according to Eaton, how many modern churches act. The language and many of the ministries of churches are not meeting the needs of the hurting, the lost, and the disconnected. These churches expect lost people to behave like them, but they can't. They don't know how, and so Hope Community exists to speak into the lives of people who feel they don't belong.

A Passion for the Hurting

Eaton has been in ministry for 21 years in various roles. He grew up as a pastor's kid and has been around church all of his life. About 10 years ago, however, he was ready to quit, feeling like he didn't fit the pattern of what he thought (and what others thought) a typical pastor should be. He felt out of place in a traditional church, where he prepared sermons, ran meetings, created programs, hired staff and so on. Something was missing.
One day, he picked up the book *Surprised by the Power of the Spirit* by Jack Deere, a former

[122] Jeff Eaton, phone interview with author, October, 2006.
[123] Steve Rose, phone interview with author, October, 2006.

Dallas Theological professor and now popular speaker and author. As Eaton read, he felt an awaking take place inside of him—an awaking of the Holy Spirit and His power. He had grown up and served in churches where the power of the Holy Spirit was absent, where there was an over reliance on what man could do for God through strategies and planning.

By reading this book, he felt like a new man—a man ready to live in the power of the Holy Spirit and live out the kingdom life that Jesus calls us to. It was at that point that Eaton began to see the needs of hurting people around him. "The people that I was drawn to," he said, "are the people churches typically reject—the poor, bikers, addicts, et cetera." With this new conviction and burden for the lost, Eaton tried to move his church away from its programs and traditions. He encouraged the congregation to reach out into the community and plant a new church. Some of the church leaders, however, resisted this move and, after four years, Eaton resigned his senior pastorate role to plant a church.

"I saw a whole lot of people dying around me and nobody going after them," he stated. So, he and a few others decided to go after them and planted Hope Community in the small, horse-farming town of Lawrenceburg, Kentucky, between Louisville and Lexington. Started in 1998, the church has grown to a membership of 650 to 750 people, making it the largest church in three counties.

Some people were skeptical of the church in its beginning. Jeff received some opposition from a few churches, who believed Hope Community was not a "real" Baptist church. There was even some who prayed against the church and ignorantly threw insults at them, saying they wouldn't last. Just as Nehemiah and the leaders of Israel experienced opposition when they rebuilt the walls of Jerusalem, Jeff and his leaders continued to move forward, working "with all their heart" (Neh. 4:6, NIV). "Some of these folks," Eaton said, "don't care if a new liquor store comes to town, but they care if a new church is planted."

Nevertheless, Hope Community Church persisted and has thrived in the midst of difficulties. Eaton doesn't think of himself as a church planter necessarily; he thinks of himself as a man who loves Jesus and loves others. To him, Jesus is the real church planter. If He doesn't show up, nothing will happen.

For eight years, Hope has not owned a building. Yet, the church uses money from its budget to help new church plants buy buildings for their church to use. Hope church recently helped a new church plant buy an abandoned Save A-Lot grocery store building to use for its ministry site. Talk about missional? Here's a church that gives most of its budget to other churches to have buildings when it doesn't have a building of its own. Hope Community has been a mobile church for eight years, meeting where it can. Currently, it is using a middle school for services. The small groups meet in various places: in homes, in restaurants, in senior citizen housing, in lawyers' offices, and even in the courthouse at the center of town. However, Hope Community has just bought 100 acres so it can have more of a permanent ministry site.

Setting the Captives Free

What is the DNA of Hope Community Church? What makes its congregation tick? First, Hope's vision is based around Isaiah 61:1-2: "The Spirit of the Sovereign Lord is on me, because the Lord has anointed me to preach good news to the poor. He has sent me to bind up the brokenhearted, to proclaim freedom for the captives and release from darkness for the prisoners, to proclaim the year of the Lord's favor and the day of vengeance of our God, to comfort all who mourn" (NIV). Jesus used this passage to speak to His hometown synagogue, announcing that He was the One who was fulfilling Isaiah's words (see Luke 4:14-21).

For Hope Community, this is their DNA. Their mission statement is simply: Healing the brokenhearted and setting the captive free. "If Christ is the Head of the Church," Eaton said, "then this is what we need to be about. This is Jesus' mission statement." Hope Community puts a strong emphasis on the belief that Satan throws a lot of lies at us. As a result of believing those lies, people become wounded and are in need of healing. It's through Christ, the Person of Truth, that we are set free to be the people God has called us to be. The cross and resurrection is preached passionately; but how that is lived out, how that takes shape, is through helping people discover the lies they believe, and then leading them to freedom in Christ.

The Gospel of John tells us, "You will know the truth, and the truth will set you free" (John 8:32, NIV). At Hope Community, that is what they are all about: helping people break free from the lies they believe and experience the life-changing truth of Jesus. "Currently," stated Eaton, "we are teaching what the world's lies are in contrast to God's truth. I'm realizing that everything comes down to either a truth or a lie. Either people live a lie-based life or a truth-based life." Hope Community, with its focus around Isaiah 61, exists to walk with people and help them live truth-based lives. So, how do they do that? What does that look like?

Hope's vision is carried out, mainly, through small groups. These groups are places where people can be in authentic community, where people's needs are met, and where they can experience true freedom in Christ. Although every Sunday the church offers a Sunday service, where God's Word is preached, the focus of the church is on helping people heal and grow through authentic community that meets off campus throughout the area.

These small groups are similar to a three-legged chair. One leg is fellowship—building authentic community where people feel valued, loved, safe, and accepted. This does not mean it is merely a place people come to get their needs met. Rather, these groups exist to help individuals become authentic disciples that *find life and health, and then are equipped and released into the harvest for the glory of the Father*. Eaton believes his role is to send disciples out to start other churches. Through authentic community, these disciples can work through the lies they've believed and live a life of freedom in Christ for the glory of the Father.

The second leg of the stool is prayer. Hope believes in the power of prayer, and that without it, nothing will happen. Those in the small groups learn to pray together, lifting up each other's needs and requests. They spend a significant time praying for each other, helping people pray through lies they've embraced. Each of the small group leaders (both staff and lay leaders) are trained in emotional healing (i.e., they are trained and resourced to understand the lies of the enemy, past traumas, hurts, etc.) and have the ability to help their group learn how to pray together and grow in their identity in Christ.

The third leg is Bible study. Often these studies are focused around emotional issues that people struggle with, again, with an emphasis on the lies that they believe. Depending on the needs of the group, some leaders will lead their group through a book, such as *The Bondage Breaker*, or perhaps, a book of the Bible. Eaton is currently leading a men's group through *Every Man's Battle.*

The emphasis is on relationships and equipping people to be fully devoted, freedom-bound disciples who can live for the glory of God. Oftentimes, hospitality is practiced by those leading the small groups, by cooking a meal, opening up their homes, and spending quality time with group members with the purpose of discipling them. Hope Community believes in the importance of using hospitality as a way to see authentic discipleship take place. Paul tells us that elder shepherds are to be hospitable, not as a suggestion, but as a requirement for their calling (see 1 Tim. 3:2).

Not only do these small groups grow and heal together, they serve together. In order to be missional, it is vital to penetrate the culture in which you live with the purpose of speaking the language of that culture while maintaining faithfulness to the Word of God. This is the idea of being contextual. Michael Frost and Allan Hirsch define contextualization as, "presenting Christianity in such a way that it meets people's deepest needs and penetrates their worldviews, thus allowing them to follow Christ and remain in their own cultures."[124]

One way Hope Community does this is by equipping and training children, youth, and adults to be missional in their different contexts. Rather than having service projects and big events, Hope Community equips people in their small groups and through teaching in the services how to live missional everyday. "People are already so busy with their schedules," said Rose, "so we coach them to recognize needs all around them. If they see their neighbor working on their roof on Saturday afternoon, rather than watching TV, we encourage them to go and help."

In the New Membership Training there is a section on what it means to be life-giving in the community (i.e., looking for ways to serve others around you). Through Sunday morning teaching and small-group study, members not only talk about being missional, but get out in their community and serve. Hope is a church committed to cultural adaptability.

Hope Community believes that if a church is to be missional, it *must* be life-giving. Instead of programs and big events, church members focus on relationships, through serving others around them with the purpose of being a witness to the community in which they live. It is releasing disciples back into the harvest so that they can reach other people,

[124] Michael Frost and Allen Hirsch, *The Shaping of Things to Come* (Peabody: Mass: Hendrickson Publishers, Inc., 2003), 83.

being used by God to set the captives free. Eaton sees Hope Community as a launching pad, sending out members for church planting. Currently a young couple is considering leaving and doing church planting in Wisconsin, and Steve Rose is prayerfully considering moving his family to Boston to start a church. Rose has shared this with the congregation and is planning on taking a short-term missions trip to the city to meet with other church planters.

These leaders (and others who have gone before) place a strong emphasis on seeking God and then responding to His call for their lives. They believe in and work toward equipping the church to respond to God's calling and be willing to go wherever He leads. "Most churches think about how they can keep their people," said Eaton. "I think being missional is giving yourself away and releasing people to give themselves away."

Hope Community desires to see its sister churches (which they have many), to be more blessed than it is. Hope members are passionate about living out the mission of God in their setting and seeing His mission spread throughout the world. Through seeking God's heart, experiencing Him through His Word, through prayer, through listening to the Spirit's voice, and through authentic community, all Christians can be life-giving. As disciples, we are called to give ourselves away and lay down our lives for others (see John 15:13). Hope Community Church is an example and inspiration for us to be committed and hungry for God by being life-giving so that His glory will spread throughout all the people of the world.

Women and Children First... Equipping Them to be Missional

Hope Community places an emphasis on women and children. For example, Hope has a ministry called Kids On Mission Serving Others (K.O.M.S.O.) for children from preschool to fifth grade. On Sunday mornings, before the regular service, kids meet to learn about how they can be missional and used by God to change their world. Recently, they had a boot camp where they had to learn to work together as a team, go through obstacle courses, and follow orders from their commanding officers (the leaders of this ministry). Afterward, the leaders had a teaching time about what it means to be a soldier for Christ in our society.

In addition to these fun and interactive events, the children also have the opportunity to be part of a mission group where they can use their gifts and abilities for the Lord. Children interested in cooking or arts and crafts, will have the opportunity to cook a meal or make a craft, and then go to the local retirement home or to visit a person in the hospital. If, perhaps, there has been a loss in a family or a recent sickness, a mission group will prepare a meal for them.

Different mission groups also use sports and outdoor activities as a way to minister to the community. The Junior High and Senior High ministries have a basketball league every winter that reaches out to the Lawrenceburg community and its surrounding towns. The purpose is to invite unchurched kids to be part of a team where they can see that their teammates and coaches (adult leaders) really do care about them.

Also, Hope has a dynamic women's ministry focusing on training women to be godly wives, mothers, and missional leaders in their communities. Steve Rose's mother heads up the women's ministry. There are seven to eight women's small groups that meet throughout the area for the purpose of healing from deep, emotional issues, such as abuse from the past and dysfunctional family lives. Many of the women prior to participation in these groups had not seen an example of what it means to be a godly woman. The leaders of these groups place a strong emphasis on modeling what a godly wife, mother, and friend looks like.

Coaching becomes a large part for how discipleship happens in both the women's, men's, and couples' groups. Eaton and Rose coach the male leaders meeting with them on a regular basis. Mrs. Rose does the same with the women leaders. The point is to model Christ to these leaders who can then model Christ to their group members.

Values to Live By

To live out their vision of healing the brokenhearted and setting the captive free, Hope Community members have certain values that they live by. These values, however, are not your typical values, they are very unique and fitting for a "misfit church."

The first value is a belief that the greatest leaders are yet to be saved. Some traditional churches believe that you have to first lead people to Christ, before discipling them, and then you can put them into leadership. Hope on the other hand, believes in working with people where they are, showing them love, investing in them, with the purpose of believing that they are going to be great leaders of the church. Although they do not put non-Christians into leadership roles, they invest in them with the hope that after they accept Christ they will step into these roles.

When asked if he would start a Christian Harley-Davidson bike club, Eaton, a long time Harley rider, turned down the offer because he believes strongly in being incarnational and riding with unsaved bikers. Too often, we as believers have the tendency to want to live in our Christian subcultures, separating ourselves from unbelievers. Hope Community looks for ways to be involved in lost people's lives, whether it be through riding motorcycles, going hunting, playing sports, and so on.

The second value is that this congregation does not believe in long-term planning but rather walking with the Father, following His leadership as they journey. That doesn't mean that they don't plan and seek the heart of God for decisions; they just don't plan years in advance. "How many people will follow a pastor who doesn't know where he's going?" Eaton asked. They don't cast off strategies and planning all together, but they don't make planning for the future their major pursuit. Rather, they wait upon the Lord, seeking what He wants and then act upon that. This requires intimacy with God. It requires faith, a willingness to adjust or even abandon your plans as the Father leads.

Think about Abraham. God called him and said, "Leave your country, your people and your father's household and go to the land I will show you" (Genesis 12:1, NIV). That's all God gave him; He didn't plan it out for Abraham. God didn't tell him what it would look like, or how he'd get there. God just told Abraham to go and trust Him, that as he moved forward in faith, God would reveal His perfect will to Abraham.

Hope Community believes that one of the biggest lies thrown out by the world is that we need to know exactly where we are going and how to get there. If you look at Scripture, however, those God called (like Abraham and Moses) didn't have it spelled out for them. Jesus walked along the rocky shores of the Sea of Galilee and said to a few fisherman, "Come, follow me, . . . and I will make you fishers of men" (Matt. 4:19, NIV). Do you think they knew exactly what that meant? The emphasis, therefore, is upon faith and walking with the Father, recognizing His voice.

The third value is the importance of risk taking. Taking risks means living by faith and trusting God to come through. We live in a comfort-seeking and instant-gratification culture. We have our microwaves to heat up our food quickly, our high speed internet, and our drive through banking to get what we want immediately. Let's face it, we want life to be easy and safe. It's hard to take risks, to do things that go against our nature, to attempt things that we've not done before. It is an inconvenience to have our schedules disrupted or to not even have one! We love our routines.

According to Jeff Eaton, "God shows up in risks, He doesn't show up in planning." Following Jesus means that we don't come up with our own agendas, but that we find out what His agenda is and join Him. When Jesus called His disciples to follow Him, they left all they had—their agendas, their careers, their comforts, their homes—and followed Him. Jesus never promised it would be easy; He did promise that He would be with us along the way. "Anybody can stand at the edge of the cliff and think they're *cutting edge*," Eaton said. "But God honors those who jump." Without faith, the author of Hebrews says, it's impossible to please God (see Heb. 11:6). Church planting is all about faith: trusting God to do that which is impossible for us to do.

An example of how Hope Community takes risks is in their budget. Most churches set their annual budget at the beginning of their fiscal year, usually in the fall. Hope Community, however, sets its budget at the end of the fiscal year (in September), looking back at what God did and using that as a guideline for the upcoming year. Hope Community is a church that puts lots of emphasis on trusting God, listening to His voice, and then planning—rather than planning and asking God to bless those plans.

The fourth and final value is that Hope Community wants to be a church that Jesus would be a part of. As stated earlier, *the goal of a missional church is not necessarily to grow larger, but rather to equip individuals to live as authentic disciples and release them into the world to live out the mission of God.* This is a very important principle to live by. Too often, churches can get distracted from their vision to make disciples and equip those disciples to live for the glory of the Father. We can become focused on meeting our needs, upon staying comfortable. Recently, Eaton went to a pastor's conference where he asked the question, "If you were not the pastor of your church, would you attend it?" To his surprise, most said no.

This is unfortunate, but true. Hope believes that if the church would follow Jesus' mission statement out of Isaiah 61, and really be intentional about making disciples that walk in the freedom of the Spirit, and then release those disciples into the world, Jesus would be glorified and would *show up* in their church. They would become a place where people, including their own pastors, would want to attend.

In Need of a Surgeon

Shortly after I was married, when I was 25 years old, I underwent major surgery on my right leg. I thought I had injured it playing basketball. After a few months, and a few visits to the doctors, an X-ray was taken and it was discovered that I had a large tumor growing in my tibia bone. Needless to say, I was scared. The doctor didn't know if it was cancer and immediately scheduled me to see a bone cancer specialist at the University of Michigan for surgery.

Thankfully, the tumor was benign and the surgery went smoothly. Without that specialist, however, and her expertise in bone tumors and extensive training, it could have been much worse. I was taken good care of and restored back to full health.

Jesus is like that surgeon. But His surgery goes way beyond our physical bodies; He heals and restores our emotional and spiritual beings. The lies we've believed living in this fallen world are malignant tumors that can wreak havoc on our spiritual and emotional lives. Hope Community Church is committed to helping people remove malignant lies and be restored back to full health, walking in the Spirit's power.

Jesus calls us to preach good news to the poor, to bind up the brokenhearted, and to proclaim freedom for the captives. In order for us to do that we have to allow Him to heal *our* hearts, to restore *our* lives, and then trust Him to use us to help others be restored. Eaton said, "I'm realizing that no matter how comfortable you get on the ladder of faith, God's always asking you to climb up the next rung. And the truth is that next rung is not for me alone, but for the good of others."

Paul wrote that the Father "comforts us in all of our troubles, so that we can comfort those in any trouble with the comfort we ourselves have received from God" (2 Cor. 1:4, NIV). That is a picture of a spiritual trauma center. That is a picture of Hope Community, trauma center in an unlikely place, with unlikely people.

CHAPTER FIFTEEN

Brentwood Baptist Church:

Finding a Missional Identity

Dr. Mike Glenn has a unique perspective when it comes to shepherding Brentwood Baptist Church, the church he has pastored for more than 15 years. It's a large church, with more than 5,000 members, but Glenn is most concerned with getting his people outside of the church walls. "We want to be the church that runs members off."[125]

His philosophy is modeled on the church at Antioch's commissioning of Barnabas and Paul, "While they were worshiping the Lord and fasting, the Holy Spirit said, 'Set apart for me Barnabas and Saul for the work to which I have called them.' So after they had fasted and prayed, they placed their hands on them and sent them off" (Acts 13:2-3, NIV).

Brentwood Baptist Church is a missional church, passionate about helping its members join in God's mission of drawing people to the Gospel and a relationship with Him through Christ. Just as the church at Antioch sent Paul and Barnabas, Brentwood Baptist is committed to train, encourage, support, and send, helping people pursue their individual missional roles while also understanding the church's corporate role in God's mission. In fact, the concept of identity is central to Brentwood's missional strategies; Glenn says a church has to be secure in its vision and place within the Kingdom in order to be missional.

"A missional church is a church that understands its unique identity in Christ, and understands its unique setting and the way that it's fashioned to fulfill its obligation or opportunity in the Kingdom. Having found its 'Yes,' it's free to live out its destiny from that identity in response to the opportunities that God opens up for it."

Brentwood has continually followed God's leading as He has created opportunities for the church to join in His mission. And they are joining Him in countless ways, not following a formula or set of steps, but listening and following and supporting as God mobilizes individuals and groups with particular passions and interests. In this chapter, you'll read about some of the ways Brentwood is reaching out. More importantly, you'll read about a church that has taken hold of the call to journey with God, wherever He leads. It is a story of how He is faithful to use those who are willing to go, to do, and to lose their own lives in the pursuit of His mission.

A 24/7 Operation

The community of Brentwood has changed since Brentwood Baptist's early days as a mission church of Nashville's Woodmont Baptist. As the church has grown, so has its neighborhood, from what Glenn calls the "bedroom community of Nashville" to a community more centrally-located in the Nashville metropolitan area. Once considered

[125] Mike Glenn, interview by author, 25 October 2006, Brentwood, Tennessee, tape recording.

a suburb for Nashville commuters, Brentwood is now a thriving, affluent community all its own. Reflecting one of the characteristics of a missional church, Brentwood Baptist has adapted to its culture; Glenn says the church has moved from a place that was heavily focused on its weekend ministry to more of a "24/7 operation." For example, Brentwood offers both weekly small groups and traditional Sunday School, giving members the opportunity to serve on Sunday mornings in a children's class or other setting while also being part of a discipleship group during the week.

Along with being sensitive to the pace of its community and people, the church is mindful of geographical needs as well. As the Brentwood community has grown, Glenn says the church has become a regional church, home to members who often drive relatively long distances to attend its services and events. In order to adapt to the sprawling nature of the community, and to encourage people to continue to bring their friends and families to church with them, the church has begun a feasibility study to investigate the possibility of multi-site venues. Though Glenn says the church is early in exploring this possibility, the hope is that eventually smaller groups can meet in communities surrounding Brentwood and worship with the church via satellite. It's another way the church is committing itself to encourage people to be on mission with God, stretching itself to meet as many needs as possible.

Offering classes, outreach events and worship gatherings throughout the week, Brentwood tries to meet the people in its community where they are and when they are, using their resources to create ample opportunities for those in their community who want to be connected and involved. You'll read more about some of these opportunities later in this chapter, but the importance here is in the church's willingness to adapt to its busy, constantly moving culture.

Glenn is mindful of the fact that Brentwood's size and reach allow it to do some things that smaller churches can't. As he says, "One of the things about being a large church is that you have the resources to be able to throw a lot of pitches." It is in taking the opportunities to throw those pitches that Brentwood models the missional life Paul writes about in 1 Corinthians 9:22 (NIV), "I have become all things to all men so that by all possible means I might save some."

Finding a PLACE in Ministry

Along with adapting to the time and place concerns within its culture, a church is responsible for paying attention to the needs of its people. Believing that the only way one is truly fulfilled is in the living of an authentic Christian life (and reflecting another characteristic of a missional church), Brentwood has developed a simple process through which people are connected to God, each other, and His mission to reach all peoples. People are expected to answer three questions within their spiritual development:

(1) How are you worshiping?
(2) What are you studying?
(3) What are you doing; how are you involved in service?

Glenn says any individual or group who is only participating in one or two of those arenas is incomplete. We've already discussed worship and small group opportunities available within the church, so we'll focus here on the third question. Brentwood is dedicated to helping people discover their gifts and passions, and how those things can be used to further the Kingdom. Like you read earlier in this book, a missional church moves away from solely being a place where people come to have their needs met, and towards a place where people learn how and are motivated to meet the needs of others. Becoming equipped to engage the harvest is a need inherent in anyone seeking to live an authentic Christian life, and Glenn says it is especially relevant in a community where people are driven to dream big dreams and achieve big things.

"You have people who are talented and creative, who love solving big problems and who are used to thinking globally. Putting the church into a position where we can take advantage of these kinds of leaders is a different challenge. A lot of our people are just bored with church. They make multi-million dollar deals all week long, they start banks, they do all of these huge things, and then we tell them to come and sit in church. They don't want to do that."

In a church with so much going on, it seems that there would be plenty of opportunities for everyone looking for a place to be involved. But as Glenn and his staff noticed people getting lost in the shuffle, they looked for a solution to draw people into the community of the church, moving them from disciples to people continually transformed by the Gospel and involved in the process of making disciples. They needed an initiative for people looking to take the next step in living the authentic Christian life.

"We have a lot of very talented, gifted people who didn't know where they fit or what they were supposed to do. And while we do a good job of getting people born into the Kingdom, we do a very lousy job helping them grow into the Kingdom. We began to try to find a place where we could help our people continue to grow in discipleship."

That place was PLACE,[126] a national ministry objective dedicated to "connect church members into purpose-driven ministry including self-discovery, individualized ministry coaching and tracking from workshop to ministry placement."[127] Through a multi-hour course (offered at Brentwood through a one-day session or over several weeks), people are invited to a place where they explore their passions and dreams and how those can be used in the church and in God's Kingdom. Brentwood began implementing the program three years ago, and has made it a major ministry objective. After an individual completes the PLACE course, he or she has a one-hour session with the consultant to discuss real, specific places within the church where that person can be involved. Glenn says most people who go through PLACE are able to quickly plug into the church, and more importantly, often gain a better understanding of who God has created them to be. That understanding can take root and impact their lives outside of the church, helping them know what to look for in a job or how they can most effectively reach out to others.

[126] Place Ministries Web site, Place Ministries, *http://www.placeministries.org.*
[127] Place Ministries Web site, "About Place," *http://www.placeministries.org.*

Each session focuses on a different aspect of a person's giftedness and passion: **P**ersonality, **L**earning spiritual gifts, **A**bilities (the ability to work in a preferred environment), **C**onnecting passion to ministry, and **E**xperiences of life.[128] Through exploring each of these areas, people participating in PLACE can learn about ministry opportunities inside and outside the church that utilize their unique qualities. Lisa Baker, who serves as head consultant for Brentwood's PLACE ministry, says the program is created to give people freedom in how they minister within the church and on "the land under your feet," a phrase Glenn uses to describe one's vocation or sphere of influence outside the church.

"We've had so many people come in and say, 'In all my church experiences, this is the first time I feel free to be who I was created to be. I can breathe,'" Baker says.

Baker once consulted with two pastors' daughters who had always been looked to as leaders in ministry and outreach. They had definite desires to serve, but their profiles didn't match up with the style of an up-front leader. Through PLACE, both girls determined that they were suited to more behind-the-scenes roles; they were freed from the tension that having to pretend to be something they really weren't had caused for several years. Another young woman working as a hospital nurse went through PLACE and found out that her personality and gifts were more socially-driven. Frustrated in her job, she eventually found a new employment opportunity at an outpatient surgery clinic. Because of who she was and how she was, she felt more fulfilled in her new, more personal environment. A successful businessman came through the PLACE program and admitted that while he felt very successful in his work, he had always felt out of place in church. After assessing his abilities and gifts, Brentwood found a place for him to serve where his mind for business could really be used. Working to help establish some new foundations that the church is beginning, the man found his place in the church, using the gifts and talents that he used in his vocation.

Baker says it is amazing to see how God not only uses PLACE to impact individuals, but groups as well. Recently, she sat in on a meeting of a mission team traveling to a poverty-stricken area of Rio de Janeiro. Baker brought in their PLACE results (everyone who goes on a mission trip through Brentwood is required to take PLACE), and watched as the group discovered how many of them had the spiritual gift of mercy, as well as the unique social ability that would allow them to bring joy, build relationships and overcome obstacles. It was evident that God had brought the team together, placing them in a context where their gifts and abilities were specifically needed.

Each quarter, the staff meets together with a list of everyone in the church who has recently graduated from the PLACE program, ready to help them get involved now that they have discovered more about their strengths. Sometimes, a PLACE graduate has decided to step down from a currently-held position to pursue another ministry to which he or she feels called. Baker says this is when the buy-in on the church staff's part is crucial. They are willing to let people explore the things God's calling them to, even if it means starting from scratch. Church planters interested in using PLACE in their ministry can register to receive more information by going to *www.DiscoverChurchPlanting.net*, clicking on "Resources," then on "Field Partner Registration."

[128] Lisa Baker, interview by author, 8 November 2006, Brentwood, Tennessee.

Whether it's children's ministry, music, recovery ministry, hospitality, or any other number of things, PLACE offers people an opportunity to realize their ministry potential. It also moves them into a position where they are more comfortable with their personalities and gifts, and more at ease with sharing their faith. Living an authentic Christian life includes sharing the Gospel with the people around us, both through our words and our lifestyles. When people are ministering in areas tailored to their gifts and interests, and are experiencing a new fullness in their relationship with Christ, they are more likely to be aware of and look for opportunities to share about who He is and how He has transformed their lives. Glenn explains that Brentwood's methods of evangelism training stem from a belief that people need to experience a dynamic relationship with Christ.

"What we have found is that there is nothing less effective than a class on evangelism. When you say, 'Sunday night, we're going to talk about evangelism,' you can hold that meeting in any phone booth in town . . . What we have found is that when somebody is excited about what Jesus is doing in their life, then they are naturally evangelistic."

As part of their small group and Sunday School ministries, Brentwood takes several opportunities each year to help people learn to share their faith, so that they can be prepared for any conversations they might have. But evangelism isn't taught as a process; it's a natural outgrowth of a life that is authentically engaged in knowing Christ, experiencing Him, and serving His church. Through the PLACE initiative, Brentwood encourages its people to stretch their faith, so that they might share it through serving others and outwardly demonstrating a life-changing relationship with Jesus.

Empowered for Ministry, Partnering with the Church

Not only does Brentwood Baptist Church seek to equip and encourage individuals to serve within the body, the church also empowers those who have found avenues outside the church through which they can minister. One of the values of a missional church is its ability to enlist, equip, and commission people to live incarnational lives, and to model the missional leadership they've observed. Those who are a part of a missional church are compelled to live out their faith in their daily lives, and to be intentional in looking for opportunities to share the Gospel within their spheres of influence.

Brentwood Baptist is full of examples of individuals and groups who have been called to minister outside of their church. Whether they are connected to a group or a ministry through their job, family or personal interest, these people have been commissioned by their church to take the missional, evangelistic principles taught within the church walls to the culture outside. They are not all missionaries, at least in the technical sense. In fact, many of their ministries aren't overtly religious in nature. But they have been encouraged to take the Gospel to people instead of waiting for people to come to them or to the church.

For example, church member Daryl Murray runs Welcome Home Ministries of Nashville, an outreach created to help individuals and families who have struggled through homelessness and drug and alcohol abuse. The non-profit organization owns a housing facility for men in recovery and also offers programs to help people secure jobs and homes.

Brentwood Baptist partners with Murray and Welcome Home Ministries, not in running the outreach, but coming alongside to reach out to people in need. Murray has brought opportunities for service into his church; Brentwood's members have responded by participating in counseling programs and inviting individuals and families from Welcome Home to church events and their Sunday School classes. On Brentwood's Web site, Murray reports: ..."My wife Glenda and I have only been attending Brentwood Baptist for the past year. We are grateful for a 'church culture' that is open and interested in helping people in need. It is our desire that we can be helpful as together we reach out to the least of these."[129]

Like Murray, Jen Gash runs a ministry that seeks to help a specific group of people. But while Murray reaches out in and around Nashville, Jen is called to reach out in the Eastern European nation of Moldova. Gash, also a church member at Brentwood, is the founder of Sweet Sleep, which seeks to meet needs amongst orphans in Moldova. Begun as a way to provide beds for Moldovan orphanages, Sweet Sleep also now provides housing, education, job training and employment for boys once they leave the orphanages.[130] Brentwood is heavily involved in the ministry, sending mission teams of every age group; the most recent team traveled to Moldova in October 2006, building relationships in the orphanages and seeking to meet needs however possible.[131]

Gene and Lynn Torti are spearheading a ministry that seeks to meet a more sudden, recent need. The Tortis visited Pearlington, Mississippi in the aftermath of Hurricane Katrina and felt an immediate burden for the town, which lost all but three of its homes. Motivated by the needs of Pearlington's residents, the Tortis took their idea to Brentwood's missions leadership. In October, the first team traveled to Mississippi to build the first Project Pearlington house.[132] Glenn says the initiative's ultimate goal is to rebuild the entire town.

Daryl Murray, Jen Gash, and Gene and Lynn Torti are partnering with their church, a church that encourages them to live out the Gospel every day, to pursue a ministry to which God has specifically called them. And they aren't the only ones; other Brentwood members minister through housing rehabilitation in Nashville and medical outreach in Rio de Janeiro and Guatemala. Mike Glenn says these kinds of partnerships are of utmost value to the church, whether the ministries began within the church, or if the partnership began because someone from the ministry became part of Brentwood. The church isn't interested in reinventing the wheel; partnerships allow everyone involved to benefit from the missional leadership of someone who has been encouraged by other leaders to be intentional about living out their faith in the world around them.

Glenn says, "Missions is not church-run or church-initiated, it is church-empowered and church-sponsored. Then, it's done by our members."

[129] Brentwood Baptist Church Web site, "News: Welcome Home Ministries," Brentwood Baptist Church, *http://www.brentwoodbaptistchurch.com/info/new/newsstory.aspx?iid=162&tid=4.*

[130] Sweet Sleep Web site, "What is Sweet Sleep," Sweet Sleep, *http://www.sweetsleep.org.*

[131] Brentwood Baptist Church/Sweet Sleep blog, October-November 2006, *http://www.sweetsleep.blogspot.com.*

[132] Brentwood Baptist Church Web site, "Missions: Project Pearlington," Brentwood Baptist Church, *http://www.brentwoodbaptist.com/groups/story.aspx?aid=21&pid=52&iid=1582&tid=4.*

Reaching Across Cultural Bounds

Brentwood Baptist Church is a church that encourages its members to dream big. They support and partner with member-driven ministries all over the world; they have also developed a corporate commitment to intentionally crossing cultures, reflecting another characteristic of a missional church discussed earlier in this book. They are reaching out to people of all backgrounds, in their community and beyond. The church has also found several ways in which they can be used specifically, filling a role in cross-cultural ministry that is tailored to their vision and resources. They are meeting needs, and most importantly, planting churches amongst the cultures into which they're reaching. For example, Brentwood is actively supporting new churches in Chicago, Canada, and Montana, providing resources and sending mission teams to help planters as they establish their ministries. Closer to home, Brentwood is one of five churches in the Nashville area that are partnering to support a Hispanic church plant in their community. In each of these instances, the church is going out into a culture different from its own and helping plant new churches that are tailored to those communities.

Earlier in this chapter, you read about various international missions opportunities available at Brentwood. Along with Moldova, Guatemala, and Rio de Janeiro, the church is heavily involved in AIDS ministry in South Africa and tsunami relief in Southeast Asia. There are opportunities for Brentwood's people to cross cultural boundaries in the United States as well; in Summer 2005, a team traveled to New York City to paint public schools, many of which haven't been painted in decades. The church is instilling in its members a "sky's the limit" mentality; it is committed to using its resources and reach to go into all the world and make disciples (see Matt. 28:19).

But going into all the world doesn't just mean Africa, or South America, or New York City. Brentwood Baptist has reached into cultures within Nashville, seeing needs and striving to meet them by creating meaningful, dynamic environments of worship, service and community. Two years ago, the single adults of the church began a Bible study called Kairos (Greek for "a unique moment in time").[133] The weekly gathering was created as a time for young adults to come together and begin to experience spiritual transformation, as individuals and as a community. Now, when up to 1,000 people meet each Tuesday at Brentwood's facilities for Kairos, the crowd includes college students, professionals, singles, couples, and anyone else who's interested. Each week, attendees are invited to worship together, hear teaching from Glenn, and draw closer to a true understanding of Jesus and what it means to have a relationship with Him. This vision is reflected in Kairos' mission statement: "Kairos exists to create an authentic community where people hear and live the Gospel of Jesus Christ in a postmodern culture."[134]

To reach out to that culture, Brentwood has created Kairos as a contemporary worship service where attenders feel the freedom to ask questions, even if that means standing up during Glenn's message and asking him right then. It's meant to be a place for people who might not experience church at any other time. In fact, Glenn says about 30 percent of people who attend Kairos report that it is the only worship gathering they are able to

[133] Kairos Web site, "What is Kairos," Kairos, a ministry of Brentwood Baptist Church, *www.kairosnashville.com.*
[134] Ibid.

attend during the week. In a news article on Brentwood's Web site, Glenn discussed the importance of the outreach within the church's overall mission.

"The contemporary church must see itself as a missionary to its own culture, and part of being a missionary is learning to communicate the Good News of Jesus Christ in the language of the culture. Music, worship styles, and preaching styles are changeable methods we use to get across the unchanging message of Jesus. If we are not intentional about reaching those who are under 30, we will lose the next 2-3 generations of Christians."[135]

Kairos is focused on both evangelism and discipleship, calling those who do not yet know God to experience a real relationship with Him. For those who do know Him, Kairos offers many of the same things as Brentwood. It's a community for people who are seeking connection with God and connection with others who know God. Like Brentwood, Kairos wants to see attenders participate through worship, community and service. Along with the band-driven, contemporary worship experience on Tuesday evenings, Kairos also offers a network of small groups (called Life Groups) who meet throughout the week, with the goal of building a sense of community amongst people who attend Kairos that extends beyond Tuesday night. Also moving toward that goal, Kairos plans and sponsors missions experiences; upcoming trips include Thailand and Rio de Janeiro.[136]

Kairos aims to be both a part of Brentwood Baptist and its own missional community, encouraging people to join in God's mission through both forums. For those looking to connect into ministry at Brentwood, PLACE is occasionally offered at Kairos, pointing people towards how their particular gifts equip them for service in the church. Glenn says another way the ministry has connected to the church is through cross-generational relationship-building. Kairos leaders and Brentwood staff noticed that many of the young people who attended on Tuesday night were lonely or lacking nearby family relationships. The church connected Kairos with its senior adult ministry, providing surrogate grandparents and making a huge impact on both groups.

Kairos is Brentwood's way of crossing into Nashville's youth and professional cultures and providing a forum for people in those communities to experience all aspects of the church. Crossing cultural bounds, Brentwood has found a way to reach out to people who might not be reachable through more traditional means.

There is another community within Brentwood Baptist that is the result of an intentional, focused cross-cultural outreach. Several years ago, a member of Brentwood became burdened for Nashville's deaf and hearing impaired community. Churches in the Nashville area, including Brentwood, had interpretive ministries for deaf members, but no church existed to meet the specific needs of the deaf community. The church member went to Brentwood's leadership and shared the need; in 1995, Brentwood expanded its interpretive ministry and began the Brentwood Baptist Deaf Church, which is run as a separate

[135] Brentwood Baptist Church Web site, "News: Kairos—A Unique Moment in Time," Brentwood Baptist Church, *http://www.brentwoodbaptist.com.*

[136] Kairos Web site, "Missions," Kairos, a ministry of Brentwood Baptist Church, *www.kairosnashville.com.*

congregation but is also closely connected to Brentwood Baptist. The Deaf Church is the second-largest congregation of its kind in the country.

Currently, the church is home to 150-200 worshipers each Sunday, and is cultivating its own missional characteristics. The church offers music and children's ministries, including an all-day gathering on Sunday. The congregation worships together in the morning and then stays together throughout the afternoon, offering people an opportunity to connect with each other in community. There are classes and events throughout the week, and the congregation periodically connects with other local and regional deaf ministries.[137]

In 2003, Brentwood Baptist Deaf Church moved into its new chapel, the only facility in North America set up specifically for deaf worship. Each seat is designed to allow the worshiper a clear view of the front of the chapel, and technical equipment allows hearing impaired individuals to sit anywhere in the chapel and use their own listening aides.[138]The congregation is reaching outward as well, using the chapel as a training facility and producing DVDs of its worship services for other deaf congregations. Pastor Brian Sims' messages are seen by 12 churches around the country that receive the DVDs each week.

Glenn says there are several families that participate in both churches; parents attend a worship service for the deaf while their children attend a hearing service, or vice versa. Although the churches are separate bodies with their own staffs and deacons, they are connected by a desire to minister to people and a vision to share the Gospel across cultures. The Deaf church is an example of how a missional church can begin new missional churches when the body is willing to step out of its culture and into another, building relationships, becoming a long-term presence in the community, and encouraging missional thinking and activity.

Still Moving, Always Stretching

Brentwood Baptist Church is a place always in motion, a "24/7 operation." There are countless training sessions, outreach events, choir rehearsals, Bible studies, small group meetings, mission team meetings and worship gatherings. As Mike Glenn says, "If you're bored here, it's your own fault." But the church is about more than providing activity for its people. Brentwood seeks to be a place where people can grow spiritually, a place where they're encouraged to live authentic Christian lives. The church has adapted to its busy, time-sensitive culture, stretching itself to provide as many meeting times and places as possible. They're also sensitive to the issue of venue, understanding that some people are more comfortable, at least at first, in a small group setting than in a large worship gathering. And they are looking for more ways to reach out, exploring possibilities that will allow smaller groups of church commuters to gather in their own communities on Sunday mornings. The church is dedicated to a simple but meaningful process of making disciples: connecting to God through worship, connecting to others through smaller communities, and connecting to the rest of the world through serving.

[137] Brentwood Baptist Deaf Church web site, "Ministries," Brentwood Baptist Deaf Church, *http://www.brentwooddeaf.org.*

[138] Brentwood Baptist Deaf Church web site, "Deaf Chapel," *http://www.brentwooddeaf.org.*

Brentwood is a place intent on helping people find their role in the ministry of the church, offering programs like PLACE to help people identify their dreams and passions and how those things fit into the fabric of the church. When church members are called to ministries outside of the church, Brentwood has been willing to partner with them, traveling across town to refurbish homes or around the world to minister in Moldovan orphanages. It is an empowering place, moving its members to a place where they have ears open to God's leading. Likewise, as God has led, Brentwood has crossed cultural lines, beginning or sponsoring new churches around the world and in its own community.

The church will continue to adapt and tailor its approach to its community, and to the cultures into which it has reached, believing that God has called the Church, and their church, to a mission to expand the Church into the world by living and declaring the gospel through witnessing and disciple-making among all *ta ethne* or peoples of the world. Brentwood Baptist Church is eager to fill its role in that mission.

CHAPTER SIXTEEN

Forerunner Baptist Church:

Wherever . . . Whatever

As the sun rises on Sunday mornings in western Tennessee you can be assured of three things. First, that the faithful will get up early and attend a local church. After all, it is the heart of the Bible Belt and church attendance is very much a part of life. Second, you can be assured that in most areas, 11:00 a.m. is the most segregated hour of the week. Anglos will worship with Anglos. Hispanics will worship with Hispanics. African-Americans will worship with African-Americans. Third, you can count on the fact that many of the local residents will not be in church. If you were to dig deeper, you might discover as well that many of those who do not attend church services are either ignored by the local church or at least, kept at arms length by area believers. It is not their ethnicity or their language that separates them. It is their lifestyle. It is their drug and alcohol use. It is their reluctance or inability to live a life marked by stability and freedom from addictions.

While this portrait may describe many of the small, rural communities throughout western Tennessee, something different is happening in Ripley, Tennessee, through the ministries of Forerunner Baptist Church. Life there is different in this missional church pastored by Thomas Bester. Pastor Bester's vision is to establish a multi-racial, multi-cultural, multi-faceted ministry that will promote a loving, trusting, and obedient relationship with our Lord and Savior, Jesus Christ. He feels strongly about the multi-racial thrust of his ministry. He says, "Here in the south, we still have the attitude of 'black church, white church, Hispanic church.' On Sunday morning, you go to your church, with people of your color. I really wanted to break those barriers, because we don't think heaven will be like that."[139] Pastor Bester admits that Forerunner Baptist Church does have an emphasis on evangelizing African-Americans, but that they do go to everyone in the area. His goal is to build a kingdom church—to see a church formed that is a true reflection of God's world and God's people."

Bester had been pastoring a medium-sized church for more than nine years when he sensed a calling away to do something he had never done before. He was being called by God to reach out to people who he felt were neglected by the traditional church . . . people who were drug-users, gang-kids, and unwed mothers. He sensed a calling from God to reach people who might not be accepted by the local church or who might feel uncomfortable if they visited a typical church in the South. His was a calling to reach people who might not be attracted to a church because that church seemed to not understand who they were or where they were in life's journey.

For a long time Bester felt that the church he had been pastoring was not concerned about the Great Commission or evangelism. The church seemed more interested in getting outsiders to become *members*, rather than seeking to help people come to Christ and become real disciples. Bester explained that God used Luke 1:17 (NKJV) to solidify his

[139] Thomas Bester, phone interview with author, 23 October, 2006.

calling. In that verse John the Baptist was "to make ready a people prepared for the Lord." He shared that he was convicted by that. He said, "I knew that was the direction God wanted me to go. We were to focus on reaching people who were not prepared to meet the Lord, as opposed to meeting the needs of people who *thought* they were prepared to meet the Lord by attending church and doing things in the church. Like Jesus said, 'I didn't come for those who are healthy, but for those who are sick." This process of God's call helped set the missional direction of Forerunner Baptist Church.

Bester became more interested in reaching people in his community who were being ignored. He developed a deep love for younger people, people from their teenage years to their thirties. He developed a passion for people who seemed to be invisible to the church. It appeared to him that the local church had given up on those people. They became his focus. Bester states, "A lot of those people are unchurched or unsaved and it seemed to me that I should target that group and specifically reach out to them." Bester no longer wanted to be a part of a congregation interested in talking people into "coming to church." Rather he wanted to focus on helping people place their faith and trust in Jesus and assist them in becoming authentic disciples of Christ. This vision propelled him to start a Bible study in a high-crime, high-drug neighborhood. The study began with five people and today, four years later, the predominately African-American church runs 120 to 140 on Sunday mornings, and includes people from all backgrounds, races, and lifestyles.

What does Bester see as the primary purpose of Forerunner Baptist Church? He says, "We purpose to win souls for Christ in our community, our state, our nation, and the world by:

1. Going wherever and doing whatever it takes to reach the lost and unchurched people with the message of the gospel.
2. Glorifying God by making and growing fully devoted followers of Jesus Christ through example and life applicable teaching.
3. Utilizing the spiritual gifts, talents, and life experiences of others to provide kingdom building ministries, to reach the lost.
4. Offering the good news of Jesus Christ to those who typically are either ignored or avoided by the local church by meeting them at their point of need.
5. Growing a healthy, reproducing church that will seek to expand the kingdom of God by starting new churches committed to reproducing themselves around the world.

Going Wherever and Doing Whatever

Forerunner Church is a sending church. This is clearly a mark of a missional church. Bester teaches that the church is the headquarters. People come to the "headquarters" to get teaching, direction, and "marching orders." At "headquarters," people are prepared and then sent back into their sphere of influence to share the gospel with their friends and neighbors as well as with people unlike themselves. They are prepared to reach people with different lifestyles or worldviews. They are sent to people from different economic backgrounds or ethnicities. The focus is on reaching out. It is a strategy of taking the gospel to people where they are.

Bester has learned what it means to connect with those outside his comfort zone. He connects with people unlike himself. He's a baby-boomer, but he works mostly with baby-busters and younger people. He seeks to connect with the troubled and with those in need of life transformation. This forces Forerunner Baptist Church to look for new and innovative ways to reach out to all people. One example is a "Pay What You Want Yard Sale." This outreach works well among local Hispanic communities. Many people there are in need of clothing or shoes. The church uses this simple ministry as an opportunity to meet people with whom they can share Christ. This involvement has led Bester to a desire to start a Hispanic work through Forerunner Baptist Church.

This go wherever, do whatever attitude has truly effected Forerunner Baptist Church's mission. Bester says, "We're constantly trying to reach other groups. We see a big difference between the hip-hop generation and the boomer generation. However, you can't be afraid of having a Christian rap artist coming in to talk to the young people. Like Paul said, 'I have become all things to all people that I might win some.'" As a result, Forerunner offers many things for the youth that are specially designed to reach them and their peers. He says, "We have a dynamic youth group that goes out prayerwalking and evangelizing their friends and neighbors. We don't have things 'for' them, we encourage them to go out and reach out to their friends and neighbors."

A few months after Bester started his first Bible study, a young man, a tough, gang-banger guy started coming. He paid attention and seemed interested. One evening after one of their Bible studies, around nine o'clock, Bester's phone rang. It was this young man. He said, "Pastor Bester, I'm at my sister's house. I need you to come here and tell people what you told me at that study."

Bester confesses, "I was tired, getting ready to go to bed. But I knew God wanted me to go. His sister lived in a mobile home. I went to the door. I stepped inside and this young man had 22 people crammed into that trailer. I knew most of them were young gang members. It was a place I didn't really want to be. The gang-banger looked at all these kids, fifteen to eighteen years old. He said, 'You all be quiet and listen to this man.' I stayed for about two hours, sharing Christ with those people. Three people received Christ that night. That got me. It affirmed to me that I was doing what God really had called me to do. I knew then, going home and praising God, that I was right in doing this missional church thing. I felt this was the first time since I had surrendered to the ministry that I was actually doing what God wanted me to do. I knew then I couldn't turn back."

Disciple Making

Forerunner Baptist Church realizes that to have an adequate missional force, the people must be properly equipped. One of the means of preparing people for ministering in the harvest is a very practical discipleship class where an emphasis is put on the "going" part of the Great Commission. They teach disciples to do door-to-door evangelism. Bester sees it as a "multiplication" ministry, not just an "adding" ministry. Disciple two people, they go out and disciple two more each. That's six disciples. Those six pick two more and disciple them. That's eighteen. And so on. Multiplication.

Bivocational pastor Bester demonstrated the multiplication principle while working at his secular job with the Tennessee Board of Probation and Paroles. Bester shares, "I had a parole hearing with a guy some years ago. A couple of years later, we were doing some door-to-door work. And this young guy came up to me and said, 'Do you remember me?' I didn't. 'Well, I had a parole hearing before the board and you recommended that they decline my request for two years.' I thought he might be mad at me, but then he told me he got saved and thanked me for putting him off for those two years so he'd have a chance to get his life together. Now he's off parole and hoping to develop a jail ministry. After his release he had problems finding a church that was willing to help him develop the jail ministry he felt called to. We're training him to do that now."

That is the kind of multiplication and "sending" that really has teeth to it. It's the kind Bester sees working every day in his church. That is the desired outcome of their discipleship process. It has become Bester's passion. "We don't call people to be members of our church anymore. When we give an invitation in the worship service, we tell people to give up their membership and become a disciple. We make it clear from the beginning that in becoming a part of this church family, we want you to commit yourself to being a disciple, a follower of Christ, not just a church member."

How does he communicate this? He says, "The most powerful way is in a class we call 'New Members Orientation Class,' we give them the philosophies, goals, and mission of our church." He lets them know that Forerunner is an active group that seeks to disciple and evangelize others and that their church my not be right for them. That has turned away some people, but that's all right with them. "We know they will fit in better somewhere else, and we try to help those people find another church that will fit them better. We may even give their contact information to another pastor and ask him to contact them. We ask him to help that person remain a member of the kingdom's work" says Bester.

Forerunner is working towards teaching people what it means to seek the heart of God. He says, "We talk about prayer and meditation, and studying God's Word. We emphasize serving one another. We work at teaching people to be merciful and compassionate, to reflect the heart of Christ." This can be problematic when you are working with people like Forerunner does. Those people believe in an eye for an eye and tooth for a tooth. They try to get revenge against those who have hurt them. Asking them to show mercy is a complete turnaround. At Forerunner they are learning a different way. Bester explains, "We teach them the value of turning the other cheek, and the value of loving one another. God's Spirit softens their hearts. God is doing His thing through His people."

Utilizing the Gifts and Talents of Disciples

Another distinctly missional aspect of Forerunner Baptist Church is its emphasis on helping newly discipled followers of Christ utilize their spiritual gifts and talents to reach the people of west Tennessee. They are encouraged to use these gifts as they live life in their communities, in the workplace, and amongst their friends and families. Bester tells us, "In our discipleship class we help people find their ministry area through spiritual gifts surveys. We ask them to commit themselves to discipleship. That's the dividing line."

Bester cites a solid example in a lady who was gifted in helps and mercy. After attending the discipleship class, she became the impetus for a meals-on-wheels program for the elderly. This missional activity led to opportunities to start individual Bible studies. That drew more people in to develop group Bible studies in homes. The church allowed this disciple to live out her passion. That was a passion to evangelize those without Christ who for one reason or another could not get to the church. Bester describes the success this has produced: "She goes out and shares Christ, and people have gotten saved. It's not about them joining the church, it's about them joining the kingdom. She's serving with all her heart and is a big plus in our discipleship ministry."

Bester says he has seen many people move out of a self-focused mentality and into a desire to live a true and authentic life that glorifies Christ and then uses that platform to reach out to others. He says, "It's all about the fruit of repentance. Many people we've ministered to are from high-crime, low-income neighborhoods many churches won't touch. We help these folks not only change from that lifestyle to living an authentic Christian life, but those people encourage others in their community to do the same. Each one teaches one is the philosophy."

This philosophy permeates the church. The example of one young man gains Bester's strongest affirmation. This particular young man was a drug-dealer. However, his biggest problem in developing his Christian walk was not an addiction to drugs, but an addiction to the money that his drug-dealing provided. Forerunner helped him come to the realization that his money addiction was what he needed to overcome. Today he's given up the life of selling drugs and is working for minimum wage at McDonald's. Going from a lifestyle where he might sell several thousand dollars worth of drugs in a day to making only minimum wage has been a difficult adjustment. He cannot buy all the things he used to buy. Even though he has a wife and children to support, which is difficult on his new income, his experience being discipled has shown him the benefits. He no longer has to worry about the police kicking in his door or people driving by and shooting bullets at his house. He is providing a safer home for his family.

Because he has a church family behind him, supporting him, this young man has confidence he can overcome this addiction. He has prayer partners working with him and others calling to encourage him. Bester says, "It's a day-to-day issue with him, just as it was with the people he sold drugs to. He knows his money addiction was destroying him. But in the process, he is becoming a witness for Christ that you can make it. It's a struggle. But the peace of mind and the peace with Christ is worth it." The young man echoes Pastor Bester in his own words: "I've come a long way and I've got a long way to go. I understand things now much better than I did when I was in that life." That's the kind of change that Bester believes a missional church is best at causing.

Connecting With People At Their Point of Need

One Sunday morning a man shared his testimony about how he came to be a part of Forerunner. He shared how two people made an impact on his life, just by talking about Christ and how He had worked in their lives. They showed him real love. They never mentioned the church. He woke up one morning and something told him to come to this church. He came and the two people who had been witnessing to him were there. He said he knew then that was the place God wanted him to be, because those two ladies had just shared Christ with him and did not try to get him to come to their church.

Bester says, "By them sharing a testimony of how God had transformed their lives and showing him the love of Christ, he was connected to the church. It surprised him that those two ladies would love him like that. He knew this was the kind of church that was concerned about him personally, not about him coming to their church. That's our philosophy. We try to help people to come to Christ first, then to come to a church."

Bester conveys that this is an important aspect of reaching out. That is because the church is trying to reach people who do not understand unconditional love. They live life where "strings are attached to everything," where the rule for life is "I do it to you before you do it to me." The believers at Forerunner Baptist Church see the importance of showing all people that while they do not deserve unconditional love, that is still the way Christ loved us and them.

That message has an impact. But Bester says, "It's hard to get these kinds of people to that point, but we have a diverse group of people here at the church who show that kind of love and it reinforces everything I say from the pulpit."

The ministry of Forerunner is also multi-faceted. Many different kinds of ministries reach different cultures and people. The church looks for practical needs and tries to meet them. This leads to ministries that include computer classes, marriage support groups, a grocery ministry, and even temporary housing for people who are homeless. Bester summarizes the outreach like this: "We try to have a ministry that meets people where they are."

In their area they encounter many young people without high school diplomas. Many of these young people refuse to go to a formal setting, so Forerunner decided to offer G.E.D. classes. They have seen a number of people from drug and gang-influenced backgrounds who have received their diplomas by taking the G.E.D. classes offered at Forerunner.

Several years ago, on the coldest day of the year, one church member stopped for coffee on his way to work. He noticed a lady sitting in a police car looking pretty down and out. After asking the police officer what had happened, he was informed that the lady had not done anything wrong but that she did not have anywhere to go and was hanging out on the street. The church member felt he had to do something.

Remembering that the church's parsonage was not being used, but did have heat and electricity, he took the day off work, took her to the parsonage, and helped the lady get settled in. The church decided to allow the lady to remain and eventually, helped her find employment at a hotel. She soon got a room at the hotel as part of her compensation and more importantly, she received Christ. The parsonage is now called the "shekinah glory house." Bester says, "We saw that it would be a great place for people in need to live until they could get on their feet, find jobs, and move on. So now we're using it for that purpose."

The most recent tenant at the "shekinah glory house" was a young lady with three children. She was able to move out on her own about a month ago and is doing well. Why do they do things like this? Bester says, "Many churches would have shied away from that lady because she was not married, had the kids out of wedlock. She wasn't into drugs or anything and she wasn't a bad lady, she just had no roots, or sense of what really matters in life. Many churches shun families like that. But we had a house with beds and heat . . . That's the whole emphasis of our ministry to help people at their point of need. That's how we get the gospel to them. This lady is a Christian now and a member of our church. We try to heal the hurts of people first and then give them the truth."

Another example is found in Forerunner's "Meals on Wheels" program. Working with a local agency that delivers food to the elderly, Forerunner takes it a step further by doing deliveries to the elderly on weekends, since the agency only delivers during the week. This gives them the opportunity to not just deliver meals, but also to conduct one-on-one Bible studies, as well as deliver tapes of sermons and Bible studies. Bester explains that while these shut-ins can not come to their church, "that's not the point. We're ministering to them at their point of need . . . It's just another chance to serve. We're learning the heart of Christ and planning to meet those needs through him." Bester says, "The greatest characteristic of a missional church is to carry out the mission of God within our immediate community and eventually around the world. This is our focus."

Another example of this is Forerunner's recent "Marriage Go-Round Ministry." This ministry began as the church sensed a need to strengthen the relationships of the people they were reaching. This support group for married people recently saw a young couple avoid a divorce. The ministry was able to show the husband how badly he had hurt his wife. The young man was able to see how God feels when we dishonor His Son and make a connection from this to dishonoring his wife. The couple is back together and he is even exploring a pastoral ministry. Through this ministry, Forerunner is helping couples see they need to be more Christlike, and as a result, lives are changed and marriages restored.

Because Forerunner Baptist Church ministers to people with simple means, it's important to identify with that lifestyle in all they do. As a bivocational pastor, Bester has managed to embrace a simple lifestyle and is teaching this concept to his congregation. He says, "I'm not an A-type personality. I deal with the 'right now.' That's a simple approach to life. Planning is fine. Goal-making is fine. But 'right now' is what you have. Those things that are behind me, in the past, they're gone. Those things before me, I haven't seen them yet. So I have to live right now. I talk about this to people, telling to learn to live right now. I ask them, 'Are you believing right now? If you died right now, would you go to heaven?' And that's the philosophy that I live. I want people to become disciples and go out and make disciples, and help those disciples make more disciples. That's the simple process."

Planting New Churches

A natural outgrowth of a missional church is helping start new churches. Planting new churches is a primary value in Bester's outlook and vision for Forerunner. Forerunner has planted one church, an "incubated church," one designed to birth church planters and new works throughout western Tennessee. Detailed plans include starting eight new churches in the rural west Tennessee area over the next five years, including a Hispanic church in Ripley. Bolivar, Tennessee, is another location they are focusing on. Fifty-nine percent of the population is African-American and yet there is no evangelical African-American church.

Having targeted under-reached communities, they plan to accomplish their goal by putting together groups of people from Forerunner who will be the "support group" or launch team for the new work. They will send these groups out to identify potential locations and then send additional people to form a core group for the new church. Just as Bester started Forerunner with a Bible study of five interested people, he thinks that process will lead to more church plants in his area. They have also initiated an intentional process for equipping those who feel called to plant a church. Prospective church planters are assessed to help them clarify their calling. If, as a result of the process, the individual has a clear sense of calling to plant a church, they are placed into their internship program until the time is right for basic training for church planters. Those desiring additional training are encouraged to attain formal training in the area through attending one of many schools in the area.

Those who discover that they are not called by God to be lead planters are encouraged to become members of a new works team. The goal of their process is not to exclude, but to assist everyone to begin living a missional lifestyle within the ministry of one of their church plants. They help them get the church started by serving in outreach events, going door-to-door, and gaining local support. This is the vision of reproduction and multiplication that Bester feels must characterize a truly missional church. His passion? That every Christ-follower be about the mission of making disciples!

Struggles That Come with a New Church

Bester learned firsthand that new churches face some struggles in implementing their vision. The biggest struggle Bester encountered was the lack of support from their sponsoring church. He had hoped to have more assistance in the areas of church administration and leadership. A common letdown, Bester, having pastored for nine years, was able to draw from his personal experience. It also taught him the importance of being a good church planting partner.

Bester said, "I also asked a lot of people for help. The Director of Missions in our association, Ray Jones, was very helpful. He offered advice and would connect me to people at the Tennessee Baptist Convention who were a big help." The Cooperative Program, training, and missions opportunities "can't be matched" by any other Baptist organization, states Bester. Jones and the Big Hatchie Baptist Association were a great help in guiding them through the process of securing facilities. "We got the parsonage and church through his efforts and directions."

Personal struggles? Bester admits to feeling rejection from the "established" religious community that did not see a need for new church starts. "You have pastors in churches who say, 'Why do we need other churches when our churches are only half-full? It's hard to find a sponsoring church because they want people to come to their church.

Why should they support a new church when their church isn't full?" He shared, "It came on two fronts. We were the first mainly African-American church belonging to the Southern Baptist Convention in our area. You get a lot of rejection from the community because you're not a member of an African-American group. They wanted us to join their associations.

"We also received a lot of flak from black churches and black pastors who felt we'd abandoned our people [blacks in particular] because we were multicultural. The church in the south is very segregated. But we reach out to everyone—black, white, Asian, Hispanic—and some people resented that. For instance, recently we had a young Hispanic girl get baptized. That got some flak. But we don't want to be a white church or a black church.

"It's more undercover than overt. I used to get a lot of invitations from other churches to do revivals and such. But that's dried up. No one has confronted me per se. No one has just walked up to me and gotten mad. But it's there. In fact, I had a young preacher when we first planted the church who apologized to me because he had been talking to others about who we were—gossiping and putting us down. He said that was wrong . . . It's a tough thing to battle, but we do all the time. And God helps us."

Looking back on all God has accomplished in building Forerunner from five people in a Bible study to more than 120 in a building, Bester has had many "great moments." "But," he says, "my greatest joy has been seeing God show His favor to me by multiplying our ministry and allowing us to see lives being turned around and changed. It's by His power that these things are possible. He's sending me into areas I never thought about venturing into as far as ministry is concerned." When you look at the baptism ratio at Forerunner, it is evident that this is a church reaching their community for Christ. For every two new members, they typically have at least one baptism. New converts quickly move to the step of baptism as part of the process of becoming a true disciple and missionally engaged follower of Christ.

Forerunner is committed to going wherever and doing whatever it takes to reach the lost and unchurched with the gospel of Jesus Christ. Their emphasis? Life transformation. Loving people unnoticed or unreached by other churches. Planting new churches. A burden for an entire region. Evangelistic passion. An intentional discipleship process. Deploying Christ-followers into the harvest. Cultural relevance. Working in the harvest. Cross-cultural intentionality.

Conclusion

The population growth rate in the United States and Canada has far surpassed the growth rate of Southern Baptists and other evangelical churches. With North America's population over 324 million, Southern Baptists have an average of one church per 6,750 people. The lost population of North America is estimated to be over 235 million! That means there is one Southern Baptist Church per 4,895 lost people! It is obvious that many new churches are needed soon to impact the lostness of North America.

The challenge grows as the lost population of North America is becoming increasingly diverse. In the United States, the international-born population numbers over 34 million. This means people who were born outside the United States account for 12 percent of the total population. One million new legal immigrants arrive each year. According to the U.S. Census, 53 percent were Latin American-born, 25 percent Asian-born, 14 percent European-born, and the remaining 8 percent in other world regions. Many more arrive illegally. These people represent a variety of religions, languages, lifestyles, and philosophies; yet most of them are open to the gospel. But there are not enough churches in North America to which most of these people can relate.

Likewise, Canada's population is made up of many people from other countries. In 2001, 18 percent of its population—5.4 million—were foreign-born. This is was the highest percentage in 70 years. Mainland Chinese were the highest percentage of immigrants to Canada in 1990's, numbering 1 million. Toronto, Vancouver, and Montreal attracted almost 75 percent of immigrants in the 1990's. Over 200 different ethnic groups were reported on the Canadian Census in 2001. Only one-half of 1 percent of French Canadians are Christian.

There are several ways your church can be involved in starting a church.

Your Church Can Help by…

Becoming a Supporting Church by providing resources such as mission groups, financial support, prayer, and equipment on an as-needed basis. Sending a mission team to work for a week or weekend with a planter or planting church will not only help the plant, it will impact your people as well. You can take up a one-time special offering to support the planting efforts of a new church. Some of your members could help with children's care or serve as a welcome team for several weeks when the new church begins public worship. You could develop a continuing prayer strategy to lift up before God the planter, new church, and their needs over the course of a year. The list of possibilities is endless.

Becoming part of a Church Planting Cluster by partnering with other churches to plant a new church designed to impact lostness among people groups or in areas where your churches cannot reach. Your church would participate in the Cluster Leadership Team. Together with the other Clustering Churches, you would: identify the people group that needs to be reached, identify the church planter who will lead the planting team, design the strategy that will guide the development of the new church, and experience the joy of seeing people brought to Christ. You do not have to do it alone—partners work together!

Becoming a Primary Church by accepting God's call to plant a church among an unreached people group or in an under-reached place. As a church leader, you recognize that God has gifted and resourced your church to be in a position to start new churches. You might need Supporting Churches to help plant the new church, but the long term process of planting can be done from within your church. You might even see this as an opportunity not only to plant a new church but to support and apprentice other existing churches so that they too might experience the joy of seeing and helping in the expansion of God's kingdom.

Whatever type of Partnering Church your church decides to become, there are partners and equipping resources available to help you be effective in your church planting endeavors. Contact the following for more information:

1. Your local association's Church Planting leadership[140]
2. Your state convention's Church Planting Team

If you are not able to make contact with these, or need information about being equipped for Church Planting, contact:

The Equipping Team of the Church Planting Group, NAMB
Phone: (770) 410-6240
e-mail: *equippingteam@namb.net*

Church planting resources also can be found at www.ChurchPlantingVillage.net.

You Can Help by...

Church planting is done most often by a team of believers called and gifted by God to plant the Gospel through planting churches. The role of the lead church planter as pastor of the new church is the most common image for church planters. However, God may have gifted you to carry out an equally significant role in church planting—that of ministry support. There are resources designed especially to assist you in finding your place in church planting by discovering your spiritual giftedness. Are you ready to explore the possibilities? Are you ready to answer God's call?

Discover Church Planting, located on the Church Planting Village, is a web-based resource designed to help you identify how God has shaped you for ministry and to encourage you to utilize your gifts and talents to advance the Kingdom of God through church planting.

DISCOVER
CHURCHPLANTING
www.discoverchurchplanting.net

[140] To identify and contact your state convention office or local association, visit *www.SBC.net.*

Discover Church Planting has links to…

- Quick Test – A test designed to help you discover if you have the attributes of a church planter.
- Finding Your Place in Ministry – This comprehensive on-line assessment will help you discover how God created you with a unique personality, spiritual gifts, abilities, passions, and experiences. This tool also includes a Leadership Assessment.
- Resources – This page contains links to Bible Studies and other resources to further guide you in your journey to discover God's will for your life.

If you are interested in serving on a church planting team or becoming a church planter please contact the following for more information:

1. Your local association's Church Planting leadership[141]
2. Your state convention's Church Planting Team

Additional church planter resources also can be found at *www.ChurchPlantingVillage.net.*

North American Mission Board Church Planting Group
Enlistment and Missional Networks Team
Phone: (770) 410-6223
Email: *DiscoverChurchPlanting@NAMB.net*

[141] To identify and contact your state convention office or local association, visit *www.SBC.net.*